AnthroN

A Study Companion to Ac

PEOPLE OF THE EARTH

ELEVENTH EDITION

BRIAN M. FAGAN

UNIVERSITY OF CALIFORNIA, SANTA BARBARA

Upper Saddle River
New Jersey 07458

Publisher: Nancy Roberts
Media Acquisitions Editor: Kate Ramunda
Director of Production and Manufacturing: Barbara Kittle
Editorial/Production Supervision: Rob DeGeorge
Copyeditor: Nicole Conforti
Prepress and Manufacturing Buyer: Ben Smith
Manufacturing Manager: Nick Sklitsis
Interior Design: Susan Walrath, Anne Bonanno Nieglos, Rob DeGeorge
Cover Design: Susan Walrath, Bruce Killmer
Senior Art Director: Anne Bonanno Nieglos
Electronic Art Creation: Mirella Signoretto
Director of Marketing: Beth Mejia
Marketing Assistant: Adam Laitman
Editorial Assistant: Lee Peterson
Cover Photo: Thera, fresco of boxing children
Cover Image: R. Sheridan/Ancient Art & Architecture Collection
Composition: Interactive Composition Corporation
Printer/Binder: Von Hoffmann Press, Inc.
Cover Printer: Phoenix Color Corp.
Text: 10/12 New Baskerville

Credits and acknowledgments borrowed from other sources and reproduced, with permission, in this textbook appear on p. 183.

Pearson Education, Inc., Upper Saddle River, New Jersey 07458

Pearson Education LTD.
Pearson Education Singapore, Pte. Ltd
Pearson Education, Canada, Ltd
Pearson Education—Japan
Pearson Education Australia PTY, Limited
Pearson Education North Asia Ltd
Pearson Educación de Mexico, S.A. de C.V.
Pearson Education Malaysia, Pte. Ltd
Pearson Education, Upper Saddle River, New Jersey

10 9 8 7 6 5 4 3 2 1

ISBN 0-13-184197-1

CONTENTS

About This Companion v

1 Introducing World Prehistory 1
2 Human Origins 8
3 *Homo erectus* and *Homo sapiens sapiens* 20
4 Europe and Eurasia 40
5 The First Americans 53
6 Africans and Australians 62
7 Intensification and Complexity 69
8 A Plenteous Harvest: The Origins 78
9 The Origins of Food Production in Southwest Asia 87
10 The First European Farmers 92
11 First Farmers in Egypt and Tropical Africa 99
12 Asia and the Pacific: Rice, Roots, and Ocean Voyages 103
13 The Story of Maize: Early Farmers in the Americas 111
14 The Development of Civilization 118
15 Early Civilizations in Southwest Asia 122
16 Egypt, Nubia, and Africa 130
17 Early States in South and Southeast Asia 139
18 Early Chinese Civilization 144
19 Hittites, Minoans, and Mycenaeans 148
20 Europe Before the Romans 154
21 Mesoamerican Civilizations 160
22 Andean States 171

Epilogue: All About Becoming an Archaeologist 177

Credits 183

About This *Companion* . . .

General Comments

This *Study Companion* is designed to make your journey through human prehistory and the course text, *People of the Earth, Eleventh Edition,* as straightforward as possible. It's a combination guide and notebook, with plenty of space for notes, designed to be used during lectures and as you complete the assigned readings. Like the textbook, the pages of the *Companion* unfold chronologically, enabling you to progress through each chapter and work each assignment in order.

Features

Format The *Companion* features a running commentary on the narrative, organized on a chapter-by-chapter basis. Many of the maps, tables, and line drawings from the text are also included at the appropriate points in the commentary. Please note that the photographs and their captions appear only in the textbook and not here. We also provide you with space for notes where we feel that you have a need to take them. There is a CD included in the textbook to provide you with additional study material and aids for navigating through the past.

Summary and Key Terms/Sites Each chapter in the *Companion* begins with a "Chapter in Review" section and also with a list of "Key Cultures and Sites" covered in the text.

Introductory Comments These comments draw your attention to the major themes of the chapter in a conversational way, designed to make studying the material easier. There are also comments on the rationale behind the organization of the chapter.

Major Chapter Topics The remainder of each chapter draws attention to major topics, dissects them slightly, and sometimes adds material or perspectives not found in the text (usually for space reasons). There are commentaries on tables and text figures, which amplify the presentation in the text. These are especially useful, as they tell you what to look for in a specific table or drawing. For instance, some are designed for reference, others amplify specific text, and so on. As we mentioned, note taking space is provided where appropriate.

Archaeology As a Career As an Epilogue, you'll find a frank appraisal of career prospects in archaeology, as well as answers to questions many people have about the subject. This is reprinted from other textbooks I have written and does not appear in *People of the Earth.* I hope it will be useful to you.

CD-ROM At intervals in each chapter, you will find cross-references to the CD-ROM provided with the textbook. Please think of this book as just one element in your tools for studying the narrative of human prehistory in these pages.

Finally. . . .

If you have any comments, suggestions, or questions, please feel free to e-mail me at brian@brianfagan.com. I will do all that I can to respond promptly.

Good luck with your journey through the past!

Brian Fagan

DISCLAIMER AND WARNING!

This *Study Companion* is written to accompany the textbook entitled *People of the Earth, Eleventh Edition.* As such, it is designed as a true companion, amplifying and commenting on the narrative and the book generally. You **cannot** take a course based on *People of the Earth* using the *Companion* alone.

This book is as user-friendly as we can make it and is intended for use in class as a combination notebook and study aide. Please be sure that you take it to class and study sessions with you!

If your instructor does not assign this *Companion* as part of your text package for this course, you can easily and quickly order it on-line from the publisher, Prentice Hall. To do so, please log on to: www.prenhall.com/anthropology, which will take you right to the Catalog and order page.

chapter

INTRODUCING WORLD PREHISTORY

The Chapter in Review

- Archaeology is the study of ancient humanity, using the material remains of past human behavior.
- These material remains make up the archaeological record, the archives of the human past.
- While historians study written records, archaeologists deal with an anonymous past. Archaeology is unique among the sciences in its ability to study culture change over long periods of time.
- Text-aided archaeology combines the evidence of archaeology with documentary sources, while prehistoric archaeology is the study of prehistory, the period of the human past before the advent of written records.
- The study of world prehistory, which developed in the 1950s, is the study of human prehistory from a global perspective using archaeological data and other sources.
- Four major chronological methods date prehistory: historical records, dendrochronology, radiocarbon, and potassium-argon dating.
- All human societies are interested in the past, but they think of it in different terms and use it for different purposes.
- Archaeologists, Westerners generally, conceive of time in a linear way, while many non-Western groups measure time by the cycles of the seasons and the movements of heavenly bodies. They use linear time only when it is of use to them.
- Archaeology is not the only way of approaching history, for many societies have oral histories, alternative perspectives on the past which are of vital importance in preserving traditional culture and values.
- Theoretical approaches to human prehistory abound, but can be divided, in general terms, into processual and post-processual approaches.
- The processual (culture-as-adaptation) approach uses multilinear cultural evolution and cultural ecology to provide a viable general framework for studying world prehistory, based on the assumption that human societies evolved in many diverse ways.
- Archaeologists conventionally make a distinction between prestate and state-organized societies as part of this framework.
- Evolutionary ecology makes use of the mechanism of natural selection and optimal foraging strategy to interpret hunter-gatherer societies in terms of energy costs and risk management.

- In recent years, archaeologists have distinguished between external constraints on cultural change, such as environmental factors, and internal constraints, created by the actions of individuals and groups.
- A new generation of research is focusing on ideologies, human interactions, gender relations, and other topics, combining processual and post-processual approaches to study both types of constraints and their influences on the past.

Key Cultures and Sites

There are no key cultures and sites listed for Chapter 1. Those mentioned are described in later chapters. Key Terms, of which there are a considerable number in this chapter, are in the main text, and are not redefined here.

Introductory Remarks

Chapter 1 introduces you to world prehistory, and covers a lot of ground in the process. This is an important chapter, for it lays the foundations for the narrative of prehistory that follows. These pages are general background for the rest of the book, so it's worth taking some time to absorb the important points that it makes.

Here's how this chapter is organized:

- The first third of the chapter sets the stage by defining archaeology and prehistory, and describing the development of world prehistory as an intellectual concept. We do not describe the flamboyant early history of archaeology here, with its headlong search for ancient civilizations and royal tombs, fossils, and buried cities. You'll find a description of these adventures in Paul Bahn's well-illustrated history of archaeology (1996) or my National Geographic book, *The Adventure of Archaeology* (1985). Here we stress that world prehistory developed from radiocarbon dating, which allowed worldwide chronologies for the first time, and from a massive expansion of archaeology in the 1960s.
- Then we embark on perhaps the most important section in this chapter, "Who Needs the Past?" Here we distinguish between cyclical and linear time and discuss written records, oral traditions, and archaeology, all of which bring different perspectives to the past. We make a fundamental point: Archaeology is very much a construction of Western science. There are other perspectives on the past as well, and we should never forget this.
- Lastly we examine some of the very basic principles of archaeological research, essential to the understanding of the narrative in this book—and how it was put together. Our primary concerns are culture and culture change. We also describe some of the basic mechanisms of culture change and major theoretical approaches that seek to explain the past.

Now You Should Start Reading the Chapter. . . . Archaeology and Prehistory

Straightforward reading, these first few pages, and I think that the definitions and points made are very clear. The site box on Vindolanda is a fascinating window into the potential of text-aided archaeology . . .

Vindolanda

Vindolanda is a compelling site to visit, if your travels take you to Britain. A day spent walking along Hadrian's Wall gives you wonderful vistas over the rolling hills of northern England and makes you realize how cold and lonely this frontier outpost of the

Roman empire must have been on a winter's day. The garrison itself is about a mile south of the wall near Housesteads, where you can see the foundations of the wall garrison, which succeeded an original timber fort at Vindolanda. There is a superb visitor's center at Vindolanda, which displays finds from the many years of excavations, including some of the documents. What with the foundations, perhaps a dig in progress and the reconstructions of parts of the site, you obtain an unrivaled impression of life on the Roman frontier. This is far more vivid and entertaining than Stonehenge and ranks up there with Viking York, not too far south.

But it's the documents which give the most vivid portrait, notes written by lonely people from a Tungrian cohort, who were suddenly uprooted and transferred to the faraway Danube in A.D. 105—and they marched there. We know more about this remote garrison than almost any other in the Roman Empire. We know, for example, that auditors visited the commander, Flavius Ceralius. They cannot have written a favorable report. Wrote one: "I have come to Vindolanda to carry out the audit—but sadly we do not know what happened." Ceralius himself set out to make life more pleasant for himself. He corresponded about hunting nets with a fellow officer named Aelius Brocchus stationed in western Scotland. His wife was asked to a birthday party on (of all days) September 11. "I will expect you sister," wrote Brocchus's wife. She probably declined, for the journey would have taken two days and required a full military escort. The frontier lands were dangerous for a solitary traveler.

Just for a moment, the veil lifts, and we enter the lives of obscure, long-forgotten folk. You'll never regret a visit to this place.

Who Needs the Past?

"Who Needs the Past?" is self explanatory and really an essay on respect for other historical perspectives.

Part of this section is concerned with cyclical and linear perspectives on the past, which means that we examine ways in which archaeologists date ancient societies. There are issues here, the first being relative chronology and the second chronometric measurement of the past—dates in years.

The Dating the Past box is very important. I strongly advise you to spend some time studying the dating methods table, for this lays out the chronological span of the various major dating methods used in world prehistory. We describe each one in more detail in later boxes, at moments when they become relevant, but here you see how they fit together to produce our global, linear chronology. One of the hardest things is gaining a strong sense of the sheer length of time humans have been on earth. This table will help.

Culture and Culture Change

These pages are of fundamental importance, especially if you are new to archaeology. They define culture and cultural process, two fundamental concepts, and then discuss the primary cultural processes, which are the mechanisms of cultural change. These are all terms we will use again and again in later chapters, and it's important that you know what they mean.

No other comments here: just go ahead and read!

Culture and Culture Change: Explaining the Past

People of the Earth is not a theoretical work, but a narrative of what happened in human prehistory and why. However, all good archaeology is based on sound archaeological theory and the prehistory in these pages is no exception. Two chapters, 8 and 14, pay considerable attention to theoretical controversies, in the context of food production

TABLE 1.1
Dating methods commonly used in world prehistory

Date	Method	Major Events
Modern times (after A.D. 1)	Historical documents; imported objects most useful	European settlement of New World; Roman Empire
4500 B.C.		Origins of cities
	Dendrochronology	Origins of agriculture
	Radiocarbon dating (organic materials)	First Americans
70,000 B.P.		*Homo sapiens neanderthalensis*
		Homo sapiens sapiens
500,000 B.P.	Potassium-argon dating (volcanic materials)	*Homo erectus*
		Homo
		Australopithecus
5,000,000 B.P.	Uranium series dating	

Note: These conventions are used in the tables throughout this book:

———	A continuous line means the chronology is firmly established.
——→	A line terminating in an arrow means the time span continues beyond the arrow.
——⊣	A line terminating with a horizontal bar means the limit of chronology is firmly established.
-----	A broken line means the chronology is doubtful.
?	A question mark beside the name of a site means its date is not firmly established.

and early civilization, as background to subsequent narrative chapters. But there are some basic theoretical approaches that need some general discussion at the outset, which is what we are doing here.

We start with the "Culture as Adaptation" approach, then discuss evolutionary ecology and, finally, what we call "People as Agents of Change." These pages offer just a sampling of the complex, and often verbose and obscure, theoretical literature of human prehistory, but I hope they are a reliable guide to the basics.

Culture as Adaptation

"Culture as Adaptation" is currently the most popular approach, involving as it does the notions of cultural ecology and multilinear evolution. A generation ago, evolutionary approaches were all the rage, especially the idea that one subdivided ancient societies into a hierarchy of bands, tribes, chiefdoms, and states. Today, we are much more cautious. The discussion here takes a careful middle ground, being concerned mainly with prestate and state-organized societies.

Figure 1.9 lays out some of the distinctions between these two general categories of society and is worth studying at some length. After all, this is fruitful test material, apart from being useful for your later understanding of the narrative in this book! There is a minor hierarchy of complexity from left to right in the table, but please understand that this is NOT chronological. There are still band societies flourishing in remote parts of the world today, and chiefdoms are commonplace.

	Band (Prestate)	Tribe (Prestate)	Chiefdom (Prestate)	State-Organized Societies
Total Numbers	Less than 100	Up to a few thousand	5,000 – 20,000+	Generally 20,000+
Social Organization	Egalitarian Informal leadership	Segmentary society Pan-tribal associations Raids by small groups	Kinship-based ranking under hereditary leader High-ranking warriors	Class-based hierarchy under king or emperor Armies
Economic Organization	Mobile hunter-gatherers	Settled farmers Pastoralist herders	Central accumulation and redistribution Some craft specialization	Centralized bureaucracy Tribute-based Taxation Laws
Settlement Pattern	Temporary camps	Permanent villages	Fortified centers Ritual centers	Urban: cities, towns Frontier defenses Roads
Religious Organization	Shamans	Religious elders Calendrical rituals	Hereditary chief with religious duties	Priestly class Pantheistic or monotheistic religion
Architecture	Temporary shelters 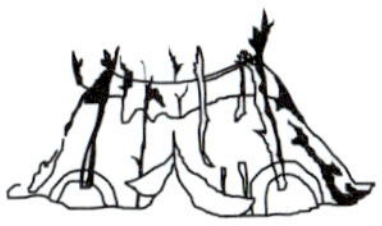 *Paleolithic skin tents, Ukraine*	Permanent huts Burial mounds Shrines 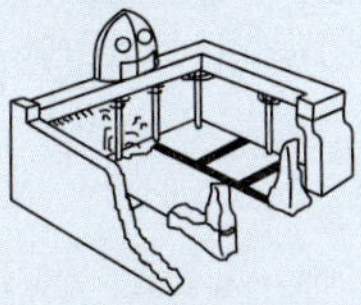 *Neolithic shrine Çatalhöyük, Turkey*	Large–scale monuments  *Stonehenge, England — final form*	Palaces, temples, and other public buildings  Pyramids at Giza  *Castillo Chichén Itzá, Mexico*
Archaeological Examples	All Paleolithic societies, including Paleo-Indians	All early farmers (Neolithic/Archaic)	Many early metalworking and Formative societies Mississippian, USA Smaller African kingdoms	All ancient civilizations, e.g., in Mesoamerica, Peru, Near East, Southwest Asia, India and China, Greece and Rome
Modern Examples	Eskimos !Kung San Australian Aborigines	Pueblos, Southwest USA New Guinea Highlanders Nuer and Dinka in East Africa	Northwest Coast Indians, USA 18th-century Polynesian chiefdoms in Tonga, Tahiti, Hawaii	All modern states

FIGURE 1.9 General categories of ancient human societies. (Modified from Renfrew and Bahn, 2000.)

Notes

Evolutionary ecology is mainly of concern to the study of hunter-gatherer societies. The discussion on different strategies is fascinating and relevant to Chapter 7, which discusses changes in human societies after the Ice Age.

People as Agents of Change

I think that "People as Agents of Change" is the most interesting part of this discussion. Clearly, individuals of exceptional ability were all-important in ancient times, whether in the context of small bands or entire civilizations—witness the Egyptian pharaoh Narmer (see Chapter 16). The issue is how we identify people or small groups in the archaeological record, which is what is loosely called "post-processual archaeology." This is a ghastly term that is effectively meaningless, but it at least makes a distinction between the rather anonymous archaeology of processual scholars and the greater emphasis on people and the intangible of the new theoretical generation. Post-processual archaeology covers a multitude of different approaches. However, many of them are concerned with the issues discussed briefly here: constraints, interactions between people, gender, and exchange.

Figure 1.10 is self-explanatory, but it shows how pharaohs and other divine rulers of ancient civilizations depended heavily on their own charisma and carefully choreographed public appearances to maintain power. Pharaoh Akhenaten appeared infrequently in public, always in a formal procession or at an audience like this one. Gods were remote. So were divine rulers. Notice how the sun's rays descend on the pharaoh, the living sun god.

FIGURE 1.10 The New Kingdom pharaoh Akhenaten, who reigned from 1353 to 1335 B.C., appears at the Window of Appearance, rewarding one of his loyal officials, Pannefer. Pannefer receives gold necklaces and other gifts, as well as provisions, being carried off at the lower right. Scenes such as this, from Pannefer's tomb, are an important amplification of the archaeological data from Akhenaten's capital, El-Amarna (Chapter 16). (After N. de G. Davies, *The Rock Tombs of El-Amarna,* vol. 6, Pl. IV [London: Egypt Exploration Society, 1908].)

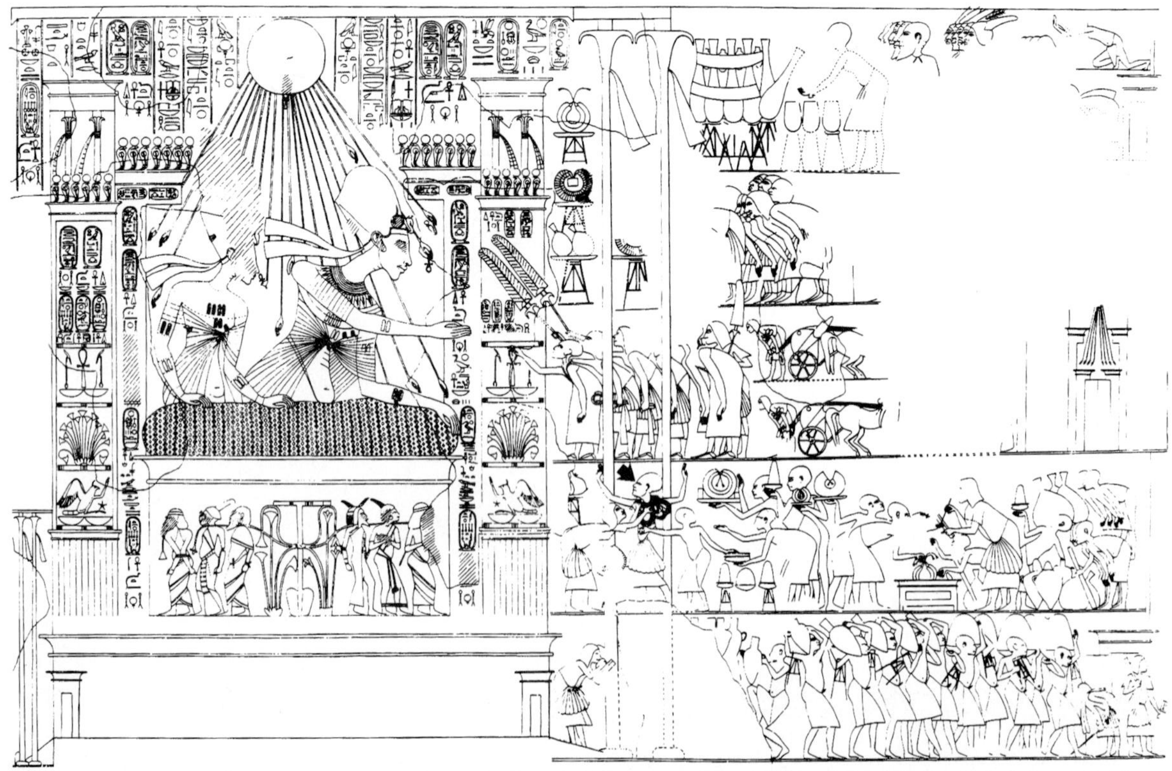

As we say at the end of the chapter, the most promising theoretical approaches marry both processual and post-processual approaches, where researchers examine such factors as climate change and environment, and also pay careful attention to ideology and to the deeds of people as individuals or groups.

If you have a clear idea of what is involved, in general terms in the "culture as adaptation" and "people as agents of change" sections, you will have a good background for later chapters in the book.

chapter 

HUMAN ORIGINS

The Chapter in Review

- The story of human evolution begins with the separation of the chimpanzee and human lines from a common, and as yet unknown, ancestor about 5 to 6 million years ago.
- The first hominids were tree-living, with long arms and legs and broad chests, who eventually became bipedal, walking on two limbs. They adapted to more open country in Africa, which resulted from global cooling over 4 million years ago, by broadening their diet to include more meat, and by achieving great mobility and behavioral flexibility.
- The earliest known possible hominid is *Sahelanthropus tchadensis* from Chad, which may date to between 6 and 7 mya.
- A small bipedal hominid named *Ardipithecus ramidus* flourished in Ethiopia 4.5 million years ago.
- A later hominid, *Australopithecus afarensis,* was ancestral to later hominids and flourished 3.5 to 3.0 million years ago.
- By 2 million years ago, the hominid line had radiated into many forms, among them robust and more gracile Australopithecines and the larger-brained *Homo habilis,* another hominid form.
- *Homo habilis* was a forager who also scavenged game meat and perhaps hunted. These hominids used a simple stone technology, had some ability to communicate, and had a very rudimentary social organization.
- New definitions of the genus *Homo* make a major distinction between the more ape-like hominids described in this chapter, which flourished before 2 million years ago, and the true humans, beginning with *Homo erectus,* which evolved after 1.9 million years before the present.
- Three lines of evidence can be used to test hypotheses about human behavior: artifact scatters, manufactured artifacts, and food remains.
- The earliest known artifact scatters were not "central places" or camps, as was once thought. They were places to which food was carried, processed, and eaten by hominids who scavenged much of their meat from predator kills rather than hunting large animals. Plant remains were also important.
- The earliest human technology, known as the Oldowan, was a simple, effective use of stone cobbles and sharp-edged flakes, which eventually evolved into artifacts flaked on both sides—bifaces.
- *Homo habilis* shared the ability of its earlier ancestors to "map" resources over the landscape, its intelligence amplified by tool making. These hominids may have lived in larger groups, something made possible by greater social intelligence resulting from larger brain size.

- Despite these enhanced skills at communicating with others, the first humans probably had only the most rudimentary forms of speech, in addition to the grunts and gestures of other primates.

Key Cultures and Sites (Hominid Fossils Are Not Included)

Allia Bay
Aramis
Hadar
Kanapoi
Koobi Fora (East Turkana)
Koto Toro
Laetoli
Oldowan Tradition
Olduvai Gorge
Taung
Toro-Menalla

Introductory Comments

Chapter 2 surveys what we know about human origins, what the Victorian biologist Thomas Huxley called "the question of questions" for humankind. A century-and-a-half later, we are somewhat closer to the answer than we were in Huxley and Charles Darwins' day. In some respects, however, the story of human origins becomes ever more confusing as more and more fossils come to light. "Human Origins" attempts to navigate through a thicket of competing theories and ever-proliferating human remains.

Chapter 2 is set entirely in tropical Africa, which was the only place where humans and their ancestors lived for over 5 million years.

Darwin's *Origin of Species* helped establish an open-ended date for human origins, far earlier than the 6,000 years or so allowed for by the genealogies in the Old Testament. But how old was humanity? One hundred thousand years, a quarter of a million, or more? The earliest estimates were little more than guesses. Even when I was an undergraduate in the late 1950s, human origins were dated to no more than 250,000 years or so.

Enter potassium-argon dating, described in the "Dating the Past" box on page 41. The first potassium-argon dates in 1960, from Olduvai Gorge in East Africa, dated humans there to about 1.75 million years ago (hereafter mya). Today, human origins date back to over 4 million years, and the first human tool making to about 2.6 million!

This first chapter of our story spans an immensely long period of time—well over 3 million years. This is the longest chronology in human prehistory: more than three quarters of all our past!

In writing Chapter 2, I had to meld together several important and competing themes to make a linear narrative. As I pointed out in Chapter 1, *People of the Earth* is a chronological narrative, "beginning at the very beginning, ending at the end, then stopping," to quote Lewis Carroll's immortal *Alice in Wonderland.* This is the only logical way to tell a story like human origins, so I unfold the tale as follows:

- Chapter 2 begins by introducing a general climatic background, for the cooling of the earth may have played an important part in human evolution.
- Then we start right at the beginning, with the Order Primates, then with the first such mammals, who flourished over 30 million years ago.
- Next, we survey the startling findings of molecular biology, which show that chimpanzees, our closest relatives, and the hominid line split between 5 and 6 million years ago.
- We describe the remarkable, recently discovered 7 million-year-old hominid from Chad that may revolutionize our thinking about early human evolution.
- Now we have set the stage for two themes: the evolving behavior and adaptations of the first humans—ecological challenges, bipedalism, and so on—and for a survey of the sketchy fossil record.

- We describe the fossil record in three stages: the very first hominids of 7 to 3 mya, including the first human footprints; the diverse hominids of 3 to 2.5 mya, then the appearance of early *Homo,* humanity, between 2.5 and 2 mya.
- Once the fossil record is covered, we discuss the overall evolutionary picture, and try and answer the question of questions: Who was the first human?
- Finally, we examine the archaeological evidence for early human behavior, the first human technology, and such issues as social organization and language.

Time to Start Reading! The Earliest (and Remote) Human Ancestors

At this point, you are probably receiving some assigned reading, so here are a few thoughts on the first part of the chapter, where we cover the very earliest primates and early human adaptation.

This is a straightforward narrative, and needs little commentary by me, as I am sure your instructor will amplify the story.

But I do want to draw your attention to the four tables in this section, which are reproduced here.

One problem confronts beginners—keeping everything in order in your head. At this point, I strongly recommend that you spend some time going over each table carefully. This will save you a lot of work later.

I've written brief commentaries on the tables to help you.

As we said in the guide for Chapter 1, the narrative of human prehistory proceeds from site to site, these being the signposts for the story. Table 2.1 is a straightforward table, which lists sites and places them in chronological order. It's at this spot in the chapter next to the map, so that you have a reference point. As you read, you might want to put a Post-it on this page, so you can flip back easily.

Table 2.2 on page 12 is another simple table, which lays out the order of geological epochs, to which we refer in the text. The climatic curve is a generalized one, which makes one point—the world's climate has been very volatile over the past 2 million years, a trend that began during the Miocene.

Now we go forward in time from Table 2.2 and cover the entire spectrum of human prehistory. We set the major developments such as human origins, the origins of modern humans, and so on against a climatic background and chronology of the Pleistocene, the last geological epoch. We name the major glaciations, too. The main purpose of the table is to lay everything out for you, so you have a general overall picture for future chapters. From our point of view, the important developments are in the right-hand column.

Table 2.4 is parallel to Table 2.3, and is directly relevant to Chapter 2. We chronicle four major aspects of human biological and cultural evolution. Notice that all the major anatomical changes are complete by the time modern humans appear, and many of them occur before 2 mya. This table will keep the various developments discussed in the chapter in chronological order for you.

The Fossil Record

The real meat and drink of this chapter is the fossil record between 7 and 2 million years ago. I wager that many test questions will come from this part of the chapter!

It's difficult for non-specialists to get a grasp of the various fossil groups and their Latin names, which seem to proliferate every time I revise this book.

Before you read a thing, I strongly recommend spending a few minutes on Table 2.5, which lays out what we know in summary about the five tentative groups of hominids known to have flourished in East and Southern Africa after about 4.5 mya. The earlier hominids and their anatomical features are still too little known for definitive statements about them.

TABLE 2.1
Major sites mentioned in Chapter 2

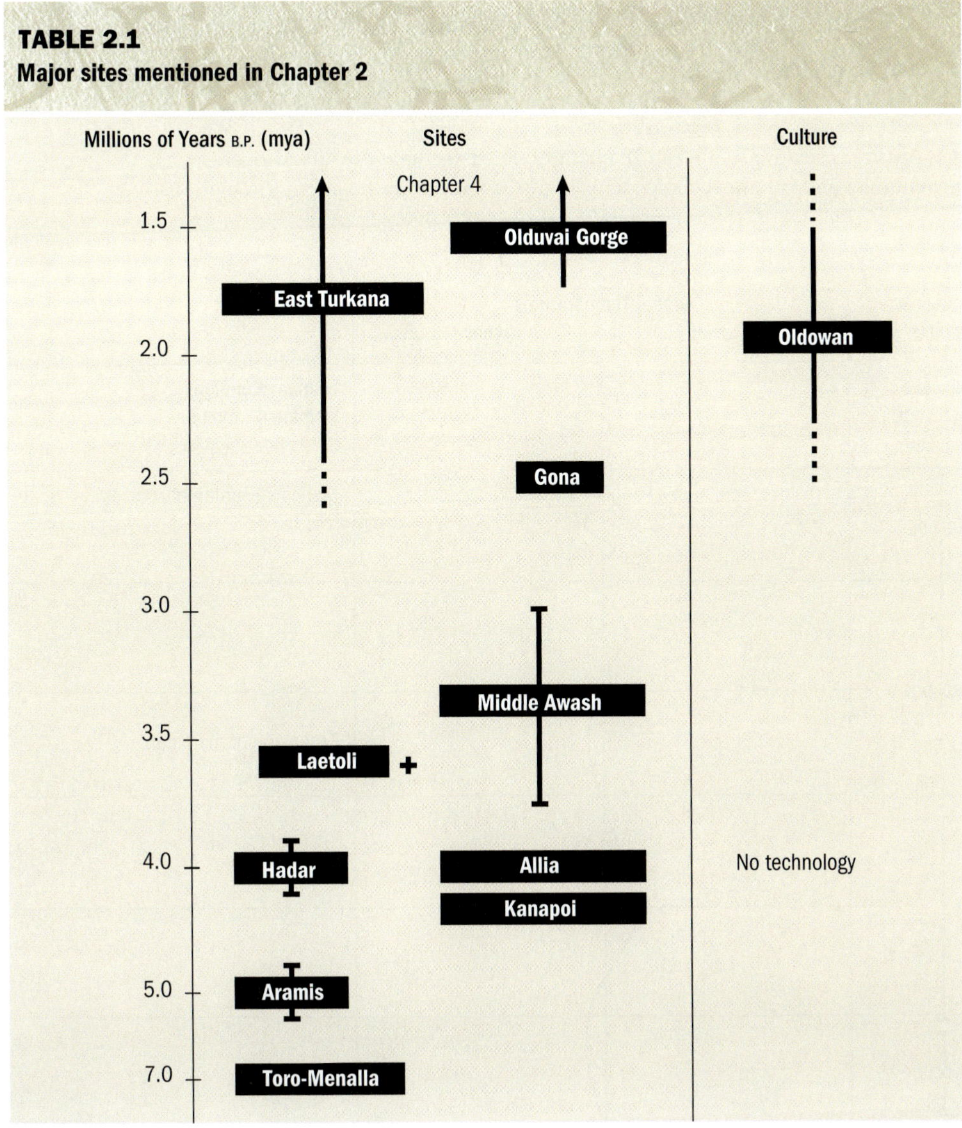

Notes

TABLE 2.2
Geological epochs from more than 60 million years ago

The curve demonstrates relative temperature changes on earth since the late Miocene. Notice that the general trend is toward cooler temperatures with more frequent fluctuations. (Pleistocene temperatures are shown in Table 2.3.)

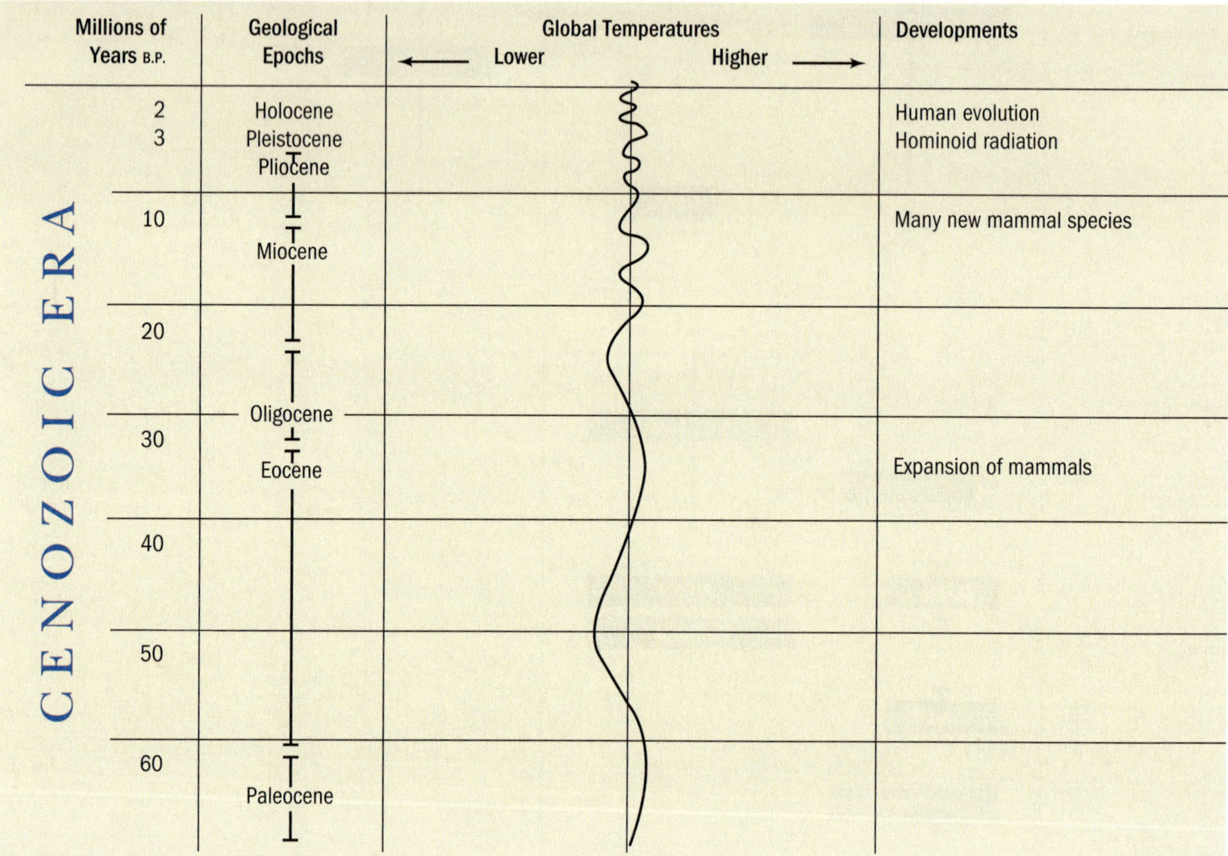

Table 2.5 summarizes a mass of descriptive information into five categories. Please realize that the table is organized chronologically from *left to right,* the earliest group being at left. Work your way up the columns, from dates, to sites and species, then anatomical features. A highlighter will work well to summarize the main points.

If you do this *before* you read, and before a lecture, you should have much less trouble with the many Latin names and sites.

A word to the wise. All of this is highly tentative, and is likely to be outdated by new discoveries at any time. Your instructor should guide you on this.

Who Was the First Human?

This section is the crux of the early and middle parts of Chapter 2. We make a number of points worth summarizing as you look at Figure 2.10:

- First, the old notions that human evolution was linear are long gone. We now know that there were many forms of hominids in East Africa between 7 and 2 million years. Many remain undiscovered, others are still wrongly classified, and yet others are too fragmentary.

TABLE 2.3
Geological events, climatic changes, and chronology during the Pleistocene (highly simplified), with approximate dates

Temperature (Lower ← → Higher)	Date (B.C.)	Epochs	Glaciations/Interglacial in Europe	Developments in Prehistory
				Origins of states
		Holocene	Holocene	
	10,000			First food production
				First settlement of Americas
	18,000		Weichsel Glaciation	Cro-Magnons in Europe
	40,000			First settlement of Australia
				Radiation of modern humans
	118,000	PLEISTOCENE		Origins of *Homo sapiens sapiens*
			Eemian	
	128,000			
			Saale Glaciation	
				Archaic *Homo sapiens*
Uncertain climatic detail			Uncertain climatic detail	
	780,000			
	1.6 Million			
				Homo erectus
		Pliocene		*Homo habilis*
				Australopithecus

Notes

TABLE 2.4
Human development: 10 million to 5000 years ago

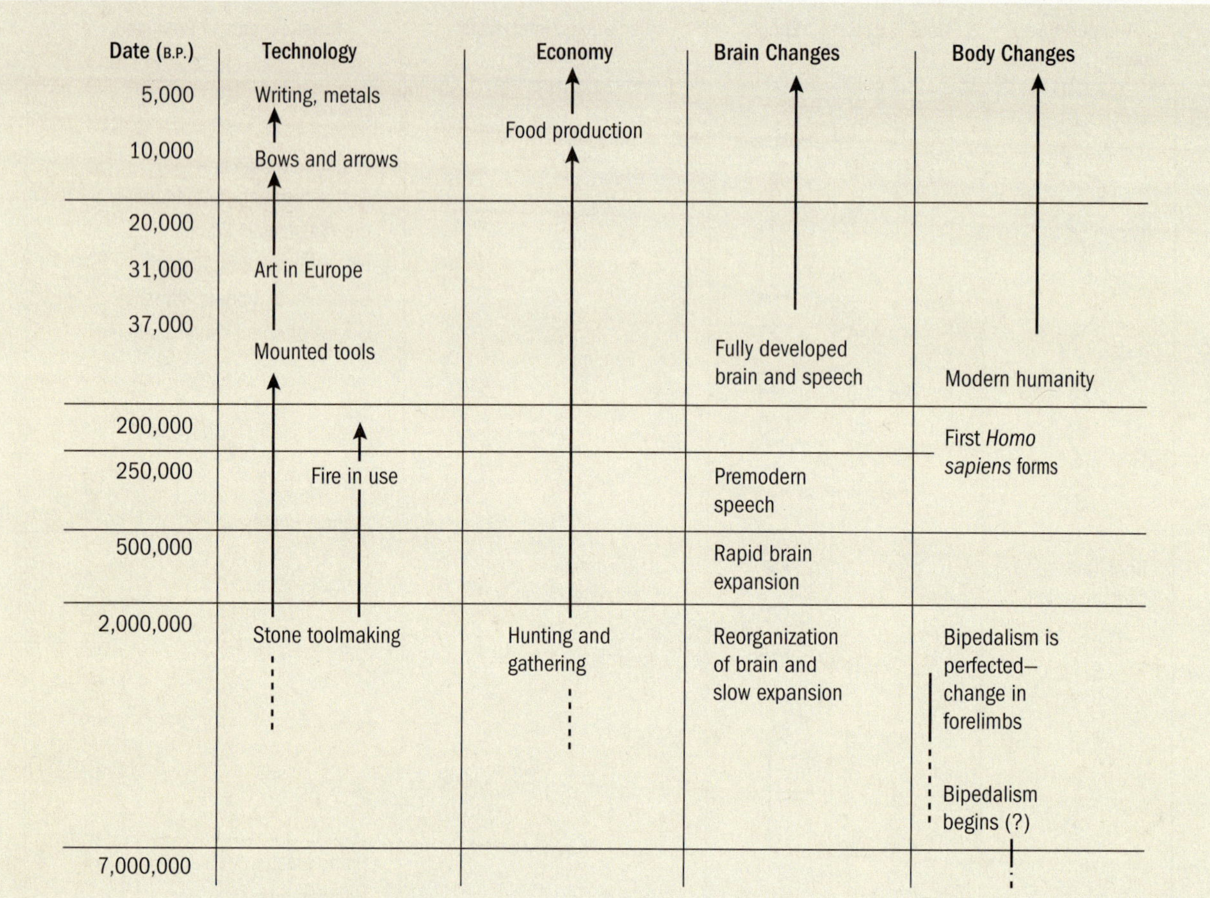

Date (B.P.)	Technology	Economy	Brain Changes	Body Changes
5,000	Writing, metals			
10,000	Bows and arrows	Food production		
20,000				
31,000	Art in Europe			
37,000	Mounted tools		Fully developed brain and speech	Modern humanity
200,000				First *Homo sapiens* forms
250,000	Fire in use		Premodern speech	
500,000			Rapid brain expansion	
2,000,000	Stone toolmaking	Hunting and gathering	Reorganization of brain and slow expansion	Bipedalism is perfected—change in forelimbs
				Bipedalism begins (?)
7,000,000				

Notes

TABLE 2.5
Five tentative groups of East and South African hominids, much simplified for this book

Variables	Aramis/Allia Group	Hadar/Laetoli Group	Gracile Group	Robust Group	*Homo* Group
Brain size	Comparable to that of a chimpanzee	Comparable to that of a chimpanzee	450–550 cc	500–550 cc	650–775 cc
Teeth	Small back teeth; large front teeth	Small back teeth; large front teeth	Large front and back teeth	Very large back teeth; relatively small front teeth	Variable; generally smaller than those of robust and gracile forms
Limbs	Bipedal; long arms	Bipedal; arms slightly longer than those of *Homo sapiens*		Some elements of limb bones differ from those of modern humans	Bipedal, but lower limbs still partially adapted to arboreal life
Species and sites	*Ardipithecus ramidus* *Australopithecus anamensis* East Africa: Allia Bay, Kanapoi, Aramis	*Australopithecus afarensis* East Africa: Hadar and Laetoli	*Australopithecus africanus* South Africa: Taung, Sterkfontein, Makapansgat East Africa: Omo? East Turkana	*Australopithecus robustus* South Africa: Swarkrans, Kromdraai *Australopithecus boisei* East Africa: Olduvai, East Turkana, Omo *Australopithecus aethiopicus* East Turkana	*Homo* East Africa: Olduvai and East Turkana South Africa: Sterkfontein
Dates	East Africa: c. 5 million to c. 4 million B.P.	East Africa: c. 4 million to c. 3 million B.P.	East Africa: c. 3 million to c. 1.5 million B.P. South Africa: no reliable dates	East Africa: c. 2.6 million to c. 1 million B.P. South Africa: no reliable dates	East Africa: c. 2 million to c. 1.5 million B.P.

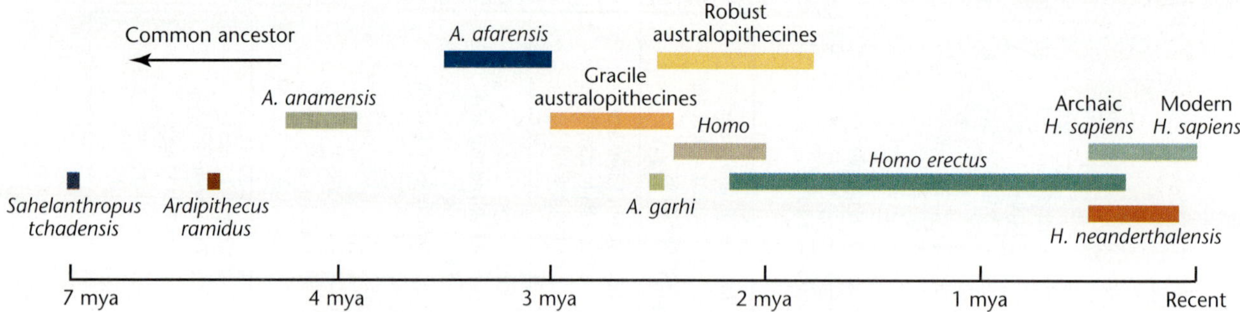

FIGURE 2.10 A highly simplified diagram showing the chronology and evolutionary status of early hominids and humans.

Notes

- Second, with so much species diversity, we have to think of punctuated equilibrium, long periods of stability, then rapid change caused by new selective pressures. Look at Figure 2.10 with this in mind.
- Third, cladistics, thinking of evolution as a bush, works well. The latest thinking, based on elaborate statistical analysis, are two main groups of hominids, the Australopithecines and *Homo habilis* and later humans like *Homo erectus* (see Chapter 3).

If you think this way, a lot of things will fall into place.

Central Places and Scavenging/Hunting

I think that the summaries of the controversies over central places and hunting are pretty easy to follow, but, again, a couple of thoughts:

Scatters of early human artifacts and food remains are very rare finds. When one comes to light, the archaeological methods used to excavate them are meticulous in the extreme. Typically, a site scatter excavation involves scientists from several disciplines, and years of painstaking laboratory work, especially on animal bones—attempts to reconstruct activities at the site.

Which brings us to Olduvai Gorge . . .

Olduvai Gorge

Olduvai Gorge has been a world famous archaeological site ever since Louis Leakey first visited it in 1931. It was dangerous, then, too. The gorge was infested with lions. Today, it's become a tourist destination with a small museum commemorating the famous Leakey discoveries here. The site's important because of its unique stratigraphy, which preserves an immensely long span of prehistoric times at one location. This is a rarity, especially with sites from earlier prehistory. Olduvai was where Leakey developed his long sequence of stone tool manufacture, beginning with crude choppers and flakes and then simple, followed by increasingly well-made hand axes, the Oldowan evolving into the more advanced Acheulian technology. Even Leakey himself pointed out that the hand axe probably developed at many locations, not necessarily at Olduvai.

At first, Louis and Mary Leakey collected stone tools from the great beds of the gorge. Then they turned to excavation of artifact scatters and kill sites, insofar as their funds permitted. Large scale investigations of individual scatters, which the Leakeys called "living floors," only began after the finding of *Zinjanthropus* in 1959. What is not generally known is that Mary Leakey did most of the excavation, for she was a far more meticulous fieldworker than Louis. She was also a gifted illustrator of stone tools and was responsible for the first monograph on the Oldowan Tradition, a standard work in the field.

It's only now, over forty years after *Zinjanthropus*, that much more refined laboratory methods have changed our perceptions of the Olduvai living floors. But we should never forget that it was the Leakeys, especially Mary, who established the basic standards for excavating these priceless sites years ago, and with practically no money into the bargain.

A shift in emphasis has come since the Leakey's day. A lot of work went into studying artifact scatters, the so-called central places, back in the 1970s and 1980s. Now the emphasis has changed to studies of entire landscapes—the ways in which early hominids used their environment and moved across it. Much of this stems from observations of scavenging by modern-day predators.

The Earliest Technology

The three drawings on page 18 cover the basics of Oldowan technology.

Mary Leakey was the pioneer researcher on the Oldowan. Alas, she is no longer with us, for she was a perceptive student of stone tools and a brilliant artist, as well as a connoisseur of fine cigars! Research into the Oldowan Tradition (named after Olduvai Gorge) has entered a new phase, with controlled experiments by Nicholas Toth and others, which have revolutionized our understanding of the earliest human technology.

We know a number of things from this new research:

- The earliest human technology was very different from that of chimpanzees, who used stones to pound nuts, and even shaped them (see the description of the "excavation" of a chimpanzee nut pounding site.)
- The first humans used quite sophisticated flaking methods from the beginning, not making choppers, as we thought a generation ago, but mining cores for flakes. These flakes were vital for cutting up meat and dismembering scavenged game animals.
- Oldowan technology was the ancestor of later human technologies. Among other things, the chopper evolved into the hand axe, a multipurpose tool flaked on both sides, which remained in use for over a million years (see Chapter 3). The flake artifacts first used by early humans also evolved into more complex knives, scrapers, and other tools.

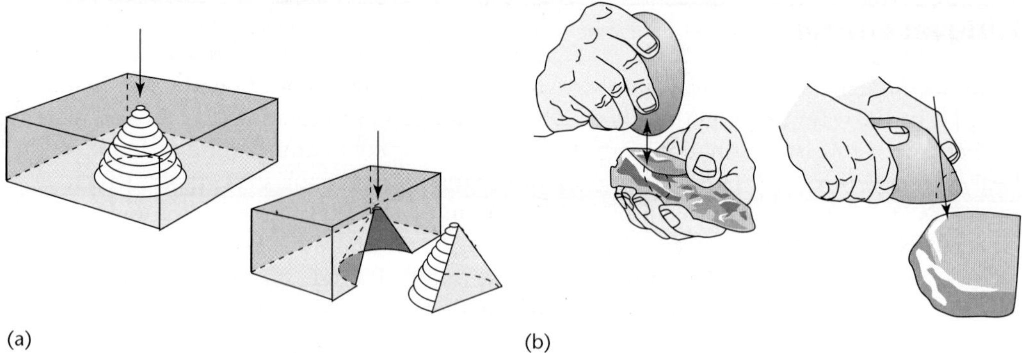

FIGURE 2.14 Early stone technology. The principles of fracturing stone were fully understood by early stoneworkers, who used them to make simple but very effective artifacts. Certain types of flinty rock will fracture in a distinctive way, as illustrated in (a). Early stoneworkers used a heavy hammerstone to remove edge flakes, or they struck lumps of rock against anvils to produce the same effect, as shown in (b). Oldowan tools were frequently made by removing a few flakes from lava lumps to form jagged working edges. Such flakes have been shown by experiment to be remarkably effective for dismembering and butchering game animals. Perhaps it is small wonder that this simple stone technology was so long-lasting. (a) When a blow is struck on flinty rock, a cone of percussion is formed by shock waves rippling through the stone (left). A flake is formed (right) when the block (or core) is hit at the edge, and the stone fractures along the edge of the ripple. (b) Using a hammerstone (left) and an anvil (right).

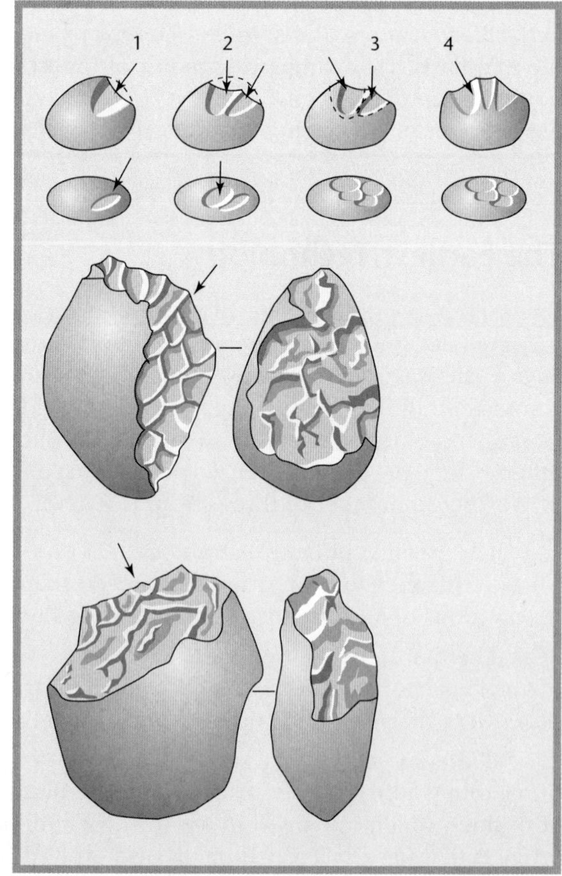

FIGURE 2.15 Oldowan technology. Many cobbles at Koobi Fora and Olduvai Gorge were used as cores to produce sharp-edged flakes. The technology was simple in the extreme. First, sharp blows were struck near the natural edge of a pebble to remove flakes. The pebble was then turned over, and more blows were struck on the ridges formed by the scars of the earlier flakes. A core with a jagged edge, perhaps used as a chopper, resulted. Many cores were "mined" for as many flakes as possible before being discarded. The figure shows Oldowan cores from Olduvai Gorge. Arrows show flake edges. Front and side views (two-fifths actual size).

Notes

Language and Mind—A Reading . . .

An enormous literature surrounds the linguistic and mental capacities of the earliest humans. Some of it is startlingly theoretical and of little scientific value, but a few studies stand out as excellent examples of science combined with good reasoning. Steven Mithen's *The Prehistory of the Mind* (1996) is a stellar example of such a work.

chapter

HOMO ERECTUS AND *HOMO SAPIENS SAPIENS*

The Chapter in Review

- This chapter covers a long period of time from about 1.9 mya to 40,000 years ago.
- We describe the climatic events of the Great Ice Age (the Pleistocene) between about 1.6 million and 128,000 years ago. These complex fluctuations between glacial maxima and much shorter interglacial periods were the backdrop to the evolution not only of *Homo erectus,* but of modern humans—*H. sapiens sapiens*—as well.
- *Homo erectus* had evolved from earlier *Homo* in tropical Africa by 1.9 million years ago, then radiated into Europe and Asia as part of a general radiation of mammalian species soon afterward. The earliest date of this radiation may be as early as 1.8 million years ago, but the chronology is controversial.
- Sometime after 1.8 million years ago, humans domesticated fire, but the date is much debated.
- The new humans used a simple technology based on hand axes and basic flake technology in the west, relying heavily on bamboo and other forest products in Southeast Asia.
- There was a gradual increase in brain size, perhaps beginning as early as about 0.4 million years ago, as archaic forms of *H. sapiens* with enlarged brain capacities evolved in various parts of the Old World.
- The best known of these forms are the Neanderthals of Europe and Eurasia, who developed more sophisticated tool-making technology than *Homo erectus,* were more adept hunters and foragers, and were the first humans to bury some of their dead.
- Two competing theories account for the appearance of anatomically modern humans. The multiregional hypothesis for modern human origins has it that modern humans developed independently in Africa, Europe, and Asia, and that the biological diversity of contemporary humankind has very deep roots in prehistory.
- The Out-of-Africa hypothesis argues that modern humans evolved in tropical Africa before 100,000 years ago, then spread into other parts of the world from Southwest Asia after 45,000 years ago (see Chapter 4).
- The long delay in this later spread is thought by some to be attributable to the later evolution of the full cognitive abilities of modern humans.
- With the appearance of modern humans, the long prehistory of the archaic world ends.

General Key Terms: Lower, Middle, and Upper Paleolithic

First, a widely used term—**Paleolithic,** meaning Old Stone Age after the Greek *paleos,* "old," and *lithos,* "stone." Conventionally, the Paleolithic is divided into three broad stages, each defined by technology:

Lower Paleolithic: From the origins of humans to the end of the Acheulian. Simple hammerstone and bone flaking technologies.
Middle Paleolithic: Covers prepared core techniques, like those associated with archaic *Homo sapiens* and the Neanderthals, and described in this chapter.
Upper Paleolithic: The blade technologies of modern humans.

These three subdivisions are still used in a generic sense, as they are in this book. Like the Three Ages described in Chapter 1, they have little significance these days, except as convenient labels. (Just so you know what we are talking about.)

Key Cultures and Sites

Acheulian culture
Atapuerca
Ban Mae Tha
Bouri
Boxgrove
Chesowanya
Clacton
Combe Grenal
Dmanisi
es-Skhul
et-Tabun
Gran Dolina
Hahnofersand
Kapthurin
Klasies River Cave
Kow Swamp
Krapina
La Ferrassie
Lang Trang
Lant'ien
Lehringen
Longgupo
Long Rongrien
Mauer
Mojokerto
Mousterian (Le Moustier)
Nariokotome
Narmada
Niah Cave
Omo Kibish
Q'en-Xia-wo
San Césaire
Sangiran
Schoningen
Shanidar
Sima de los Huesos
Swartkrans
Tautaval
Teshik-Tash
Torralba-Ambrona
Trinil
Ubeidiya
Vertésszöllös
Zhoukoudian

Introductory Comments

Chapter 3 covers nearly two million years of the past, from the first appearance of *Homo erectus* in tropical Africa to the moment when anatomically modern humans—ourselves—spread out of southwestern Asia into Europe some 45,000 years ago.

These two million years span the later history of what we call the archaic world, when the predecessors of *Homo sapiens sapiens* appeared in Africa, then radiated over much of Asia and Europe, but not very far into northern regions of the world. Nor did they settle in the Americas.

We describe two critically important developments in this chapter:

- The first appearance of *Homo erectus* in East Africa, and its subsequent radiation across the Sahara into other parts of the world;
- The emergence of modern humans after 150,000 years ago, probably also in Africa.

Controversy surrounds both of these major events, for our understanding of both is based on a very inadequate fossil record, and on little more than thousands of stone artifacts, distributed from South Africa's Cape of Good Hope to Europe and deep into East and Southeast Asia. In fact, Australopithecine fossils are more numerous than those of the elusive and probably diverse *Homo erectus.*

Whereas most of what we know about *H. erectus* comes from fossils and artifacts, a new player comes on the stage with the advent of molecular biology, and particularly mitochondrial DNA—DNA inherited through the female line. But the origins of modern humans pits those who believe that we emerged in tropical Africa against an opposing school of thought, who argue that we evolved from ancestral *Homo erectus* populations in several parts of the world.

Chapter 3 is set on a much wider stage than the previous one, which was confined to Africa. By about 1.6 million years ago, archaic humans, in the form of *Homo erectus,* had spread from Africa into Southeast Asia, and probably China. By at least 800,000 years ago, there were also archaic humans in Europe.

How do we achieve these chronologies? In most cases, the dates come from potassium-argon tests, although paleoanthropologists also rely on paleomagnetism and other lesser known methods. By the standards of later dating methods, they are at best statistical approximations, but they do give some chronological perspective to a world where little happened, and what did happen happened very slowly.

For convenience, I divide this discussion into two large parts, first dealing with *Homo erectus,* then with modern humans. Once again, I followed Alice in Wonderland, and began at the beginning, 2 million years ago, before progressing gradually through time. But think of this chapter as a branching tree, with the trunk as the main thrust of the narrative, and the branches as side tracks that bear on the central story. The sections on the domestication of fire and technology are good examples.

- We begin by introducing the Pleistocene, or Great Ice Age, the ever-changing scenery for our play. We point out that the earth's climate has been in a constant state of transition for the past three quarters of a million years, alternating between periods of extreme cold and shorter warmer intervals. It's important that you think of global climate as always changing, never constant. And, for your information, despite the reality of humanly-caused global warming, we are still in a warm period of Ice Age! Trust me! One day the world will get cold again, even if human activity modifies the effects somewhat!

- Next, we survey what little is known from East Africa of the evolution of *Homo erectus* from earlier *Homo* (perhaps *Homo habilis*). We also survey the general anatomical and behavioral characteristics of the new humans.

- At some point, perhaps about 1.8 to 1.5 mya, *Homo erectus* radiated out of Africa into Asia, and perhaps into eastern Eurasia, as part of general mammalian movements at the time. We point out that how and why this happened is a mystery.

- A branch of our narrative tree now comes along, as we discuss what little is known about the domestication of fire, one of the most important innovations in human life. As you will see, we do not really know when this first happened.

- Now we move to Southeast Asia and China and look at what we know about the first human inhabitants of those regions. We look at them in the context of a simple technology that may have relied heavily on bamboo and wood.

- Then we examine the controversies surrounding the first settlement of Europe, which may not have taken hold until some 800,000 years ago.

- We end our coverage of *Homo erectus* with a look at Acheulian hand axe technology and the evidence for big-game hunting, and also the linguistic abilities of these archaic humans.

- Finally, we describe the famous Neanderthals of western Europe and Eurasia, tough, cold-adapted hunter-gatherers descended from the earliest Europeans.

You Should Now Start Reading . . . *Homo erectus*

The narrative on *H. erectus* covers a lot of quite complex ground, and, again, I am sure that your instructor will amplify the story. But here are some additional points and commentary:

Figure 3.1 encapsulates the Ice Age in simple terms.

In Figure 3.1a, we display the constant shifts of Ice Age climate since the Matuyama/Brunhes boundary of about 780,000 years ago. Look at the jagged line, which documents the shifts from warm to cold and back again. This curve is reconstructed from fluctuations in the frequencies of sea-temperature sensitive diatoms and is remarkably accurate, considering the ages involved. Deep sea cores are proving very effective for studying more recent climate change. In Southern California's Santa Barbara Channel, they actually have a 3,000 year core that provides accuracies in the order of 100 years or less. This means that you can study the impact of short-term climatic change on nearby human societies—very useful! However, this Ice Age curve gives just a general impression of the changing world of human prehistory.

FIGURE 3.1a Climatic events of the Pleistocene. Stratigraphic record of the Pleistocene from deep-sea core V28-238, from the Solomon Plateau in the Pacific Ocean (Shackleton and Opdyke, 1983). The Matuyama-Brunhes boundary occurs at about 780,000 years ago, at a depth of 1200 cm (39.3 feet). Above it, a sawtoothlike curve records the relative size of the world's oceans and ice caps and identifies eight complete glacial and interglacial cycles, a more complete record of the Middle and Upper Pleistocene than comes from land sediments. The Vostok ice core from Antarctica covers the past 335,000 years and documents a periodicity of about 100,000 years for transitions from cold to warm conditions.

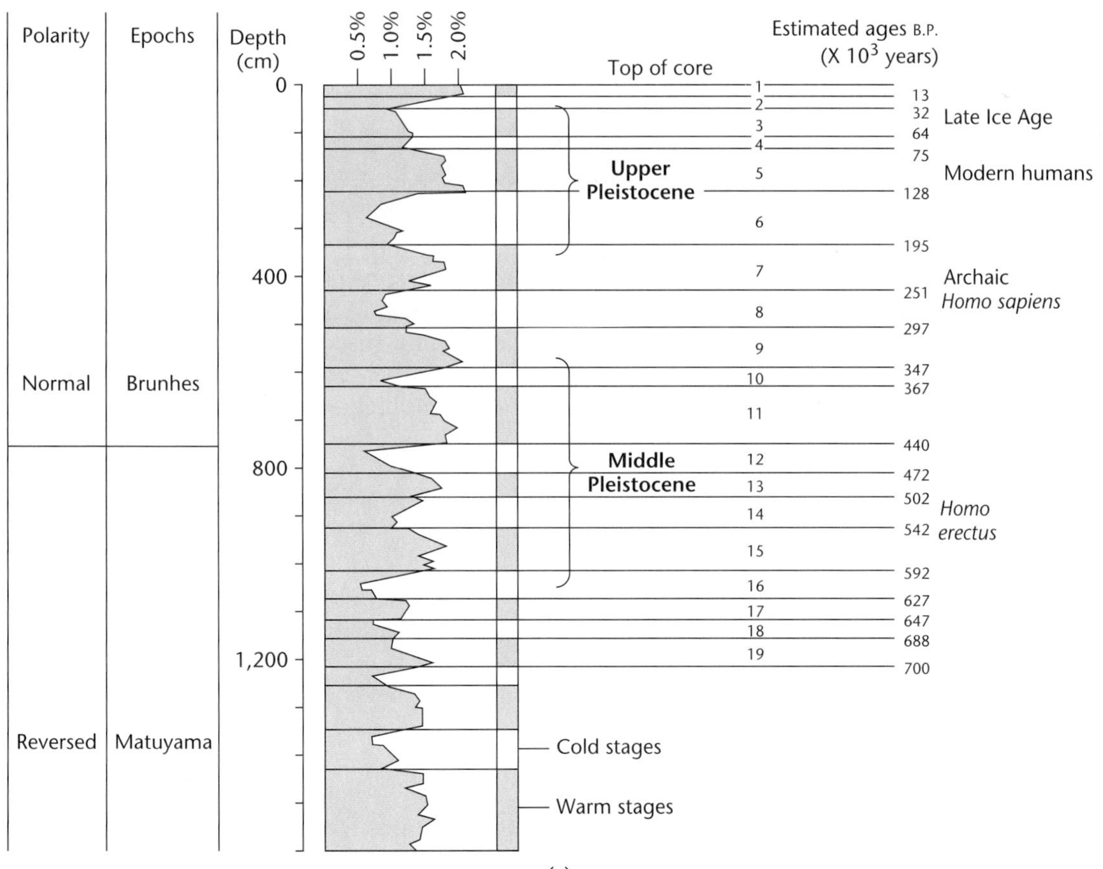

FIGURE 3.1b Pleistocene glaciers in the Northern Hemisphere at their maximum extent. Shorelines caused by low sea levels are not known.

Figure 3.1b plots the extent of the vast ice sheets that mantled the northern hemisphere at the height of cold intervals during the Ice Age. This diagram shows how much of the northern world was covered with deep ice sheets as recently as 15,000 years ago. Northern North America was effectively covered with ice and uninhabitable for long periods of time, an important factor in studying the first Americans (see Chapter 5). It's worth taking a close look at the distribution of ice sheets here: we refer to this constantly later on in the book.

And now the Chronological Table. This one is a biggie, which spans four continents and 1.3 million years, starting with the radiation of *Homo erectus* out of Africa. Again, take a little time to study this, for it incorporates key sites, which are the signposts in the chapter narrative. Notice that by three quarters of a million years ago, humans are active on all continents. Again a Post-it might be helpful for later reference.

Please note that the Chronological Tables in this book are cumulative, which is another good reason for a series of Post-its, so you can find them. Some ambitious souls Xerox all of them and put them up on a bulletin board or some other suitable surface, just like I did when writing the book.

This is a site map and entirely straightforward. Note that Neanderthal sites are the subject of a separate map (Figure 3.16).

Some Thoughts on *Homo erectus*

Inevitably, things are more complicated than they seem. For years, scientists described *Homo erectus* as a single human species, which varied somewhat through time and

TABLE 3.1
***Homo erectus* and early modern humans**

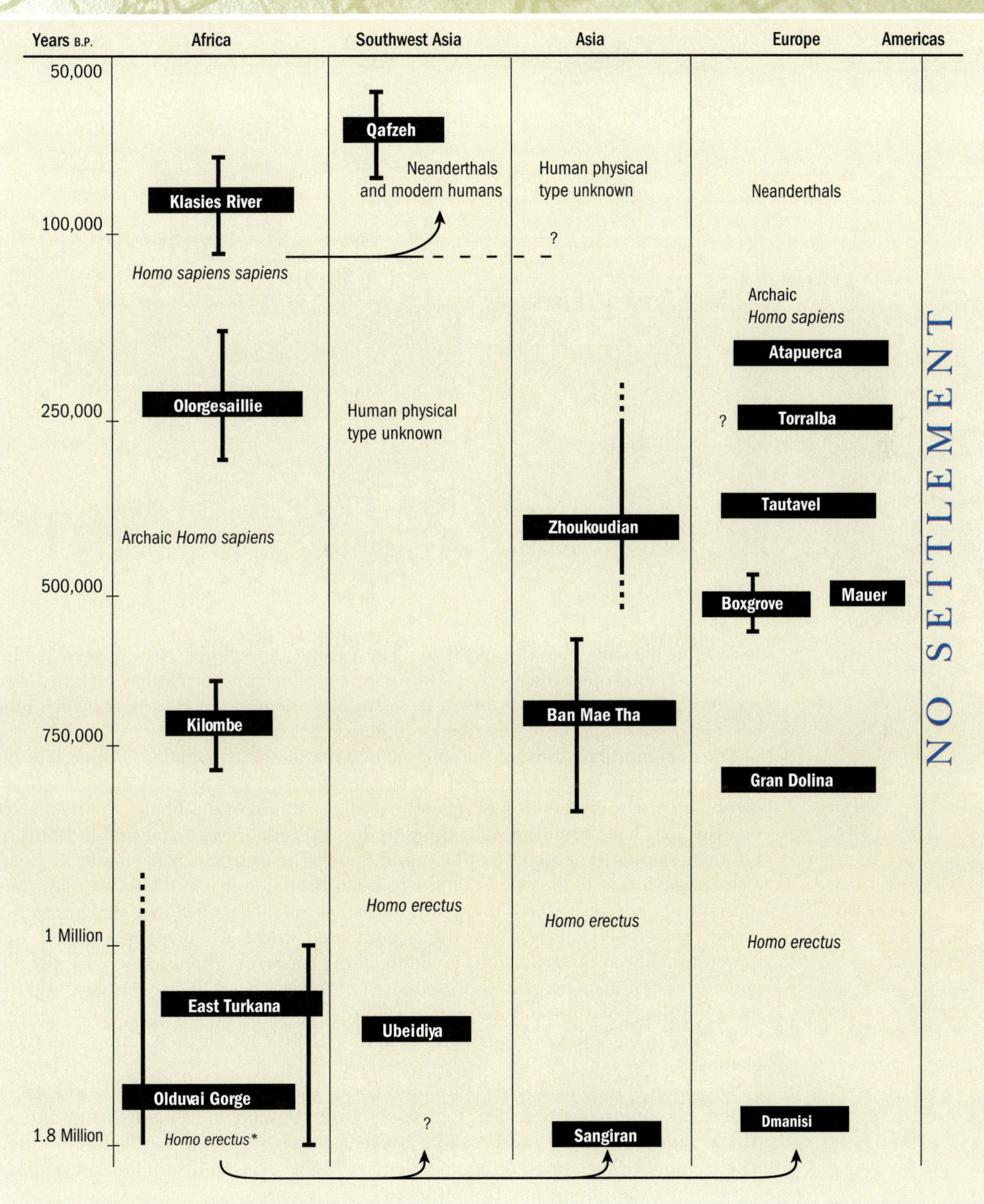

* The term *Homo erectus* is used generically here.

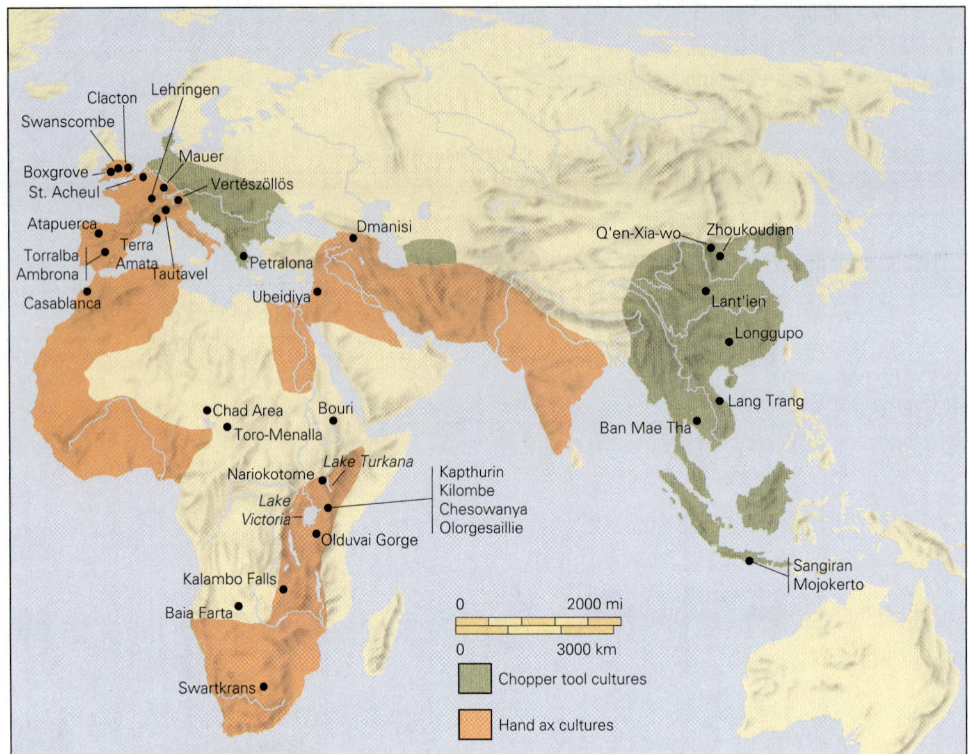

FIGURE 3.2 Archaeological sites mentioned in this chapter. (For Neanderthal sites, see Figure 3.16.)

space, but basically was a single form. Then came the splitters, as opposed to the lumpers. They proposed several new forms, one of which was the earliest African *Homo erectus,* known from Nariokotome in West Turkana, Kenya, and elsewhere, which now became *Homo ergaster* (and described in the text).

The anatomical reasons for the split seemed reasonably convincing, although by no means every expert was convinced. In fact, I went so far as to keep the term *Homo erectus* for the (brief) mention of *ergaster* in earlier editions of this book. Now it appears that this may have been the right thing to do. A recent *Homo erectus* find at Bouri in Ethiopia, dating to between a million and 800,000 years ago is very similar to Asian *Homo erectus* forms, to the point that the paleoanthropologist Tim White, among other specialists, is now disinclined to use the *Homo ergaster* label at all. So we are back with a single *Homo erectus* species, in a thinly populated world, where people ebbed and flowed in and out of Africa, interbreeding along the way—which led to basically the same form of human over an enormous area of the world a million years ago, and for some hundreds of thousands of years afterward.

It's nice to be right sometimes, and to have a simpler, rather than a more complex, picture!

This map shows, in grossly simplified form, the radiation of *Homo erectus* from Africa. It's important to realize that there were constant movements from and to Africa, with subsequent interbreeding between widely scattered populations—which may account for the apparent homogeneity of *H. erectus* around a million years ago—witness the recent Bouri find from Ethiopia.

Unfortunately, Zhoukoudian was almost completely dug out, so there is no way to check the early findings. Modern thinking believes it was more of a sink hole than an occupation site. The chopping tool in Figure 3.6b is typical of the crude stone artifacts used by many Asian groups relying on wooden artifacts.

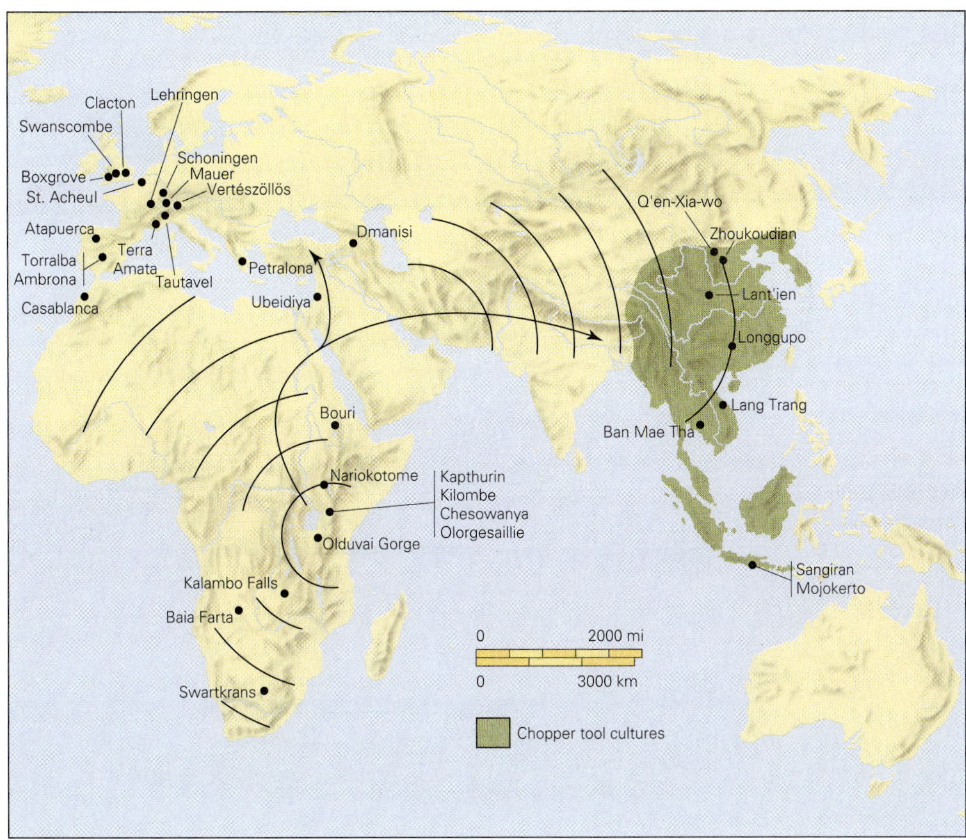

FIGURE 3.4 The radiation of *Homo erectus*. Map shows key sites and the major technological provinces of the world of *H. erectus*. The radiating lines are meant to give an impression of radiation outward from tropical Africa. A recent fossil discovery of *H. erectus* in Ethiopia dating to 1 mya strongly suggests that there was movement both in and out of Africa after the initial radiation.

Notes

The First Settlement of Europe and the Neanderthals

From Asia, we turn to the first settlement of Europe, a highly controversial subject. I've taken a pretty conservative position here, and argued for somewhere around 800,000 years ago in the west. The Dmanisi find in Georgia puts humans in Eurasia by 1.7 mya, as if settlement came from the east as well as the southeast. We need many more finds before we can even begin to solve this problem.

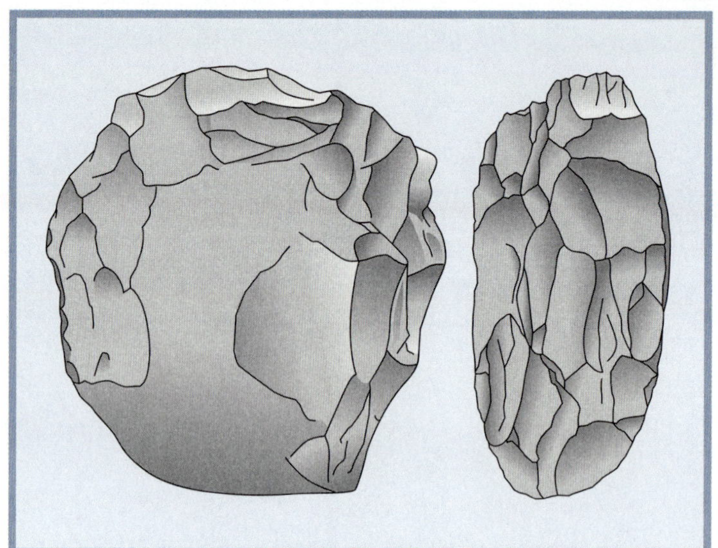

FIGURE 3.6b A crude chopping tool from Zhoukoudian, front and side views (one-half actual size).

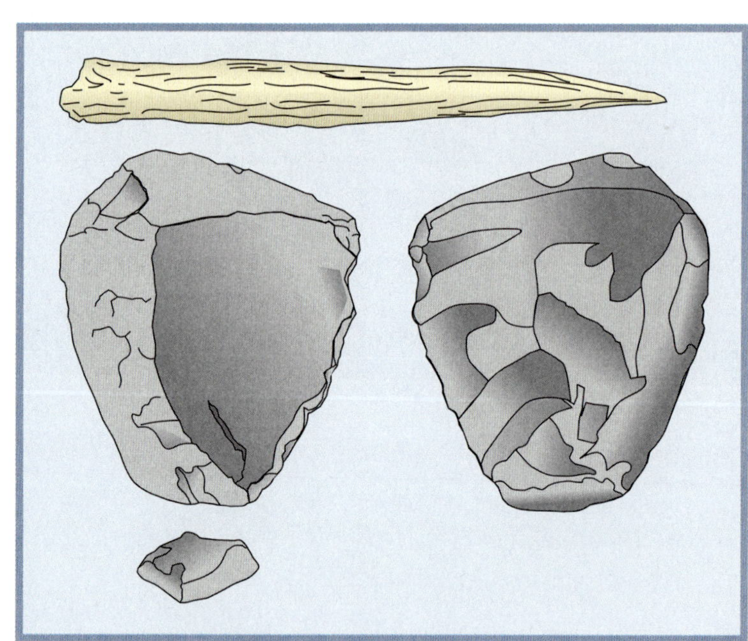

FIGURE 3.9 European wood and stone tools. Top, a wooden spear tip from Clacton, England, dating to about 200,000 years ago (approximately one-eighth full size). Bottom, views of a flake from the same location. The upper surface is shown at the left, the flake (lower) surface on the right. The striking platform is at the base (one-third actual size).

We know a great deal more about the technology used by the first Europeans, thanks to numerous stone axe finds from large river valleys. There are some wooden artifacts, too. I was unable to find a photograph of the Schoningen spears (see text), but here is one of the tip of a wooden spear found with some simple flakes in eastern England three quarters of a century ago. It is obviously part of a longer weapon. Judging from the Schoningen spears, hunters used long throwing weapons, which must have been surprisingly effective. But you would have to have been an expert stalker to get close enough to kill or wound even a small animal. Spears have a very limited range.

Thousands, if not millions, of stones write the early chapters of human prehistory, simply because they are the most durable of all finds. These three drawings tell the story of what is called Acheulian technology. Study them carefully, as we will ask you to compare later technologies with them down the line.

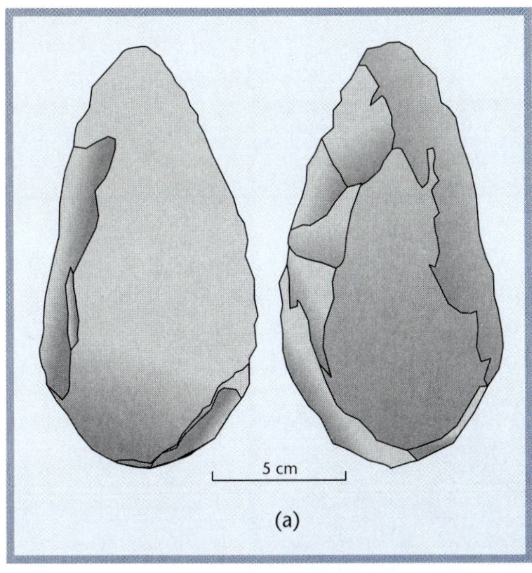

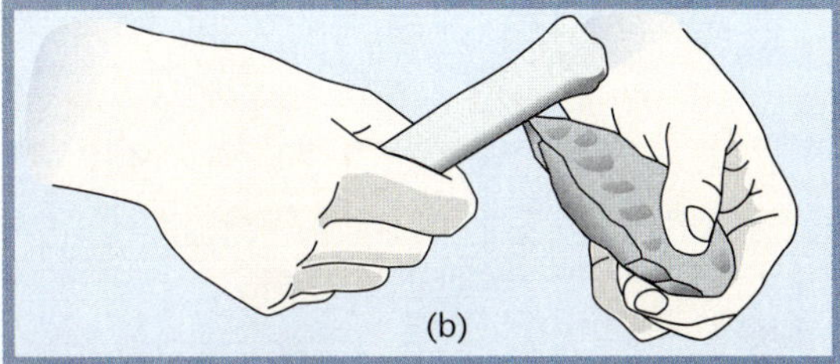

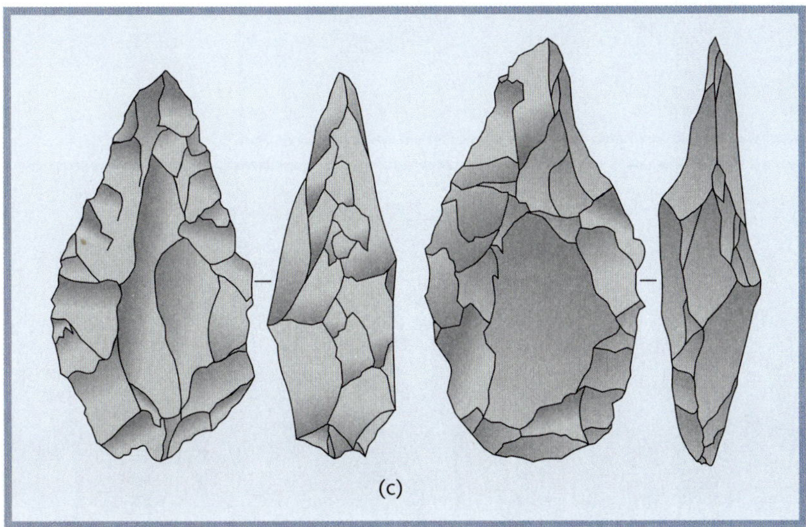

FIGURE 3.10 Acheulian technology. Hand axes were multipurpose artifacts that were shaped symmetrically around a long axis. (a) As the hand axe from Kilombe, Kenya, of 700,000 years ago shows, the stoneworker would sometimes use a minimum of blows with a simple hammerstone to achieve the desired shape. (b) Sometimes a hammer made of animal bone served to strike off the shallower flakes that adorn the margins of these tools.

Later hand axes assume many forms, among them the finely pointed shape in (c), which shows front and side views of two early hand axes from Bed II, Olduvai Gorge, Tanzania (three-quarters actual size). As time went on, the stoneworkers used carefully prepared cores to fashion large flakes that served as blanks for axes and other artifacts. They also produced flakes that were used as opportunistic artifacts, for woodworking and for many other purposes.

Notes

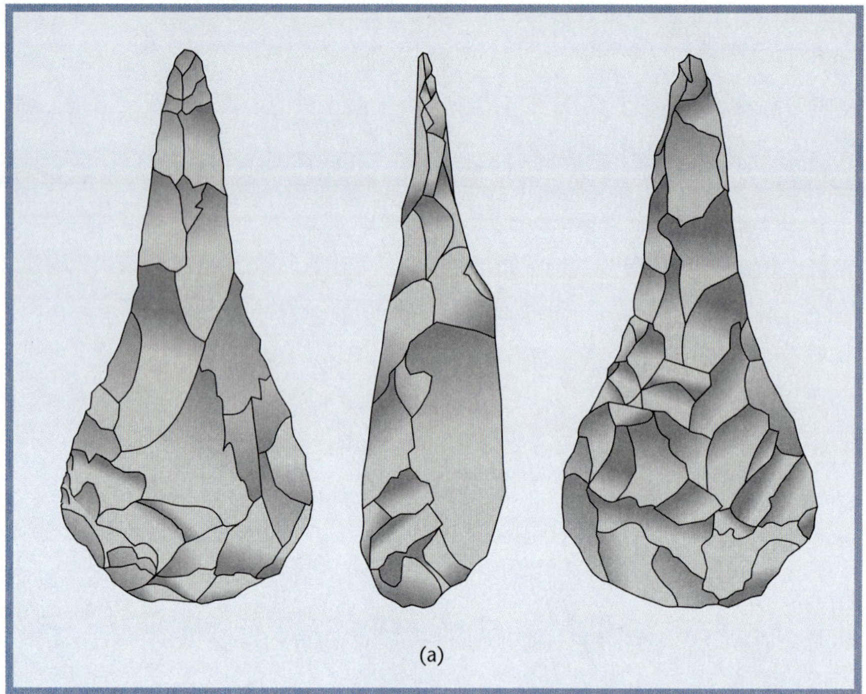

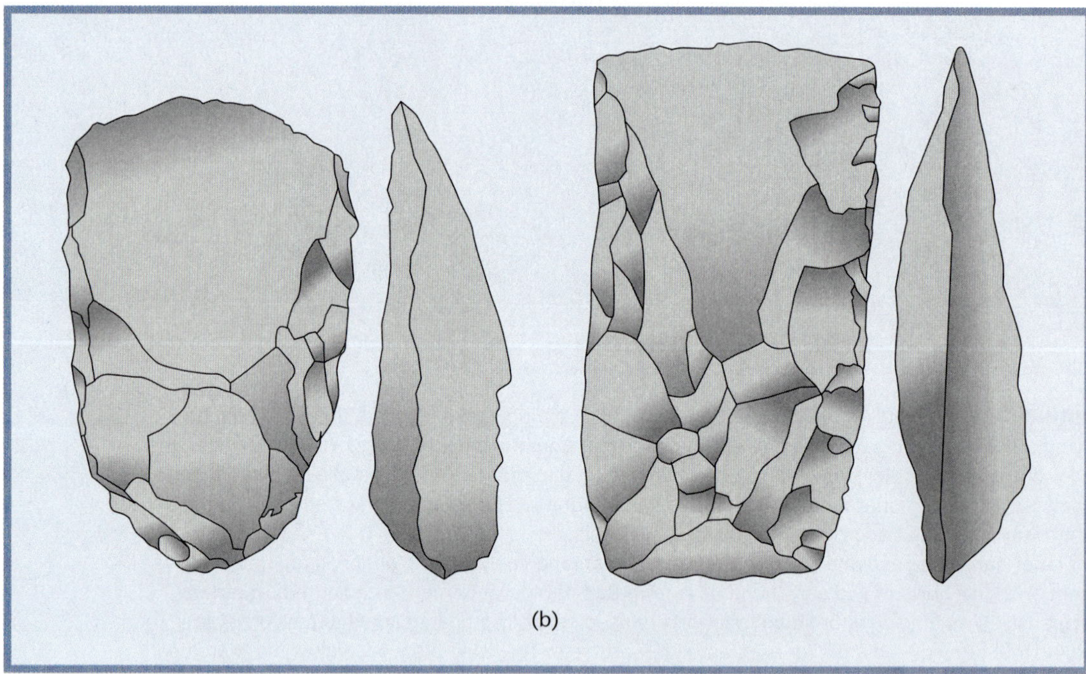

FIGURE 3.11 Hand axe technology. (a) Acheulian hand axe from Swanscombe, England (one-third actual size). (b) Two Acheulian cleavers, from Baia Farta, Angola (left), and Kalambo Falls, Zambia (right) (both one-half actual size). Cleavers are thought to have been butchering tools, artifacts with a single unfinished edge that modern experiments have proved effective in skinning and dismembering game.

Notes

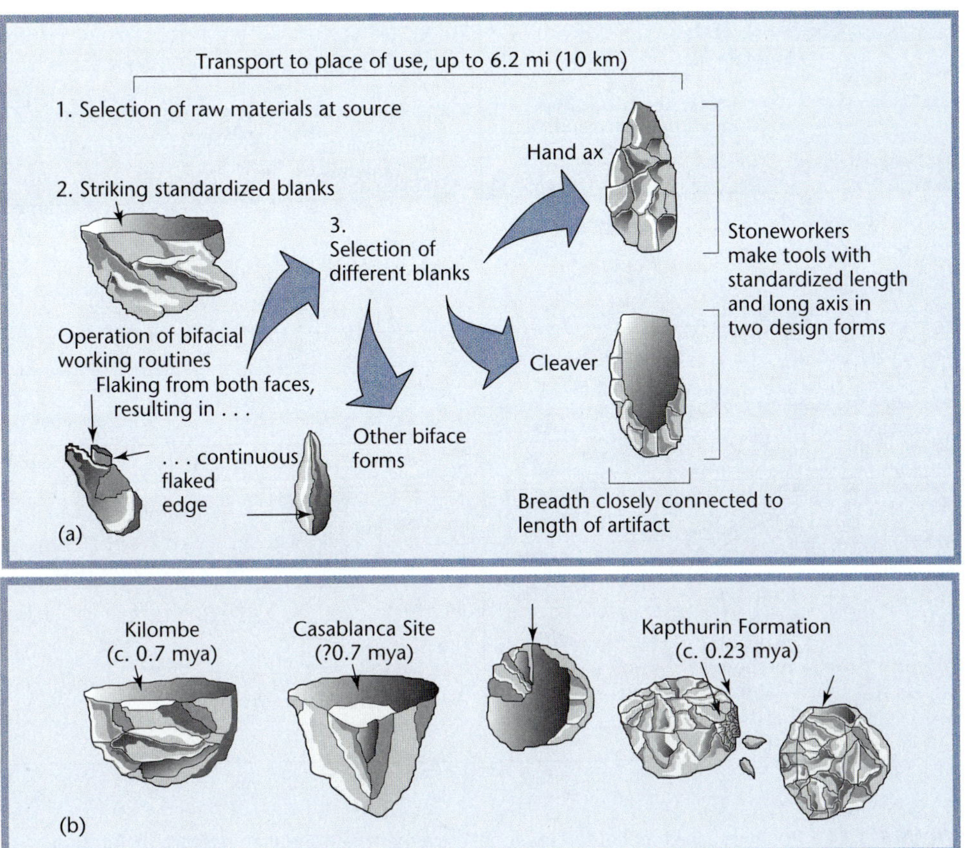

FIGURE 3.12 Making Acheulian bifaces. (a) The axe-making process used about a million years ago. (b) Early and late methods. The simple flaking process of 700,000 years ago (left), used in East and North Africa, compares with the expertise of the stoneworkers at Kapthurin, Kenya, 230,000 years ago (right). They prepared elaborately shaped cores to create flakes about 16 cm (6 inches) long as hand axe blanks.

Notes

Boxgrove

Boxgrove is important because it documents hunting methods some 500,000 years ago. The Boxgrove site may be the smoking gun, which shows that *Homo erectus* or archaic *Homo sapiens* was capable of hunting large animals. To hunt any animal on foot armed merely with a spear requires great skill, not only in aiming and thrusting a weapon, but in stalking. You would literally have to be able to touch the animal to inflict a fatal wound. This may be why the Boxgrove people preyed on animals at a waterhole, perhaps driving their quarry over the nearby cliff. Unless one rendered the animal helpless by enmiring it (as may have been the case at Torralba), driving it over a cliff, or using a deep pit as a trap, the chances of killing a beast of any size were small indeed.

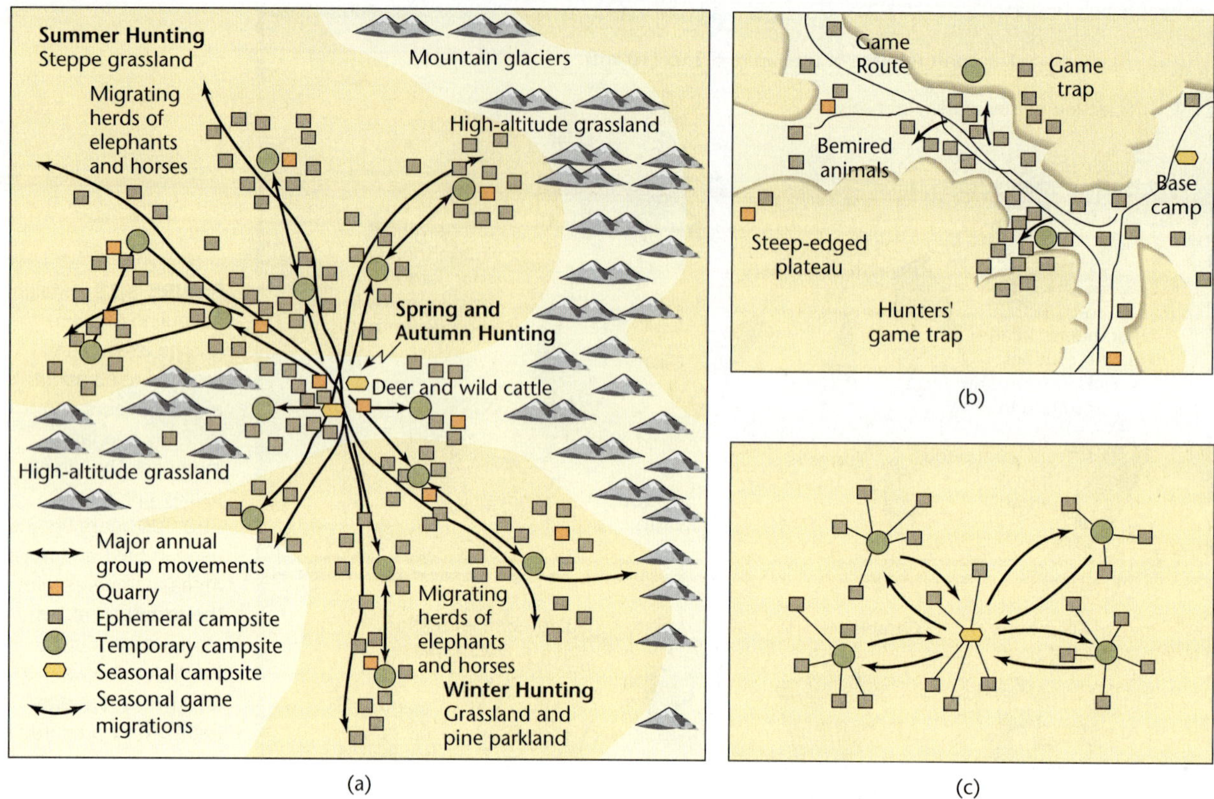

FIGURE 3.14 Reconstructed model for seasonal movement by Acheulian hunters at Torralba-Ambrona, Spain. (a) Interception of migrating animals in spring and fall. (b) Use of topography to secure game. (c) Schematic model of how the populations moved. The reconstructions were based on information recovered from excavations (Butzer, 1982).

Nothing much more to say about Figure 3.14, beyond remarking that this painstakingly reconstructed model is probably the best interpretation of a site where people may have actually just come across stranded elephants and killed them. At this time range, we cannot be sure, because so much of the hunt is intangible.

Figure 3.16 is self-evident, but it's important to get the distribution of Neanderthals into your mind.

Figure 3.17 simply gives an impression of the variation in Neanderthal anatomy. The point: not all Neanderthals were squat, beetle-browed, and adapted to extreme cold.

The useful side-by-side comparison of a Neanderthal and modern human shown in Figure 3.18 is a good way to study the salient features of the former for a test!

Figure 3.19 shows the increasing efficiency of human stone technology, the prepared core techniques used by Neanderthals, and a selection of the artifacts. For an exercise, compare and contrast this technology with the Acheulian equivalent (Figures 3.10 to 3.12). Again, this is good test studying material. If you are lucky, your instructor may demonstrate stone tool making (a surprising number of archaeologists know the basics). However, I wager he or she will not be able to make Levallois or disc cores. It's hard. All I acquire is cut fingers!

Modern Human Origins

Now we really enter a controversial arena, where scientist is pitted against scientist in an often passionate debate over a small collection of fossils. In recent years, molecular biology has really changed the landscape.

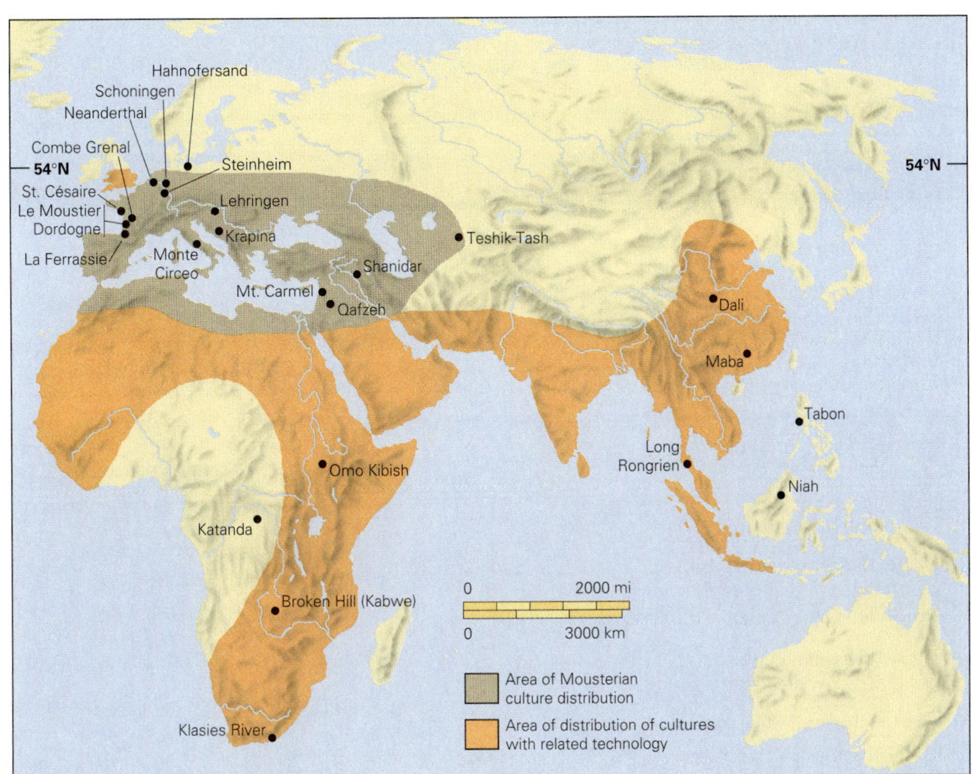

FIGURE 3.16 Distribution of the Neanderthals, their culture, and related technologies. Also shown are sites mentioned in the remainder of Chapter 3.

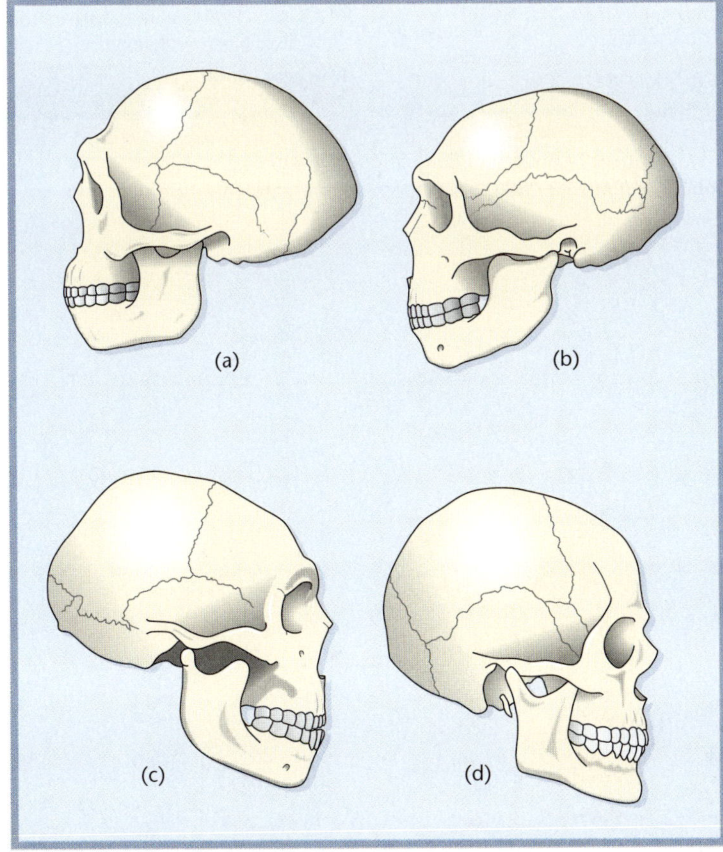

FIGURE 3.17 Comparisons of four fossil skulls and jaws. (a) The reconstructed skull has prominent brow ridges, a bun-shaped rear to the cranium, and a retreating chin. (b) A "classic" Neanderthal skull found at Monte Circeo, Italy, still has well-marked brow ridges and a bun-shaped cranium but an increased brain capacity. The skull is lower and flatter than those of modern humans, and the jaw is chinless. (c) The Shanidar Neanderthal from Iraq is a less extreme example, with a higher forehead, somewhat reduced brow ridges, and a much more rounded skull. (d) A modern skull, with well-rounded contours, no brow ridges, a high forehead, and a well-marked chin.

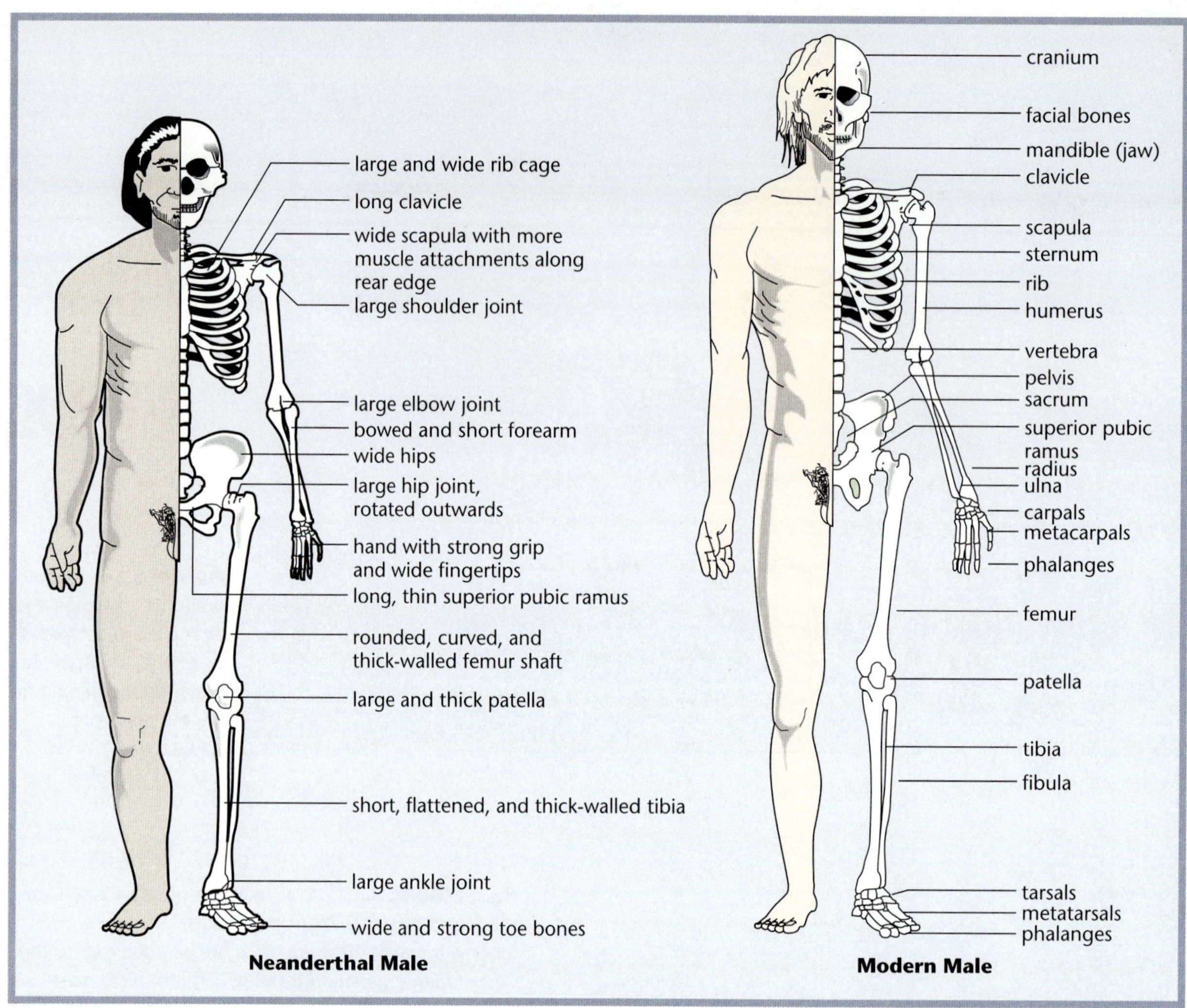

FIGURE 3.18 The skeleton of a male Neanderthal (left) compared with that of a modern male. The Neanderthal is more robust and stockier than his modern counterpart. (After Stringer and Gamble, 1993.)

Notes

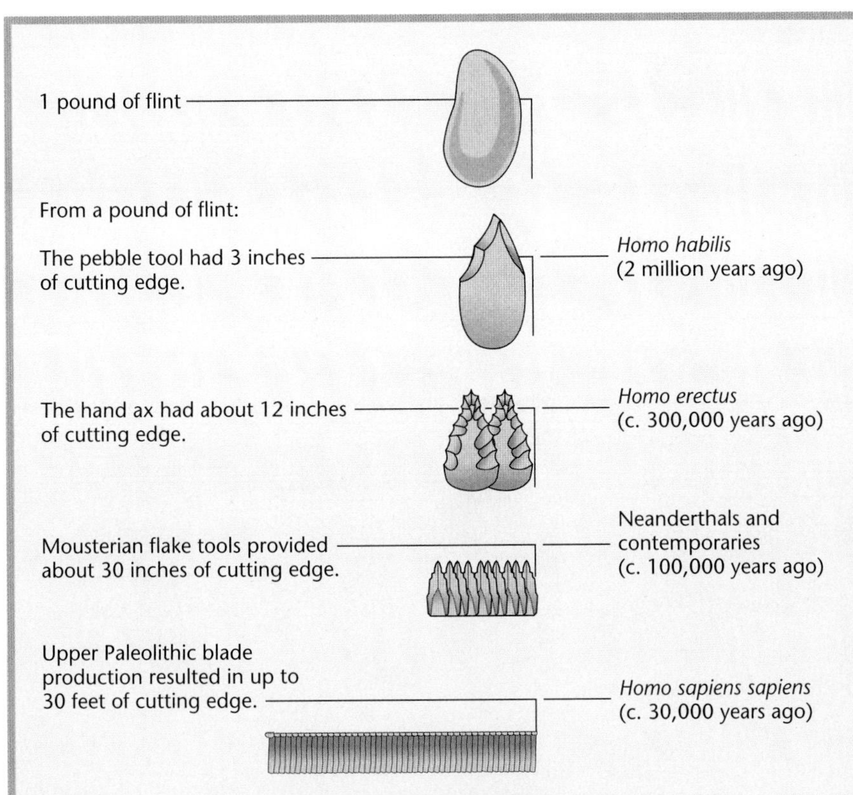

FIGURE 3.19 The growing efficiency of Stone Age technology is shown by the ability of ancient stoneworkers to produce ever-larger numbers of cutting edges from a pound of flint or other fine-grained rock. The Neanderthals were far more efficient stone artisans than their predecessors. By the same token, *H. sapiens sapiens* used a blade technology (see Figure 4.4), which produced up to 9.1 m (30 feet) of blades per pound of flint.

Notes

This is the first moment in prehistory where we see a synthesis emerging between archaeology, genetics, and paleontology, with the genetics suggesting a possible model for where and how modern humans originated and dispersed through the world. There are other, even more elaborate syntheses to follow, which meld archaeology, human biology, genetics, and the history of languages, but this is the first, and arguably most important.

Here's how I tell the story:

- First, we describe the two competing models: the Multiregional hypothesis and the Out-of-Africa theory.

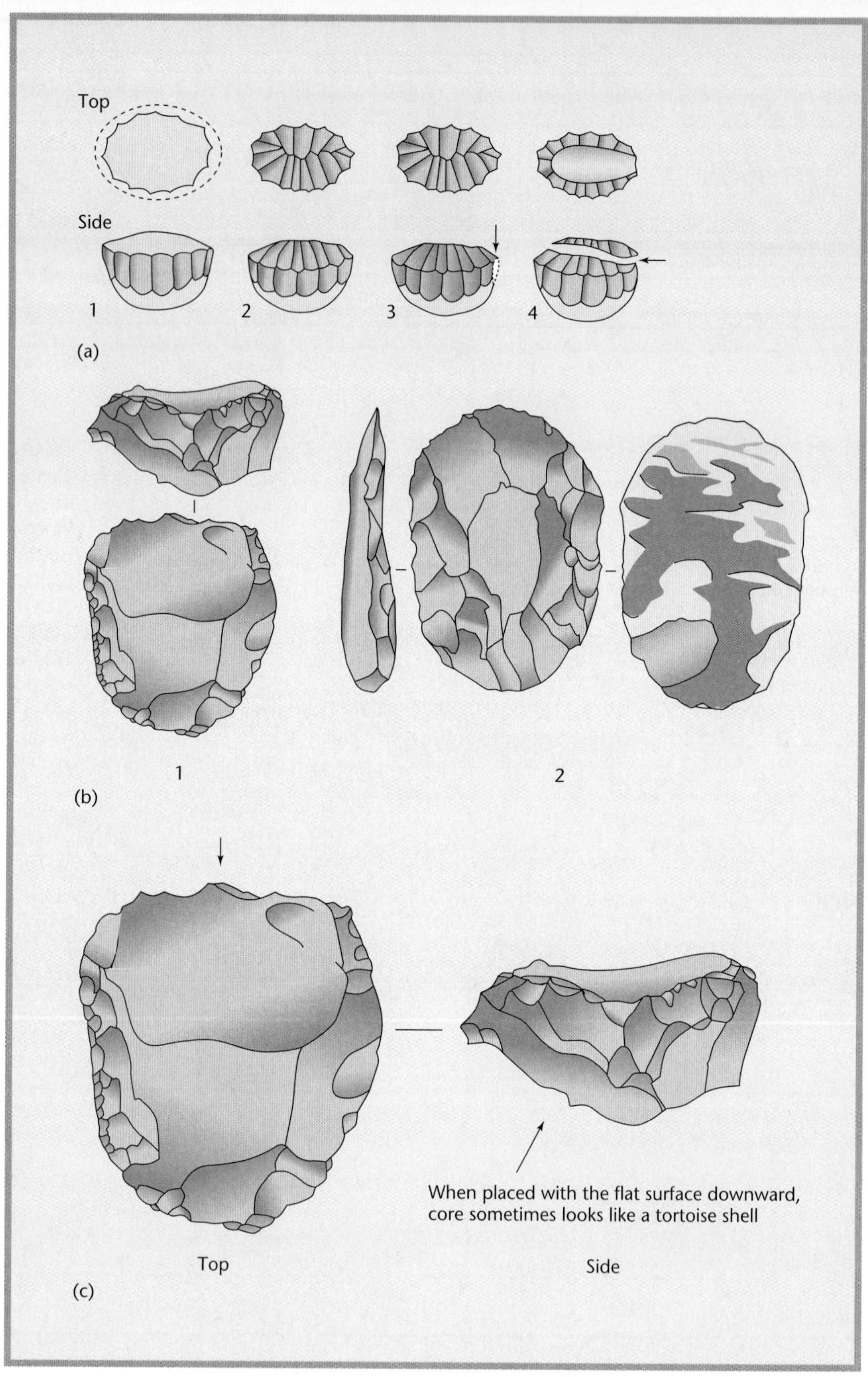

FIGURE 3.20 Prepared-core techniques. Prepared cores were carefully flaked to enable the toolmaker to strike off large flakes of predetermined size. The Levallois technique meant that the stoneworker would shape a lump of flint into an inverted bun-shaped core (often compared to an inverted tortoise shell). The flat upper surface was struck at one end, the resulting flake forming the only product from the core. Another form was the disk core, a prepared core from which several flakes of predetermined size and shape were removed. The core gradually became smaller, until it resembled a flat disk. Disk cores were often used to produce points and scrapers. (a) Making a Levallois core: (1) The edges of a suitable stone are trimmed; (2) the top surface is trimmed; (3) a striking platform, the point where the flake will originate, is made by trimming to form a straight edge on the side; (4) a flake is struck from the core and removed. (b) (1) A Levallois core from the Thames Valley, England, with a view of the top of the core (top left) and the resulting flake (2). (c) When placed with the flat surface downward, the core sometimes looks like a tortoise shell. One-half actual size.

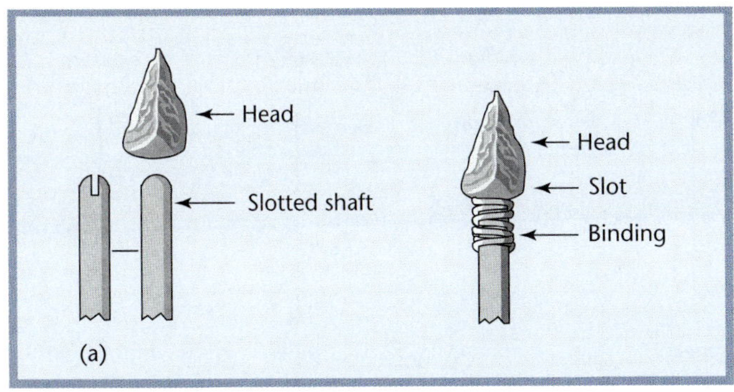

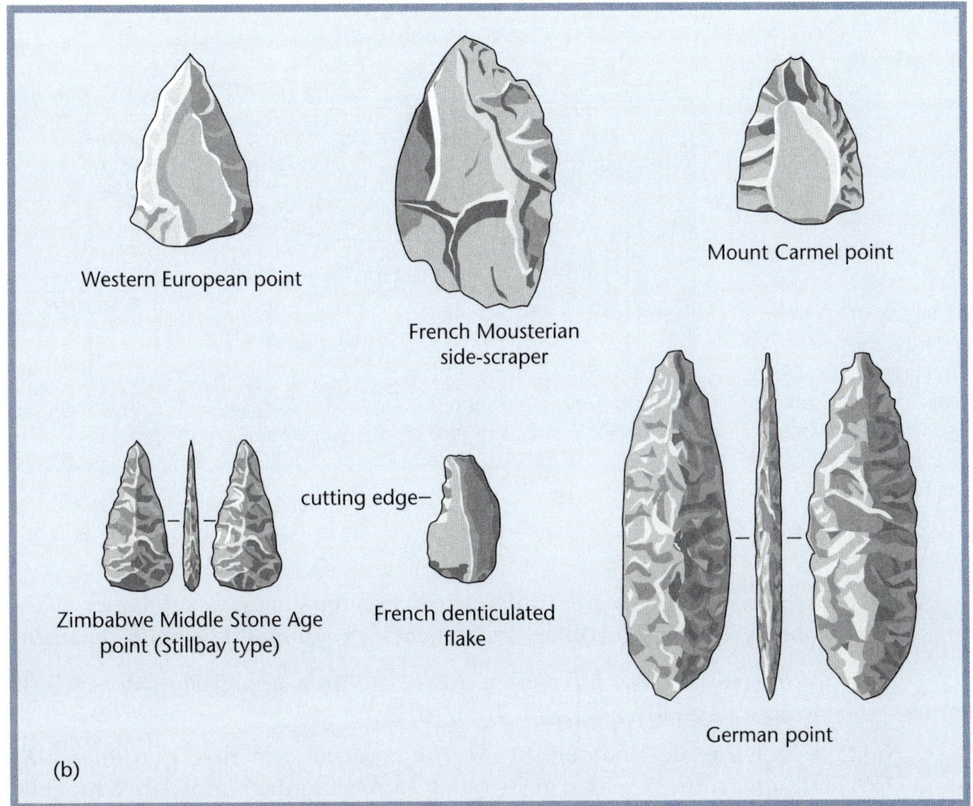

FIGURE 3.21 Middle Paleolithic tools and technology. This technology was based on simple stone techniques that were used for tens of thousands of years before the emergence of early *Homo sapiens*. By 100,000 years ago, artifacts of many types were of composite form, that is, made from several different parts. A wooden spear might have a stone tip, a flint scraper a bone handle. Unfortunately, we know almost nothing about the bone and wood tools used. (a) Stone-tipped Mousterian spear (a hypothetical example). The spear was made from a pointed stone head attached to a wooden handle to form the projectile. The head probably fitted into a slot in the wooden shaft and was fixed to it with resin or beeswax; a binding was added to the end of the shaft. (b) Mousterian artifacts.

Notes

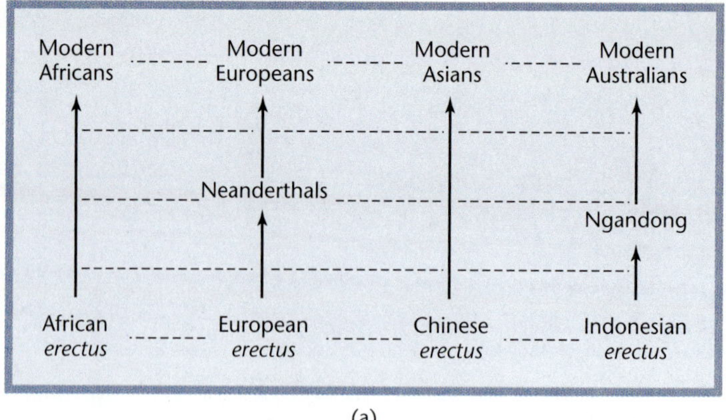

(a)

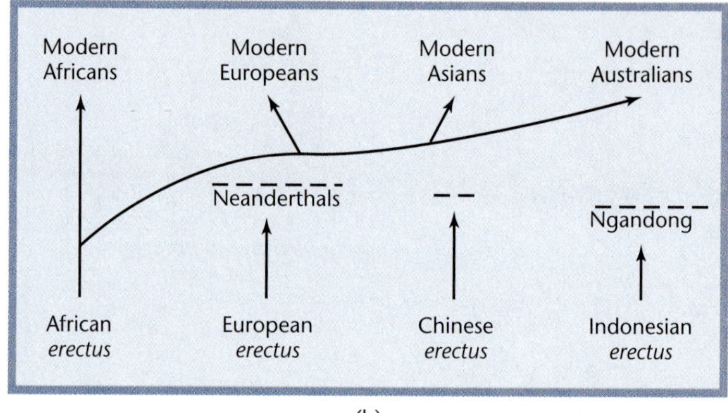

(b)

FIGURE 3.22 Theories of the origins of modern humans, each of which interprets the fossil evidence in very different ways. (a) The multiregional model, which argues for the evolution of *H. sapiens sapiens* in many regions of the world. (b) The out-of-Africa model, which has modern humanity evolving in Africa, then spreading to other parts of the world.

As this figure shows, there is a great difference between them. As we emphasize in the text, the two models represent extremes. Indeed, their proponents are highly polarized.

- Then we discuss the very incomplete fossil and archaeological evidence from Africa, notably the Klasies River Cave in South Africa.

- Next, we examine the compelling and controversial evidence from mitochondrial DNA and other sources, which gives strong support to the out-of-Africa model. I think this is now widely accepted in outline, with the greatest controversy surrounding the date of first emergence. According to the latest research, the first modern humans emerged in a population of about 10,000 Africans.

Figure 3.24 charts a family tree from mitochondrial DNA. This was compiled some years ago, and has been bolstered with numerous new samples. The general picture still prevails.

- We then briefly discuss the ecological background, before looking at the spread of modern humans out of Africa around 100,000 years ago. I like the notion of the Sahara Desert as a giant pump, sucking in people, then ejecting them. The Sahara really did behave like this in much later times, at the end of the Ice Age, as we discuss in Chapter 11.

- Then there is the question of questions, which we discuss only briefly. When did modern humans acquire their formidable cognitive skills? Was it in Africa when they first appeared? Or did these abilities develop over many thousands of years, after 100,000 years ago, when southwestern Asia became, in human biological terms, part of Africa for a while? There's a growing suspicion from recent genetic research that modern humans did not develop their full intellectual horsepower until somewhere around 45,000 years ago, when they were then equipped to settle in the bitterly cold

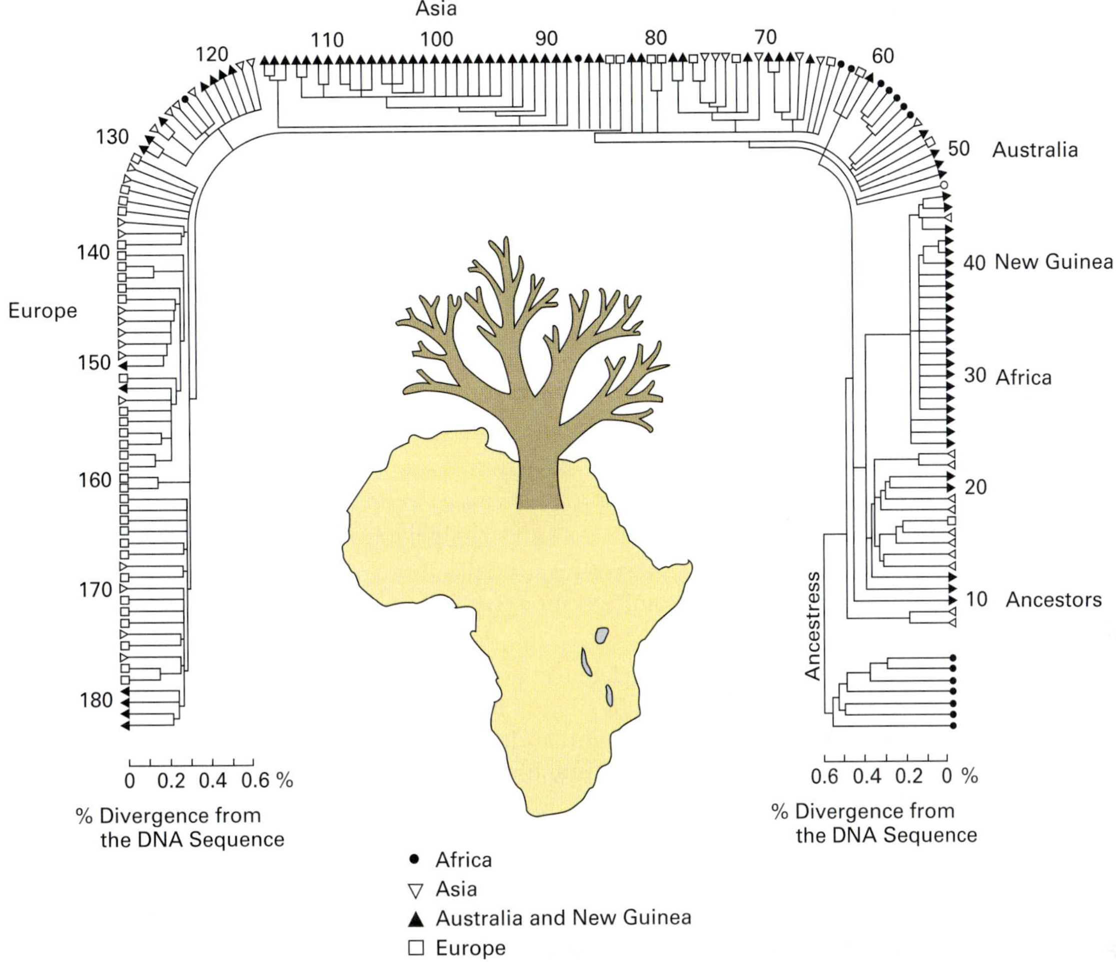

FIGURE 3.24 Allan Wilson and his research team used mitochondrial DNA from 182 women around the world to develop this family tree of modern human origins.

environments of the north—but this is all intriguing guesswork. That's what makes for controversy—which is the fun of all this!

Is there a future for the past? Yes, but only if we all help, not only by influencing other people's attitudes toward archaeology but also by living by this simple code of ethics:

- Treat all archaeological sites and artifacts as finite resources.
- Never dig an archaeological site.
- Never collect artifacts for yourself or buy and sell them for personal gain.
- Adhere to all federal, state, local, and tribal laws that affect the archaeological record.
- Report all accidental archaeological discoveries.
- Avoid disturbing any archaeological site, and respect the sanctity of all burial sites.

From: Brian Fagan. *Archaeology: A Brief Introduction.* 8th ed. Upper Saddle River, NJ: Prentice Hall, 2003. Pp. 316–318.

---

chapter

EUROPE AND EURASIA

The Chapter in Review

- Chapter 4 documents the spread of *Homo sapiens sapiens* into Europe and Eurasia from Africa and Southwest Asia after 43,000 B.C., during the late Ice Age.
- This time, there was increasing specialization and flexibility in human hunting and foraging, as anatomically modern humans replaced Neanderthal groups by 33,000 B.C.
- The sheer diversity of the late Ice Age environment gave the Cro-Magnon people of western Europe great flexibility. They developed more complex societies and developed elaborate bone and antler technology, as well as a complex symbolic life reflected in intricate artistic traditions.
- These cultures reached their apogee in the Magdalenian culture, which flourished after 16,000 B.C., and for about 5000 years.
- Cro-Magnon art traditions developed before 30,000 years ago and involved engraving, painting, and sculpture, as well as the adornment of portable objects. The motives behind the art are much debated. Some of the cave art may be connected with shamanistic activity and initiation ceremonies.
- The Eastern Gravettian cultural complex of eastern Europe and Eurasia was contemporary with Cro-Magnon societies in the west and was based on the exploitation of open plains and steppes.
- The many groups within this complex spread slowly eastward from the Czech Republic onto the Russian plains, relying heavily on game of all kinds.
- Far to the northeast, western Siberia was settled at least as early as 28,000 B.C., but the extreme northeast was devoid of human settlement until the very late Ice Age, perhaps as late as 13,000 B.C.
- Most experts agree that northeastern Siberia was the stepping off point for the first settlement of the Americas. From there, humans first crossed the Bering Land Bridge into Alaska, either during the late Ice Age or when global warming began after 15,000 B.C.

Key Cultures and Sites

Afontova Gora
Altamira
Chauvet
Dolní Vestonice
D'uktai
East Gravettian complex
Kostenki
La Madeleine
Laugerie Basse
Lascaux
Laugerie Haute
Magdalenian culture
Malaia Siya
Mal'ta
Mezhirich
Niaux
Pavlov
Shugnou
Tolbaga
Zafarraya

Introductory Comments

Now we have moved into Part II of *People,* which covers probably the most significant development in human prehistory—the spread of modern humans across the Old World and into the Americas. To remind you: we cover this great diaspora in four chapters. Chapters 4 and 5 take us from Europe and Eurasia into the Americas. Chapter 6 describes developments in tropical Africa and the first settlement of Australia and New Guinea, the latter an important stepping stone for the Pacific islands. Finally, Chapter 7 looks at what happened to hunter-gatherer societies during the great global warming after the Ice Age.

Chapter 4 tells the first part of this story—the arrival of modern humans in Europe and Eurasia. We still cover a long period of time, but nothing like that of the previous two. Here the narrative begins about 45,000 years ago and finishes at the end of the late Ice Age, c. 15,000 B.C.

Once again, the chapter has a chronological gradient, beginning with the first spread of modern humans out of southwestern Asia into southeastern Europe. But thereafter, we tell the story regionally, so that you get a sense of what happened over time in different areas.

Chapter 4 is concerned with three general issues, two of which involve fairly passionate controversy, although we have to skate over them superficially, given the enormous scope of this book.

- Most experts agree that the first modern humans appeared in Central Europe around 45,000 years ago and some millennia later in the west. But what happened to the Neanderthals? Proponents of the multiregional hypothesis believe that *Homo sapiens sapiens* evolved from earlier (Neanderthal) populations in Europe itself, which now seems unlikely, given the lack of both fossil and genetic evidence to this effect. Almost all scholars would argue that the first moderns came from outside, from southwestern Asia, and settled in Europe, where they lived alongside Neanderthal bands for some time. As we have seen, DNA tests suggest that interbreeding did not take place. Most likely, the Neanderthals were marginalized, pushed from their ancient territories, survived in some isolated enclaves until about 30,000 years ago, then became extinct.
- Cro-Magnon painting and engraving appears with flamboyant suddenness, before 30,000 years ago, perhaps the oldest art tradition in the world. Controversies over the meaning of the art have raged for more than a century. Was it art for art's sake, or did it have some deep, symbolic meaning which now eludes us. Again, controversy rages, especially around the issue of shamanism. In recent years, extensive research into San hunter-gatherer art in southern Africa (see Chapter 6) has highlighted the close association between much rock art and shamanism. At the same time, we have learned much more about altered states of consciousness and hallucinogens, research which also bears on ancient rock art. Experts debate fiercely as to the extent to which shamanism lies behind the art—as you will see, I tend to favor such an explanation.
- The third, less debated controversy in Chapter 4 is really a set up for the extended discussion of the first settlement of the Americas in Chapter 5. The debate's been rather muted until recently, because we knew so little about the archaeology of the region. Now a stream of new research is confirming what many people suspected—Stone Age hunter-gatherers did not settle in the extreme northeast Asia, close to Alaska, until very late. The climate may have simply been too cold for human occupation earlier than about 13,000 years ago. In our narrative, we discuss the earliest human colonization of Eurasia, then examine what little archaeological evidence there is for late Ice Age humans in northeastern Siberia, the jumping off point for the Americas.

All this has fascinating implications for the debates over the first settlement of the Americas, discussed in Chapter 5. Stay tuned for interesting new developments in coming years.

Again, I have divided the chapter into two halves for you. We begin with the Cro-Magnons of Central and western Europe.

- First, we introduce the Upper Pleistocene, or late Ice Age, which began about 128,000 years ago.
- The story itself commences in southwestern Asia, where we take up the thread from Chapter 3. You'll recall that we had Neanderthals and modern humans living alongside one another until about 45,000 years ago. Once, again we face the issue of a cognitive explosion, discussed in Chapter 3.
- Then we describe what little we know about the first modern Europeans and trace their journey into the west. This is sometimes called "the Upper Palaeolithic Transition," marked by major technological changes. We introduce the Cro-Magnons and describe their increasingly elaborate societies, which developed between about 45,000 years ago and 8000 B.C.
- Cro-Magnon groups may have settled in more permanent camps, and certainly enjoyed complex spiritual beliefs, reflected in their art, described in the next section. We examine some of the theories that seek to explain the motives behind the paintings and engravings.

Now It's Time to Start Reading . . .

The Cro-Magnons

The text figures provide a useful signpost through the Cro-Magnon narrative.

Figure 4.1(a) is a reference map, showing the sites mentioned in the text. Herein lies a trend throughout the rest of the book—many more sites, often from areas that are geographically unfamiliar to most people. It's worth having a small atlas close by, in case you want to get a sense of where mountain ranges and other natural features lie. You see, world prehistory is an exercise in the broad sweep of human geography, in a world where the most important developments often occurred in what we think of as "remote" areas. The word "remote" is, of course, a way for us to talk about places that are not close to home and is totally artificial. In this book, the world is your oyster—enjoy it! I would suggest a Post-it on the map for reference purposes, as you read on.

Figure 4.1b is very important, for it gives you an overall impression of the great diaspora discussed in Chapters 4 through 7. It's worth spending a few minutes examining this, to get the major features of the diaspora into your mind. Notice, for example, how early people spread to Australia and New Guinea, how much later they settled in the Americas (through bitterly cold northern regions), and how the settlement of the offshore Pacific Island came only within the past 3,000 years, a function of proper watercraft, easily stored foods, and the need for open water navigational skills (see Chapter 12).

Table 4.1 on page 45 covers much more than just Europe, for it summarizes the chronology of all the cultures and sites mentioned in this chapter. The cultures and sites are plotted against late Ice Age climate, and a chronology that now comes from AMS radiocarbon dating, much of it calibrated with coral or tree-rings. It's a simplified table, but useful for general reference.

Figure 4.2 on page 46 provides a fascinating environmental contrast between Europe and Eurasia in interglacial (a) and glacial (b) times. Study this carefully, as I assume that you have done in the narrative. In the context of this chapter, the glacial map (b) is especially important, because it shows how the great ice sheets of Scandinavia and the Alps dominated the environment. A vast periglacial landscape of open steppe extended from the Atlantic into Eurasia at a time when sea levels were 90 meters (300 feet) lower than today. The only forests were in deep, sheltered river valleys, notably in southwestern France and southern Germany (not shown on the map) and in what today are Mediterranean countries. Contrast this glacial map with the one

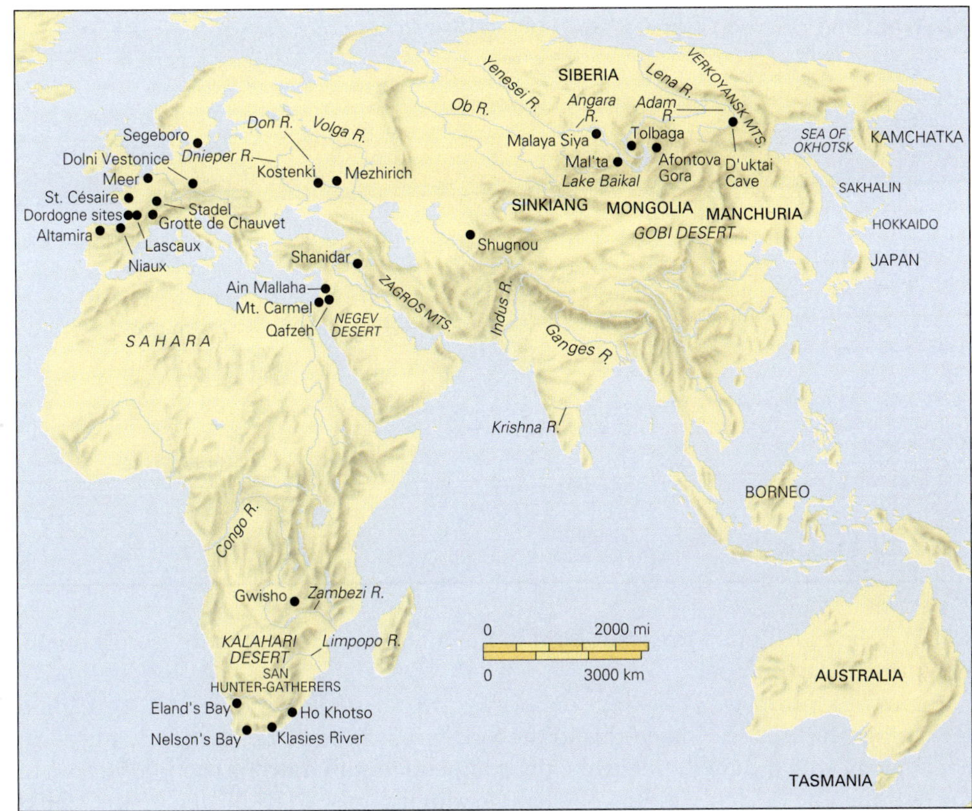

(a)

(b)

FIGURE 4.1 (a) Map showing archaeological sites mentioned in this chapter and in Chapters 6 and 7. Some minor and little-known sites are omitted for clarity, but their general locations are clear from the text. (b) The spread of *Homo sapiens sapiens* in the late Ice Age and after.

Notes

---

showing the much more forested world of the interglacial, which more closely resembles present-day Europe.

Figure 4.5 (on page 47) is very important to your understanding of Cro-Magnon technology. In the text, I liken this to the Swiss army knife or Leatherman effect—an apt analogy, which came to me while drinking coffee with a writer friend one day! In the drawing, the flint core is the knife handle with its hinges. The blades are the blanks for the attachments, which, in turn, allow the making of antler and bone artifacts. Particularly important is the chisel-like burin, which allowed people to groove deep into antlers and detach splinters for making spearheads and other tools. One of them was the needle, used for tailoring layered clothes—these, in turn allowed people to work outside effectively in the depths of winter. The layers served just like backpacker's clothing layers—the Cro-Magnons were as savvy about survival, if not more so, than modern outdoorspeople. They had to be! But it all goes back to the Swiss army knife effect.

Now take a look at Figure 4.6 (on page 48), which displays some of the major tool categories made by the Cro-Magnons. The burins appear at bottom right, small arrows showing the chisel ends. By far the finest stone tool was the so-called Solutrean point,

Notes

TABLE 4.1

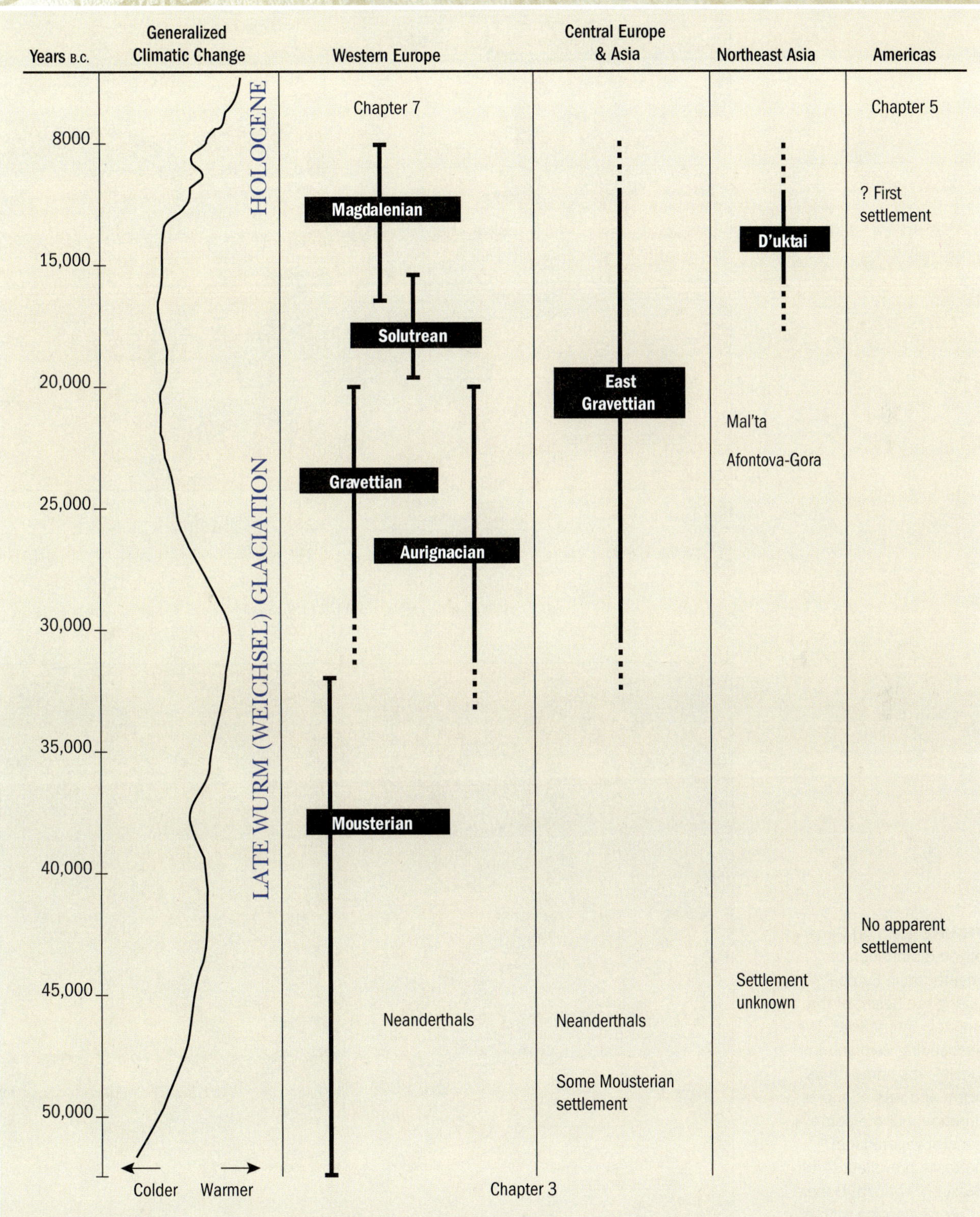

There was considerable overlap between European cultures. Climatic changes are approximate, as they are subject to considerable controversy among experts.

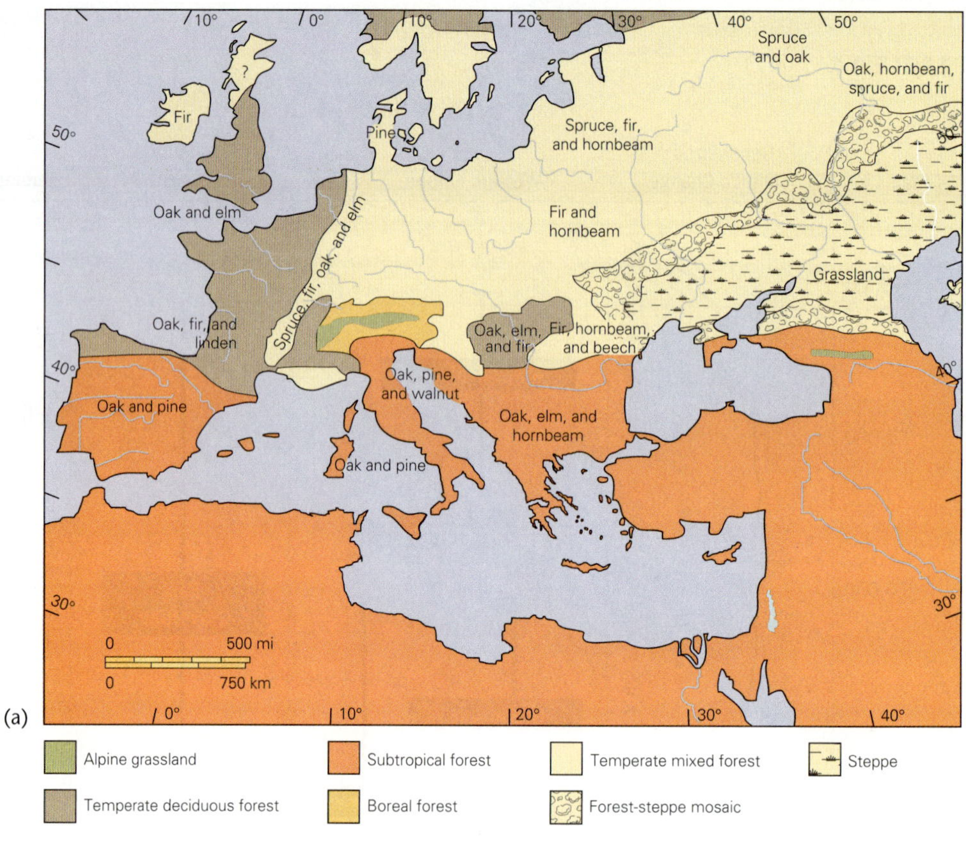

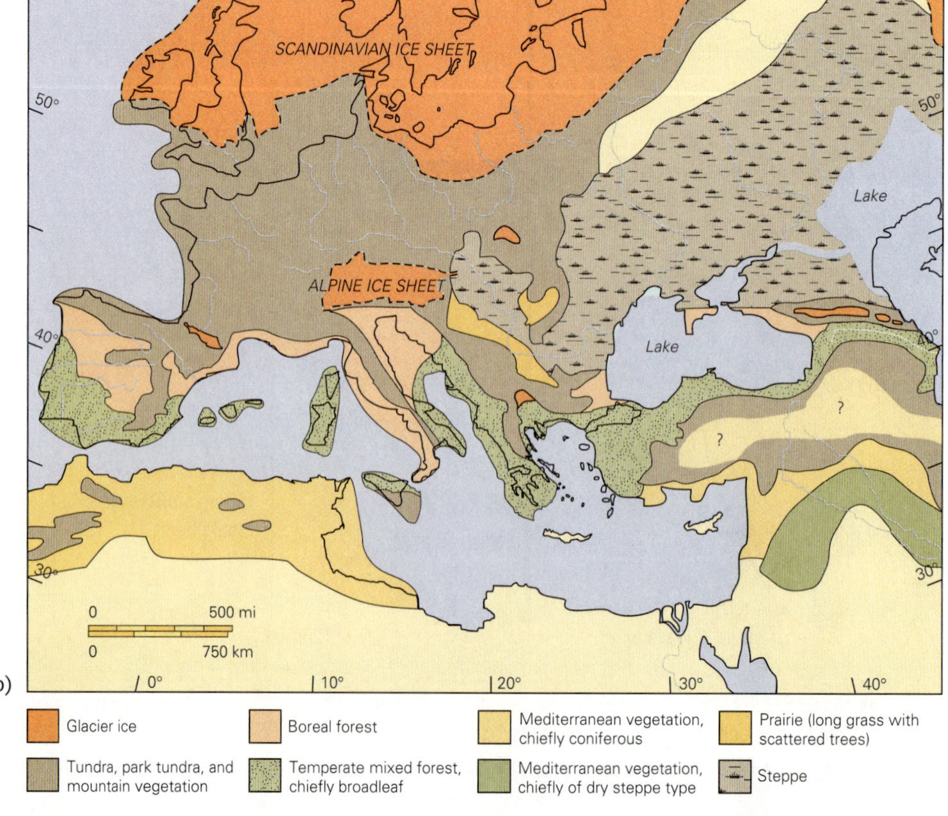

FIGURE 4.2 (a) Generalized distribution of vegetation in Europe during the height of the Holstein interglacial. The succeeding Eemian interglacial was not quite as warm and was of shorter duration, but the same general vegetational patterns prevailed. (After Butzer, 1974.) (b) Generalized vegetation map of Europe at the height of the Weichsel glaciation, showing ice sheets. (After Butzer, 1974.)

Notes

a leaf-shaped spear head, presumably used for pursuing larger game. These remarkable tools were only in use for a few thousand years. Why they appeared, then suddenly vanished, is unknown. The upper rows show a variety of small antler tools and the spear thrower, basically a hooked stick that enabled a hunter to propel a spear further, with greater force, and considerable accuracy—a major innovation.

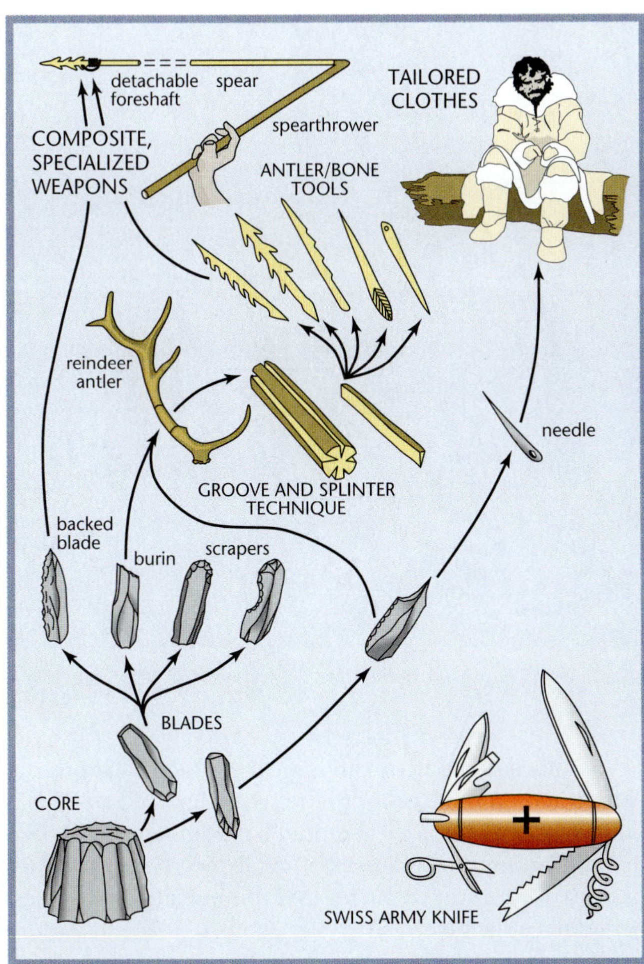

FIGURE 4.5 The Swiss army knife effect. Blade technology acted like the celebrated Swiss army knife, producing blanks for making many specialized artifacts for working bone and antler.

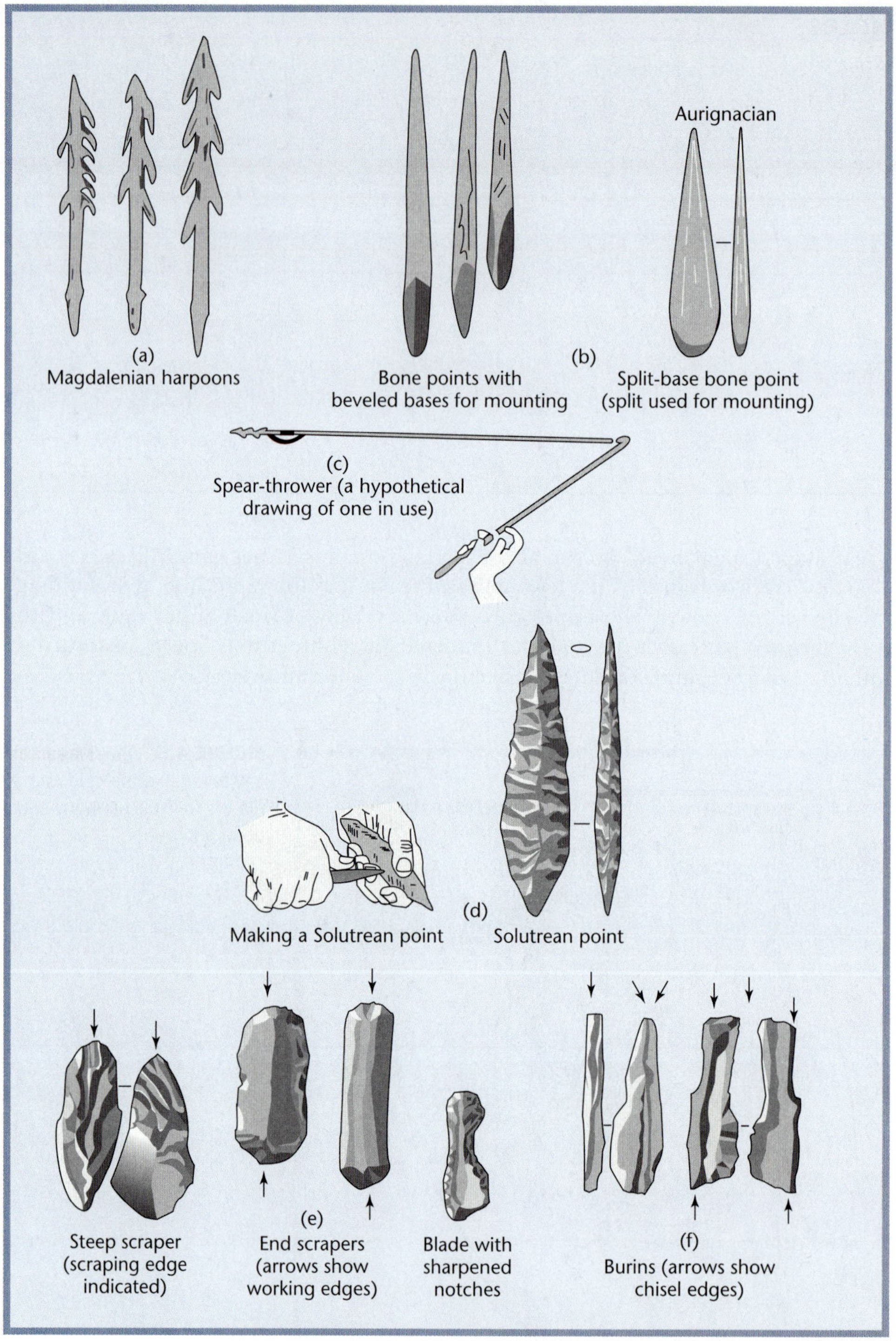

FIGURE 4.6 Characteristic artifacts used by Upper Paleolithic groups in western Europe. Antler and bone artifacts were of vital importance, especially harpoons (a) and bone points (b) mounted on wooden shafts. The spear-thrower (c) was a hooked shaft, used to propel a spear a longer distance with great accuracy. Upper Paleolithic stone tools were made from blades for the most part, reaching their highest degree of sophistication about 20,000 years ago, with pressure-flaked Solutrean points (d), named after the Solutré site in southwestern France. Every group relied heavily on scrapers (e), used for processing skins, for working bone and antler, and for woodworking. The most important artifact was the chisel-ended burin (f), employed for grooving wood, bone, and especially reindeer antler.

I designed Table 4.2 to give you more detail than can appear in the text about the various Cro-Magnon cultures identified on the basis of their changing artifacts. This is a mixture of a chronological table and a technological guide, based on an old French archaeological notion of two parallel cultural traditions. You really need only be aware of the traditions, so this table is more for reference purposes. I doubt if anyone will test you on it, unless they cover the details in lecture!

TABLE 4.2
Much simplified outline of the Upper Paleolithic traditions of western Europe from 40,000 to 10,000 B.C.

The most commonly accepted scheme has two parallel cultural traditions: the Gravettian, characterized by backed knives, and the Aurignacian, favoring scrapers and sharpened blades. The Gravettian, with increasingly finer backed knives, became dominant after 30,000 years ago. Thereafter, there were considerable regional variations, reflected in different tool traditions.

The Solutrean, a culture that relied on sophisticated "cooking" of large pieces of flint so that they became porcelainlike in texture, flourished in France and Spain. The stoneworker could exert pressure on the flake edge to produce magnificent leaf-shaped spear points. Many variations of the Gravettian culture are found in central and eastern Europe. In the west, the Magdalenian tradition, which relied heavily on antler and bone, emerged about 18,000 years ago. (For artifacts, see Figure 4.6.)

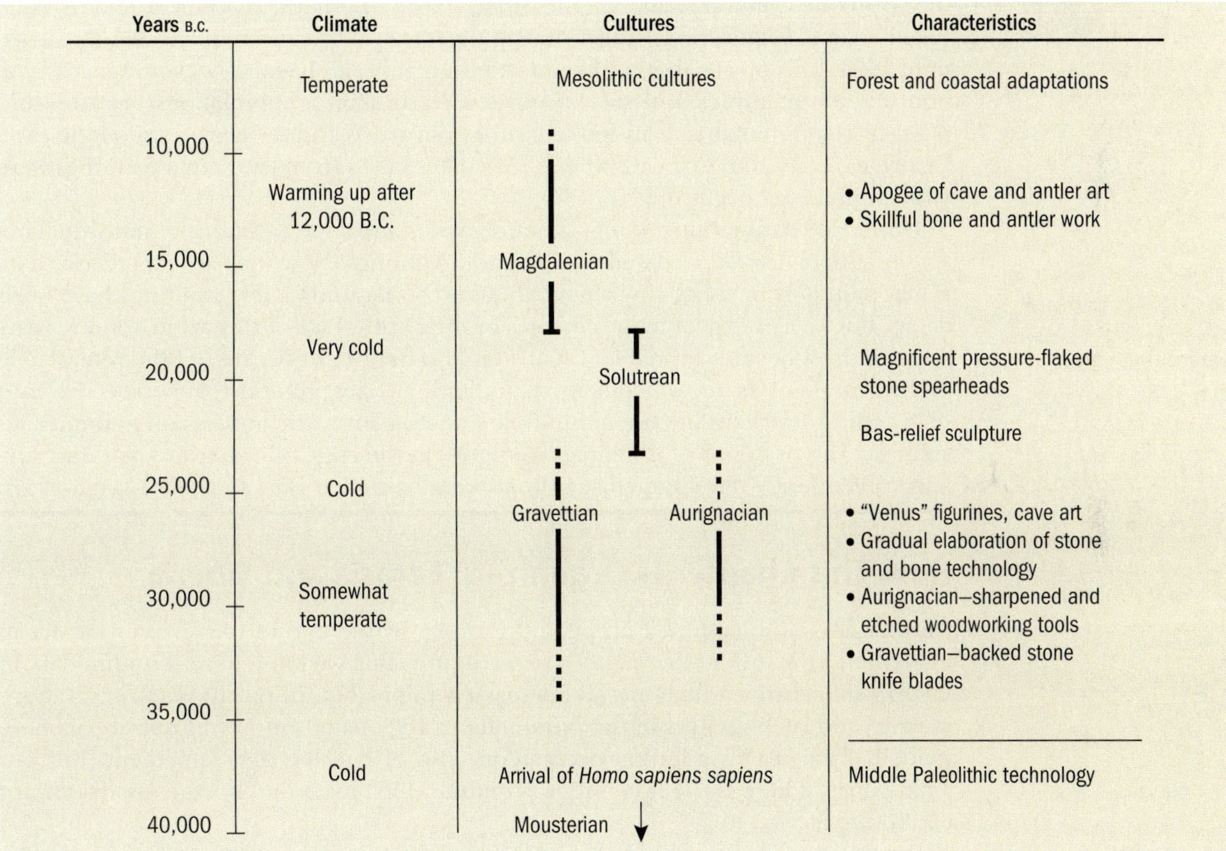

Years B.C.	Climate	Cultures	Characteristics
	Temperate	Mesolithic cultures	Forest and coastal adaptations
10,000			
	Warming up after 12,000 B.C.		• Apogee of cave and antler art • Skillful bone and antler work
15,000		Magdalenian	
	Very cold		
20,000		Solutrean	Magnificent pressure-flaked stone spearheads
			Bas-relief sculpture
25,000	Cold	Gravettian Aurignacian	• "Venus" figurines, cave art • Gradual elaboration of stone and bone technology
30,000	Somewhat temperate		• Aurignacian–sharpened and etched woodworking tools • Gravettian–backed stone knife blades
35,000			
	Cold	Arrival of *Homo sapiens sapiens*	Middle Paleolithic technology
40,000		Mousterian ↓	

Notes

Cro-Magnon Art

Major debate surrounds the meaning of the remarkable art of the Cro-Magnons, which we can only touch upon here. The discussion, "Explaining Upper Palaeolithic Art," touches the high points and is self-explanatory. The shamanism hypothesis enjoyed great popularity until very recently, when some scholars rebelled against a theory that was being applied promiscuously to all rock art. The debate continues, especially over applying approaches based on relatively recent South African rock art to an art tradition that is over 20,000 years old. The Grotte de Chauvet provides some interesting clues.

Grotte de Chauvet

There have been some spectacular Cro-Magnon art discoveries in the past century, but the Grotte de Chauvet dwarfs all the others except, perhaps, Lascaux, found in 1940. Like Lascaux, Chauvet was sealed during the late Ice Age and remained undisturbed until 1994. This means that, unlike most other caves, archaeologists could investigate not only the paintings, but such features as bear skull accumulations, hearths, and other traces of human activity left behind by the artists and those who visited the cave. Chauvet was also the first cave where AMS dates taken from the actual paintings were taken right at the beginning.

Until AMS dating came along, changing styles and superpositions of individual images one upon the other dated Cro-Magnon paintings. Now rock art experts can date actual paintings by using tiny charcoal flakes. So far, only a few paintings have been dated, but we can expect many changes in the chronology of this art in coming years as more dates become available. Chauvet is also important because of the remarkable sophistication of its art, which features multiple images, good use of perspective, and such artistic devices as the use of multiple lines to convey the impression of numerous animals. The presence of a shamanlike figure at the edge of one frieze may add support to the theory that shamanistic rituals were behind at least some Cro-Magnon art.

How This Chapter Is Organized: Eurasia and Siberia

Now we cross into eastern Europe and Eurasia. By the end of the chapter, we are in extreme northeastern Siberia. Let's stress at once that we know almost nothing about this enormous area, which was always sparsely populated. In recent years, excavations in caves and rock shelters in the mountainous regions of southern Central Asia have yielded traces of Neanderthal occupation, also of late Ice Age settlement. But our main concern here is the huge steppe-tundra, which extended northeastward toward the Bering Strait.

We begin with describing the hunter-gatherer societies of Central and eastern Europe, where big and small game were especially important, known specifically from excavations at Dolní Vestonice and Mezhirich.

Then we move into the northeast, to Siberia's Lake Baikal and beyond, to a then frigid world where cultural influences came from both the west, and more often the south, from the Mongolian and Ordos deserts. This area is vitally important for our understanding of the first settlement of the Americas, discussed in Chapter 5. In recent years, archaeological research has expanded in the inhospitable reaches of far northeast Asia, from which it is becoming apparent that few, if any, people lived in this region before about 15,000 years ago—which makes a relatively late settlement of the Americas very likely.

This is all straightforward narrative description.

These drawings amplify the text. Figure 4.15a is a diagram of an East Gravettian house reconstructed from an archaeological site in the Czech Republic. Here the builders used a hide roof and timber uprights. Interestingly, the same people used

FIGURE 4.15 Late Ice Age houses. (a) An artist's reconstruction of a winter house excavated at Dolní Vestonice, Czech Republic, dating to c. 25,000 B.C. The timber-and-bone structure supported a hide roof. This dwelling contained an oval oven used to bake clay figurines.

woven fibers for nets and other purposes, of which only tiny fragments survive (Figure 4.16). It's naive to think that Cro-Magnons and others relied on antler, bone and stone alone. Like all other hunter-gatherer peoples, they used what materials were abundant, convenient, and to hand—whence the mammoth bone houses at Mezhirich, further east in the Ukraine.

Now we are well to the north and east, in Siberia. Figure 4.18 shows two forms of artifact, which were commonplace among the tiny hunter-gatherer populations of this sparsely inhabited region. Both bifacially flaked projectile points and microblades occur not only in Siberia, but, as we shall see in Chapter 5, on the Alaskan side of the Bering Strait. Whence a question: was this the primordial toolkit used in the Americas? The answer is that we simply do not know. Microblades were highly effective when used as barbs and points for hunting weapons, but when they first appeared in Alaska is still uncertain. They were probably carried over at the very end of the Ice Age, but

FIGURE 4.16 An impression of a woven fragment preserved on clay: an open diagonal twining with an S twist weft, from Pavlov, Czech Republic.

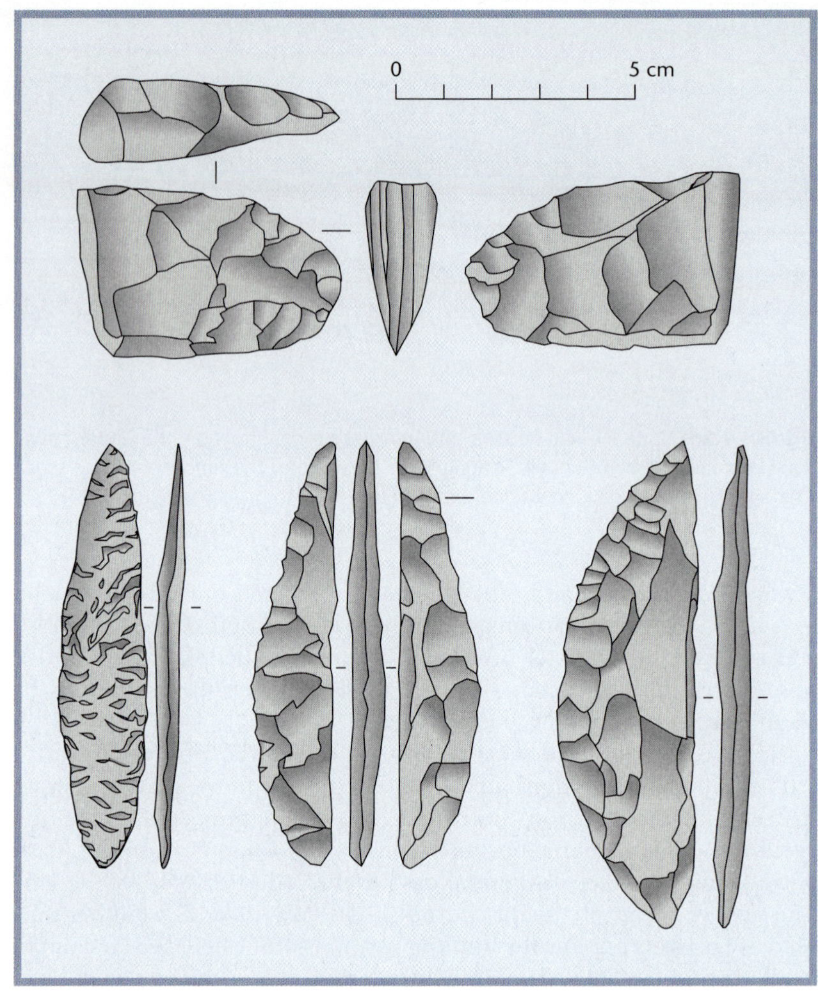

FIGURE 4.18 Artifacts of the D'uktai tradition. Top, four views of a wedge-shaped core, used to make tiny blades. Bottom, two bifacially flaked projectile points. The wedge-shaped core is a characteristic artifact found on both sides of the Bering Strait in contexts of about 8000 B.C. It is, of course, a by-product of the production of fine microblades.

their first known occurrence in Alaska is about 11,000 B.C. That is not to say that they were not made earlier: again, we do not know. Up in this area of the world, archaeology is very difficult, and sites are often near impossible to find. We are lucky to have anything to work with at all.

c h a p t e r

THE FIRST AMERICANS

The Chapter in Review

- The first humans to settle the Americas crossed from northeast Asia, probably across the Bering Land Bridge (central Beringia), but the date of their arrival is highly controversial.
- No archaic humans ever settled in the Americas, which were colonized by *Homo sapiens sapiens* alone.
- Some scientists claim that archaeological evidence from South America proves that Native Americans were flourishing in the Americas as early as 40,000 years ago, but this is a minority view.
- Most experts believe that first settlement occurred much later, perhaps at the very end of the Ice Age, as early as 13,500 B.C. or possibly even earlier.
- There is evidence for human occupation in Alaska by 11,700 B.C., while the Clovis people of North America flourished between 11,200 and 10,900 B.C.
- After 11,000 B.C., many species of Ice Age animals, large and small, became extinct, so Native American hunter-gatherers diversified their economies to take full advantage of local resources.
- Paleo-Indian groups continued to hunt bison on the North American Plains, this being the only area where any large animals survived. Big-game hunting flourished in this area until historic times.
- An always sparse population of hunter-gatherers adapted to the harsh desert conditions of the west and flourished there right into historic times. Most such groups "anchored" themselves to reliable water supplies such as small lakes and marshes.
- In the Eastern Woodlands, hunter-gatherers subsisted off deer and other small game, also a wide variety of plant foods. As time passed, both fishing and birds assumed greater importance, as did fall nut harvests. The densest populations flourished in fertile river valleys, along estuaries, and by lake shores, where more sedentary settlements developed and hunting territories became more circumscribed.
- More complex hunter-gatherer societies arose in the Pacific Northwest and in midwestern river valleys, as well as along the California coast. All cultures depended on abundant, seasonally predictable aquatic, animal, and plant resources.
- In other parts of the Americas, Archaic cultures based on hunting and foraging survived until the adoption of native plant cultivation or maize agriculture within the last 6,000 years.
- In the Arctic and extreme South America, hunter-gatherer societies flourished until historic times. In the far north, there was regular interchange of ideas with people in Siberia, and, much later, with the Norse in the east, the only contacts between ancient America and the Old World until Columbus's day.

Key Cultures and Sites

Anagula (and Chaluka)
Archaic Tradition
Arctic Small Tool Tradition
Beringia
Blackwater Draw
Broken Mammoth
Caverna da Pedra Pintada
Clovis Culture
Dalton Tradition
Danger Cave
Dry Creek
Folsom
Gypsum Cave
Hogup Cave
Indian Knoll
Koster
Lovelock Cave
Meadowcroft Rockshelter
Modoc Rockshelter
Monte Verde
Murray Springs
Naco
Olsen-Chubbock
Paleoarctic
Paleo-Indian
Swan Point
Thule
Walker Road

Introductory Comments

Now we plunge into stormy academic waters, where passions flare and personalities clash! I don't know what it is about "the first" of anything that sets people off, but there always seem to be violent arguments about the initial colonization of anywhere—Europe by the first humans, the first settlement of Australia, the earliest seafaring, and above all, the first Americans. The debates over the first settlement of the Americas are remarkable for their pettiness and often vicious personal attacks, and for their far-ranging theorizing, usually on the basis of virtually no data whatsoever! It's an academic minefield by any standards, where the pressures to take sides are enormous. So we navigate a somewhat conservative course, which the very sketchy archaeological evidence justifies.

This chapter takes us for the first time into the Americas, a vast continent uninhabited by human beings until very recent times by prehistoric standards. Even if you were to buy into the early settlement theories, you are talking about a mere 40,000 years, a blink of an eyelid by the standards of 2.5 million years. I've divided the chapter into two parts. The first surveys the evidence, and theories, for first settlement. The second part describes what happened to hunter-gatherer societies in different parts of the Americas after initial colonization. (In this chapter, we're concerned only with hunter-gatherers. For later societies, see Chapters 13 and Part V.)

Obviously, the major issue in this chapter is first settlement. At the most basic level, the controversies surround four topics:

- When did people first settle the Americas?
- Which route did they take to do so?
- What were the ancestral roots of the first settlers?
- What do we know about their life ways and societies?

I do all I can here to examine the evidence dispassionately. However, as you will soon find out, I tend to favor a later date for first settlement, in the order of 15,000 to 20,000 years ago or so—but, unlike some participants in the debate, I do so because *the weight of the scientific evidence* favors such a chronology. You see, in the final analysis, we have to rely on data, and, despite a century and a half of intensive search for the first Americans in North America, there are still no sites that date earlier than some 15,000 years ago.

I believe that a conservative perspective is the responsible way to approach this important issue.

Another factor is also involved. Everyone agrees that the extinction of the Ice Age megafauna in about 11,000 B.C. was a turning point in ancient North American life. But did climate or human overhunting cause this extinction?

After this extinction, hunter-gatherer societies diversified into all manner of local environments. In some resource rich areas, they developed much more sophisticated social and political mechanisms, sometimes to cope with unpredictable climatic shifts, or to help in the redistribution of food and wealth through society. The causes for this emerging sophistication are much debated, but lie beyond the brief scope of this chapter. So I have contented myself with a brief description of what happened, knowing that we will address these issues in more detail later on in *People.*

Now It's Time to Start Reading. . . .

First Settlement

As I said, I try and chart a calm and judicious course through a swampy abyss of controversy and passionate argument. Again, it's a narrative, organized as follows:

- First, I lay out the fundamental questions, to focus the narrative.
- Then, we move on to the geography. Many people do not realize just how much the geography of North America has changed since the Ice Age. Huge ice sheets mantled Canada and the Great Lakes, which were formed by retreating glaciers, reaching as far south as Seattle. And sea levels were 100 meters (300 feet) lower than today—whence the Bering Land Bridge.
- Now the first settlement of Alaska, which links to the Siberian story in Chapter 4. At this point, we deviate slightly into the rather compelling biological evidence for the ancestry of the ancient native Americans—very much part of the story.
- Next, we face the issue of routes southward: overland through the parting and retreating ice sheets or along the now-sunken coast?
- By now, we are ready to examine the archaeological evidence in the heart of the Americas. First, we chase the elusive evidence for Late Wisconsin glaciation settlement—that is occupation before 15,000 years ago. Then we put forward a possible scenario for first settlement immediately after the Ice Age, which segues into . . .
- The Clovis Culture of c. 11,200 to 10,900 B.C., which is when human settlement is well documented. We make the point that there were equivalent and different societies south of North America. (If your instructor tells you that my Clovis dates are 2,000 years too early, please refer him to the article by Stuart Fiedel in the text bibliography (1999), which is the latest word on the subject!)

The narrative is fairly straightforward, so most of my running comments refer to the text figures.

I hope Figure 5.1 (page 56) and Table 5.1 (page 57) are reassuring baselines for you. They are purely for reference, and a Post-it on the page might be useful as you read along. As always, the chronological table is cumulative, with climate to the left and a useful column of contemporary developments to the right. Notice, for example, that first settlement was taking hold as the Magdalenians flourished in western Europe and megafaunal extinctions occurred just before farming appeared in southwestern Asia.

Figure 5.2 is especially important, as it shows the extent of the now-vanished Bering Land Bridge. The low-lying, tundra-covered plain really was a nasty place climatically, swept by perishing cold winds, dry, dusty, and treeless. Even during the brief summers, conditions were inhospitable to animals, humans, and plants, except, perhaps, in the shallow river valleys, which dissected the plain. I suspect populations were always very sparse and widely scattered—and anyone who thinks of a single migration that settled the Americas is deluding themselves. There were probably dozens of such movements back and fro, by tiny groups of people just doing their hunter-gatherer thing. No one just decided to "move to Alaska." They did not think that way.

In recent years, a few experts have wondered whether the Beringians came east along the ice-strewn seacoasts. In my other life, I am a small boat sailor. I must confess that I would be very leery of paddling skin boats or kayaks in these bitterly cold, pack congested waters. The danger of hyperthermia was constant, and the maritime environment much more severe than it is today. In later times, Eskimo and Inuit of the far north were,

FIGURE 5.1 Ancient hunter-gatherers in the Americas. Sites mentioned in the text are indicated. (For the Bering land bridge, see Figure 5.2.)

indeed, expert sailors, helped by a sophisticated, well-adapted maritime technology. But there are no signs that Paleo-Indians had the same expertise: certainly their terrestrial toolkits do not reflect a level of sophistication that allows for specialized kayak manufacture. Unfortunately, thanks to the higher sea levels of today, we have no evidence of course, but I would not bet the farm on maritime settlement. These are not the tropical waters of southeast Asia and northern Australia! It was very cold on the water!

It's important to understand that we know *almost nothing* about the first Americans. If you delve into the more specialist literature, you sometimes get the impression that we know a lot more than we do. Contemplate the Alaskan evidence as an example: a mere handful of tiny sites, each little more than a scatter of stone tools and a few animal bones.

There's a lot of talk these days of a "new synthesis" of archaeology, genetics/biological anthropology, and linguistics. We've already talked about this with the appearance of the first modern humans in Chapter 3. I think that the new synthesis is going to be a powerful approach for studying the first Americans in future years. Figure 5.3 summarizes some interesting points about dental morphology described in the text. This dental evidence, and the emerging mitochondrial DNA data, firmly anchors the primordial Paleo-Indian populations in Siberia, with a predominantly

TABLE 5.1

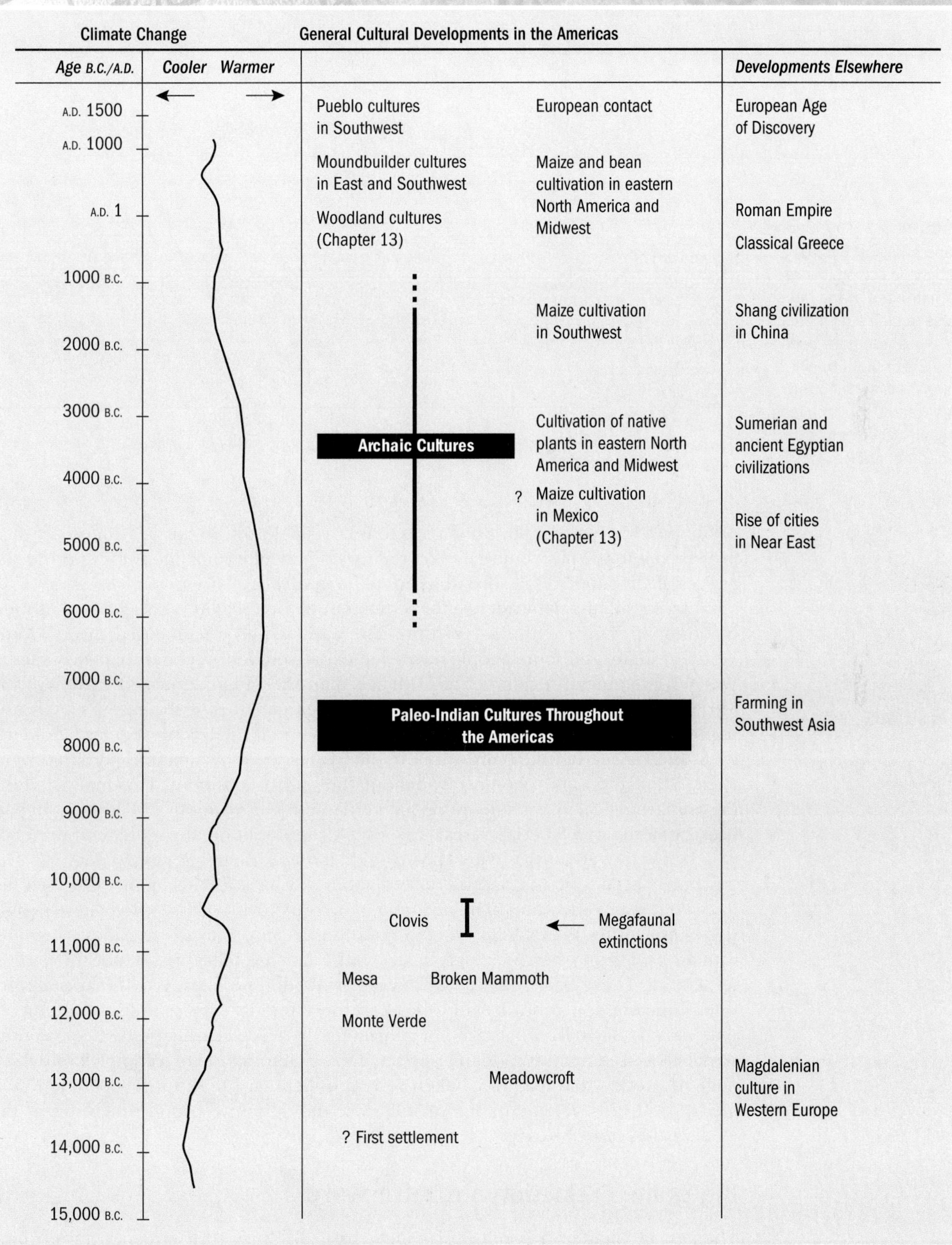

Climate Change		General Cultural Developments in the Americas		
Age B.C./A.D.	*Cooler* ← → *Warmer*			*Developments Elsewhere*
A.D. 1500		Pueblo cultures in Southwest	European contact	European Age of Discovery
A.D. 1000		Moundbuilder cultures in East and Southwest	Maize and bean cultivation in eastern North America and Midwest	
A.D. 1		Woodland cultures (Chapter 13)		Roman Empire Classical Greece
1000 B.C.				
2000 B.C.			Maize cultivation in Southwest	Shang civilization in China
3000 B.C.		**Archaic Cultures**	Cultivation of native plants in eastern North America and Midwest	Sumerian and ancient Egyptian civilizations
4000 B.C.			? Maize cultivation in Mexico (Chapter 13)	Rise of cities in Near East
5000 B.C.				
6000 B.C.				
7000 B.C.		**Paleo-Indian Cultures Throughout the Americas**		Farming in Southwest Asia
8000 B.C.				
9000 B.C.				
10,000 B.C.		Clovis	← Megafaunal extinctions	
11,000 B.C.		Mesa	Broken Mammoth	
12,000 B.C.		Monte Verde		
13,000 B.C.			Meadowcroft	Magdalenian culture in Western Europe
14,000 B.C.		? First settlement		
15,000 B.C.				

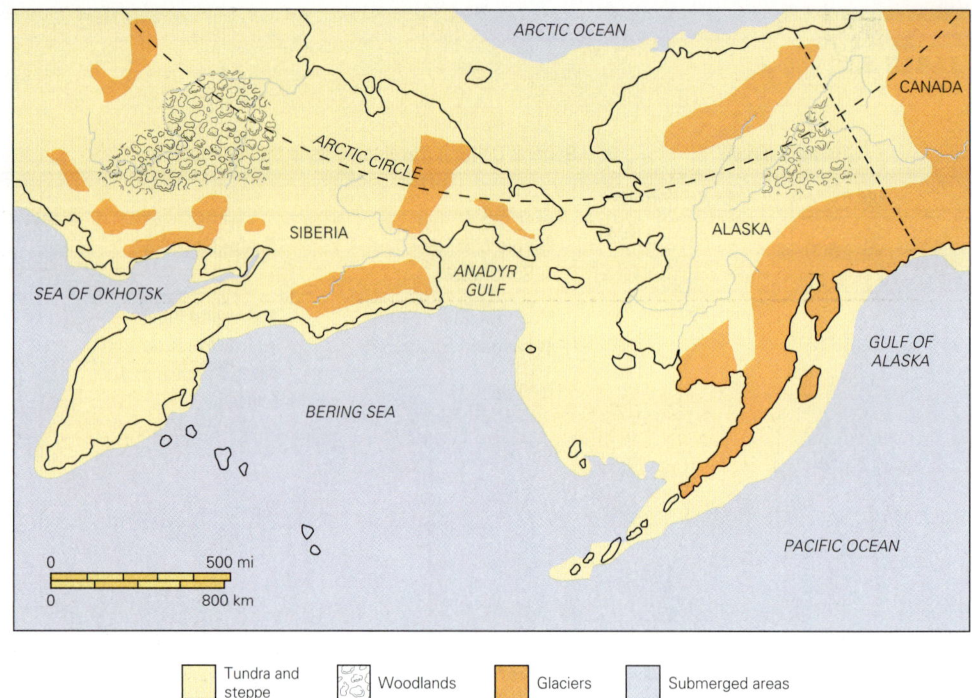

FIGURE 5.2 The Bering land bridge at the last glacial maximum, as reconstructed by the latest research. The land bridge is thought to have been the major route by which humans first colonized Alaska and the Americas, during or immediately after the late Ice Age.

Asian ancestry. I am frankly dubious as to how reliable any linguistic evidence is when projected into the past, but there is certainly a powerful homogeneity to Amerind languages, if Greenberg's classifications are to be believed.

Next, we discuss the evidence for settlement before 15,000 years ago, and, it must be admitted that it is thin—very thin. The earliest well documented site is Monte Verde in Chile, and some people have even expressed doubts about that. New sites in West Virginia may provide better evidence than the much contested early levels at Meadowcroft shelter. If there was human settlement during the late Ice Age, the populations must have been very sparse indeed—and if the few sites we have hold up, then the archaeological record supports such a scattered occupation, perhaps, at the most, a few thousand people throughout the entire continent. Personally, I think the archaeological jury is still out on any settlement before about 12,000 B.C.—in part because of the new Siberian researches, which cast doubt on any settlement in northeast Asia before about that date. Having said all this, I hope that I am wrong!

There's been a lot of nonsense talked about a "Clovis barrier," a media-driven distinction that pits advocates of no occupation before Clovis to those who believe people were here earlier than 11,200 B.C. No question that the Clovis occupation coincides with an explosion of archaeological sites, but I am sure that this was not the earliest settlement. There were some groups here earlier, but, perhaps, Clovis marks a point when human populations began to expand more rapidly—for reasons we do not yet understand. But talk of barriers, of reluctance to accept earlier settlement, is nonsense. Clovis did not just suddenly appear, it was a culmination of a complex initial settlement process that may have taken several millennia. I doubt if few people would quarrel with this statement, *but* we still await the definitive proof, which is why the media babble about barriers.

Big-game Extinction and Afterward

The rest of Chapter 5 is self-explanatory, basically straightforward narrative, which needs little comment from me.

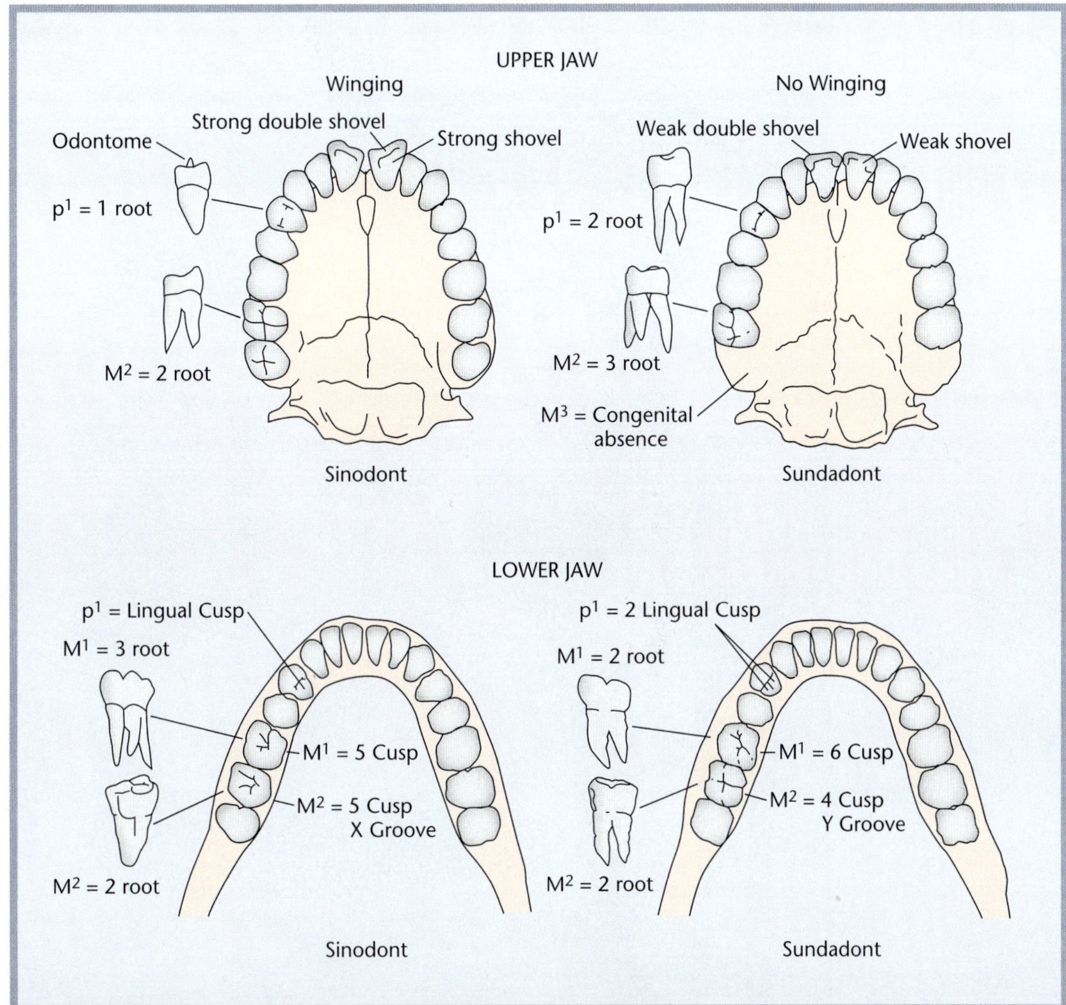

FIGURE 5.3 Dental morphology and the first Americans. Some of Christy Turner's theories about the peopling of the Americas are based on differences between the teeth of the so-called "sinodonts" (northern Asians and all Native Americans) and "sundadonts" (eastern Asians). Sinodonts display, among other features, strong incisor shoveling (scooping out on one or both surfaces of the tooth), single-rooted upper first premolars, and triple-rooted lower first molars.

The megafaunal extinction leapt into prominence during the 1960s, and, as an issue, has attracted attention sporadically ever since. I think that most people agree that humans may have played some limited role in the process, especially in accelerating the demise of slow-breeding animals like the mammoth and mastodon. But the blitzkrieg model proposed by Paul Martin is too extreme. Current thinking plays down human intervention to practically zero.

The rest of Chapter 5 surveys, very briefly, the changes in hunter-gatherer society after the extinction. This carries the story forward to modern times in some areas like the Plains, the Pacific coast, and the Arctic, and to the arrival of farming economies in other areas. I've subdivided the narrative into broad regions, starting with the Plains, where bison survived, then covering the desert west and the Eastern Woodlands.

Figure 5.9 gives a sample of the extremely simple and mobile toolkit used by desert societies over many thousands of years. We know a great deal about life in areas like the Great Basin, thanks to finds in dry caves.

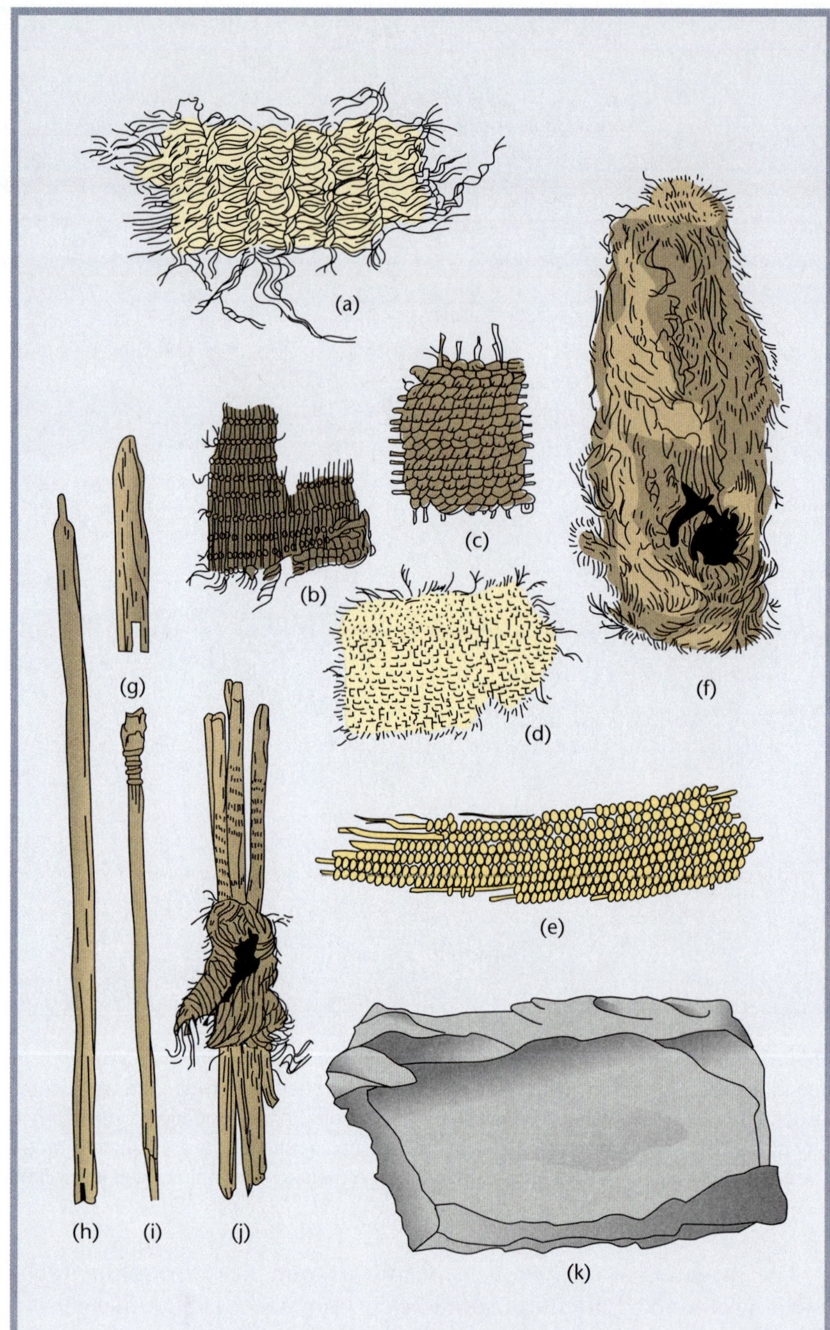

FIGURE 5.9 Artifacts from Danger Cave, Utah, preserved by the dry climate: (a and b) twined matting; (c) twined basketry; (d) coarse cloth; (e) coiled basketry; (f) hide moccasin; (g) wooden knife handle, 7.4 cm (4.5 inches) long; (h) dart shaft, 41 cm (16 inches) long; (i) arrow shaft with broken projectile point in place, 84 cm (33 inches) long; (j) bundle of gaming sticks, 29 cm (11.5 inches) long; (k) milling stone.

The big issue with hunter-gatherers is that of complexity, the dramatic contrasts between small, egalitarian bands in areas of sparse population like the California desert or Great Basin, and the much more elaborate societies which developed in places with more abundant and diverse food supplies: Midwestern river valleys, epitomized by Koster, the Pacific Northwest, or the Southern California coast. Gallons of ink have been spilled in a search for explanations. Did greater social complexity arise because of smaller territories, higher population densities, or food shortages? Or were other factors at work? Like so many academic debates, this one is unresolved. But there is little question that the need to reduce conflict over food supplies and to mediate disputes in an increasingly crowded world was a powerful catalyst for change.

Koster

Koster was excavated a generation ago, but it remains a classic example of a large-scale excavation on a stratified North American site, which is why it is included here. It's important because the settlement lay in the heart of a very diverse river valley environment, with an abundance of birds, fish, nut harvests, and grasses, as well as winter deer hunting in the nearby woodlands. At Koster, you can chronicle the gradual trend toward more permanent settlement and toward larger encampments, occupied for most, if not all the year. The latest settlement, dating to as late as 2800 B.C., was occupied just before the first experiments with the deliberate cultivation of native grasses began elsewhere in the Midwest and Southeast. The sheer elaboration and intensity of exploitation of food resources such as shallow water fish and nut harvests pre-adapted the Koster people for cultivation, an issue we explore in Chapters 7 and 8.

With its deep, stratified occupations and rich food remains, Koster is a remarkable chronicle of the intensification of hunting and gathering over thousands of years.

Chapter 5 ends with a brief discussion of arctic hunter-gatherers, where the intensive hunting of sea mammals resulted in dramatic changes in human life after about 1500 B.C.

chapter

AFRICANS AND AUSTRALIANS

The Chapter in Review

- As the Ice Age ended, hunter-gatherer groups living in Africa and Asia adapted to increasingly diverse adaptations to local environments.
- In sub-Saharan Africa, people turned their attention to smaller browsing animals, continually adapting to changing environmental conditions, a change well documented at Eland's Bay in South Africa. They focused heavily on edible plant foods.
- The densest populations were probably concentrated in areas of abundant water and diverse animal and plant resources. It was from these diverse societies that modern-day African hunter-gatherer groups are descended.
- The later hunter-gatherers of southern Africa are well documented from rock paintings and archaeology.
- Controversy surrounds the interpretation of San art from this region, which may be connected with shamanistic rituals and altered states of consciousness.
- During much of the last glaciation, New Guinea and Australia formed a single landmass, called Sahul. Sahul was settled perhaps as early as 50,000 to 70,000 years ago, but the earliest documented settlement is about 38,000 B.C. People using open-water craft had settled in the Solomon Islands of the southwestern Pacific by 26,000 B.C.
- First settlement of Australia dates to at least 33,000 B.C., but may be as early as 60,000 years before present. The controversy over first settlement continues. Securely dated sites proliferate after 35,000 years ago. Late Ice Age hunters flourished in Tasmania by 29,000 B.C.
- The later archaeological record shows that the Australian life way changed little over the millennia, except for some significant innovations in tool technology.

Key Cultures and Sites

Bobongara
Devil's Lair
Eland's Bay
Gwisho
Kilu
Klasies River
Koonalda
Kutikina
Lake Mungo
Lene Hara
Nelson's Bay
Parmerper Meethaner
Purritjara
Sahul
Sunda
Warreen

Introductory Comments

Chapter 6 surveys the first settlement of tropical regions in the Old World by modern humans, specifically Africa, offshore Southeast Asia, and Australia. These are unfamiliar archaeological stamping grounds for all but a small number of archaeologists living outside these areas, but both regions are of great importance and interest for anyone studying the great diaspora of *Homo sapiens sapiens.*

The chapter is divided into two parts:

- First, we survey what is known about sub-Saharan Africa, where San hunter-gatherers and other forager groups thrived into modern times. We also examine the controversies over the interpretation of San rock art, some of the most spectacular ancient art in the world.
- The second half of Chapter 6 examines the first settlement of Australia and the Pacific in the context of the major changes in geography in Southeast Asia during the late Ice Age. There may be evidence for the human settlement of Australia as early as 60,000 years ago.

This is necessarily a brief account, but one which covers the important issues and controversies. More detailed syntheses appear in the Guide to Further Reading at the end of the chapter.

Now Start Reading . . .

African Hunter-Gatherers

In both sub-Saharan Africa and Australia, the hunter-gatherer groups of modern times have deep roots in the remote past. This allows judicious use of ethnographic analogies for interpreting prehistoric sites and artifacts, and gives the archaeology an immediate relevance that it might not otherwise have.

Table 6.1 on page 65 places the sites and societies described in this chapter in a broad chronological perspective, with climatic changes to the left and developments elsewhere to the right. As we found in Chapter 3, the deepest roots of modern humans lie in tropical Africa. Thus, the settlement of offshore Southeast Asia and Australia was the work of modern humans, not more archaic people.

Figure 4.1a on page 48 shows the distribution of the African sites described in Chapter 7.

The African journey begins with the baseline of Klasies River, described in Chapter 3, and one of the seminal locations for the study of the origin of modern humans. From there, we discuss the increasing specialization in hunter-gatherer cultures, which may be due, in part, to rising sea levels (Eland's Bay) and climatic change during the Holocene, including a trend toward increasing aridity. The Site Box describes the Gwisho hot springs site in Zambia, Central Africa, where there are definite links in terms of subsistence practices with modern-day San groups. The exceptional level of preservation at this Central African site left an unusually complete picture of late Stone Age life on the savanna.

Gwisho, Zambia

The ego of an excavator reigns here! Yes, I excavated this site with Belgian archaeologist Francis Van Noten many years ago, which means that the excavation and analytical methodology is somewhat dated. But the general conclusions, summarized in the box, have stood the test of time. That's not why Gwisho appears here. The site is

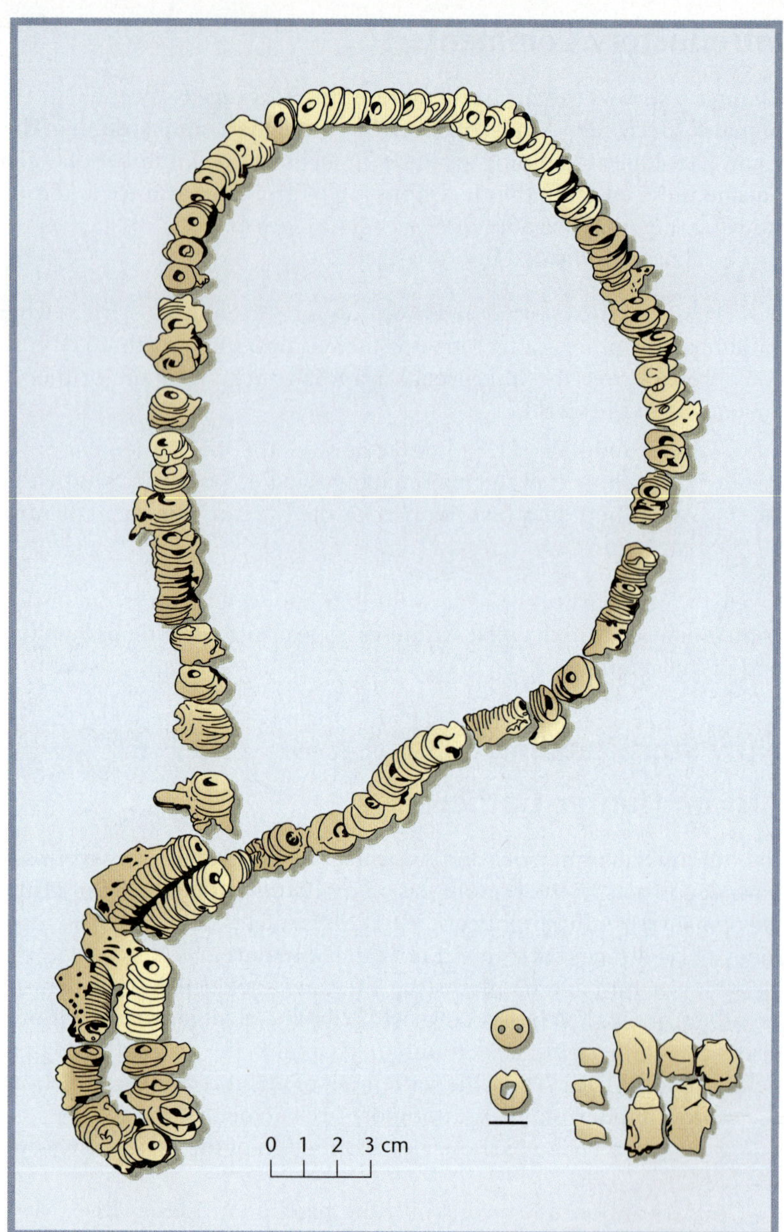

FIGURE 6.1 An ostrich-eggshell-bead necklace from a burial at Gwisho, Zambia, Central Africa (c. 1500 B.C.). The bead maker cut the beads to a roughly circular shape, then ground them against a fine, rocky surface to produce beads of even size.

important to this chapter for three reasons:

- The excellent preservation allowed survival of highly perishable artifacts and food remains. This enabled us to document a plant gathering economy, which focused on relatively few plants in the environment, when dozens more edible ones were available.
- The connection between the living !Kung San visitor and the food remains found in the site, suggests a continuity of hunter-gatherer culture over many centuries, millennia.
- The site is an excellent example of the controlled use of ethnographic analogy, and demonstrates the continuum between prehistoric and living hunter-gatherers in Southern Africa.

Burials from Gwisho wore shell-bead necklaces like the one depicted here. But the material remains from this and other sites do not adequately reflect the elaborate ritual and symbolic life enjoyed by these and other hunter-gatherer groups.

TABLE 6.1

Years B.C./A.D.	Climatic Change	Sub-Saharan Africa	Southeast Asia & Offshore	Developments Elsewhere
A.D. 1000	*Colder* ← → *Warmer*	Saharan gold trade	Settlement of offshore islands in Pacific (Chapter 12)	Maya civilization
A.D. 1		Spread of farming and iron technology	Rise of states in Southeast Asia (Chapter 17)	Shang civilization Sumerian civilization
		Cattle herding in Sahara (Chapter 16)	Rice cultivation	Food production in Southwest Asia
10,000 B.C.				
				First settlement of Americas
		Late Stone Age cultures	Increasingly specialized hunter-gatherers	
20,000 B.C.				Cro-Magnons in Europe
			Settlement in Solomon Islands	
			Hunter-gatherer settlement in Tasmania	
30,000 B.C.				
		Middle Stone Age cultures		
40,000 B.C.				Radiation of modern humans
			? First settlement of Australia	Neanderthals
50,000 B.C.				

Chapter 3

Notes

Controversies over Rock Art

About the only manifestation of these beliefs are the superb rock paintings found in caves and rock shelters throughout much of central and southern Africa. I describe the cutting-edge researches of rock art expert David-Lewis Williams, who delved into long-forgotten Victorian notebooks and ethnographies to produce new and, to some experts, controversial interpretations of the significance of the rock art. He believes that many paintings were connected to shamanistic activities and were painted by shamans emerging from states of trance—altered states of consciousness.

No question, Lewis-Williams's researches have opened a new chapter in rock art interpretation, to the point that similar interpretations have come into fashion in parts of North America, even for the Cro-Magnon art of southwestern France. Some experts are skeptical, and feel there is a real danger in considering all rock art to be the work of shamans, when it may well not be. The debate continues.

Hunter-gatherer societies flourished in East and Southern Africa right into the late twentieth century and have been the subject of classic researches by Richard Lee (the !Kung San), James Woodburn (the Hadza of Tanzania), and others. References will be found in the Bibliography.

Sunda and Sahul

The archaeology of Sunda and Sahul is a phenomenon of the past twenty years. Until the 1970s, almost nothing was known, except for a few isolated probes into caves and rock shelters, like the 40,000 year-old occupation at Niah Cave in Borneo. In recent years, Australian archaeologists in particular have been active not only on the islands, which are all that remains of Sunda, the late Ice Age continental shelf, but also in New Guinea and the nearby Pacific Islands.

At this early stage in research, we can do little more than report a handful of sites and radiocarbon or other dates. These provide tantalizing clues of early settlement. Thanks to dated sites, we know that Stone Age settlers lived as far offshore as the Solomon Islands by 30,000 years ago, possibly 10,000 years earlier in New Guinea, and about 30,000 years ago in East Timor. There is an emerging consistency in the dates here, which does not fit well with claims of 60,000 years or more for the first settlement of Australia to the south. Again, the dating issue is unresolved. Perhaps by about the Thirteenth edition of *People,* we will have a better idea of what happened!

One important point to remember: the furthest out people sailed in the Pacific during the late Ice Age was the Bismarck Strait and the Solomons in the extreme southwestern Pacific. It was not until about 1,000 B.C. that Lapita voyagers ventured further offshore to Polynesia and Micronesia (see Chapter 12). Such voyaging required outrigger canoes, sails, methods of navigating out of sight of land, and both root crops and edible animals that could be carried or stored on long canoe voyages. Until about 1,000 B.C., all navigation was line-of-sight, from landmark to landmark, island to island.

The First Settlement of Australia and What Happened Later

The map shows the major site locations mentioned in the Australian section of Chapter 6.

The first human colonization of Australia is as controversial as that of the Americas, even if the controversies do not enjoy such visibility. Once again, there are two schools of thought: those who think that humans settled on Sahul (the continent that included both Australia and New Guinea) as early as 60,000 years ago, and those who espouse a later settlement, about 35,000 years ago.

The claims of very early settlement are based on thermoluminescence dates from northern Australia and on a date of 60,000 years for one of the early Lake Mungo human skeletons from the south. Both datings are not universally accepted, and there are certainly no other sites to back up these two isolated, and unusually early, sites. Add to this the lack of sites earlier than 35,000 to 40,000 years ago on Sunda, already mentioned, and I wonder just how early settlement was.

Just as is the case in North America, the archaeological record suddenly expands, in this case after about 35,000 years ago, after which we can be certain of human settlement.

The jury is still out on this controversy, as it is in North America. In many respects the situation is eerily similar. In recent years, the earliest dates for human settlement in extreme northeast Siberia have come out around 13,000 years ago or slightly earlier. If this chronology is correct, then North America was settled as the Ice Age ended, not before. In the case of Sahul, much depends on whether future research reveals sites in the 60,000-year range on the Southeast Asian islands. At the moment, the evidence from Sunda tends to support a later Australian settlement—but archaeology has hardly begun and surprises are likely.

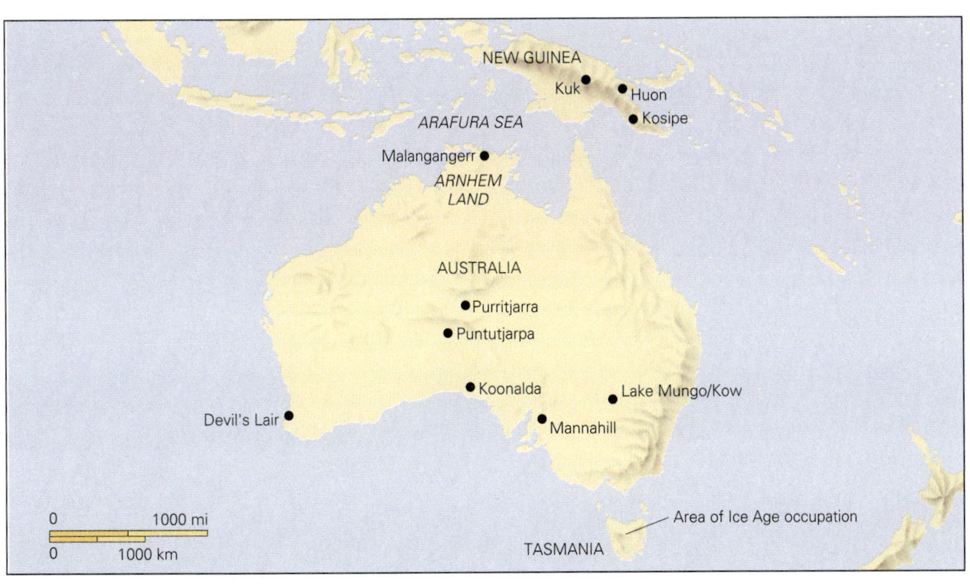

FIGURE 6.9 Archaeological sites in Australia and Tasmania.

Some of the earliest human occupation comes from Tasmania, where a series of rock shelter excavations have reconstructed the life way of wallaby hunters based on the southernmost Stone Age sites on earth, dating to before 30,000 years ago. These interesting sites show us that the earliest Australians were capable of adapting to climatic extremes.

The later prehistory of Australia is largely self-explanatory from our point of view, and needs no comment here. The interpretation of Australian rock art is made easier by rich repositories of oral tradition about the Dream Time, the supernatural world of the Australian Aborigines. The interpretative problems are very different from those surrounding San art.

chapter 7

INTENSIFICATION AND COMPLEXITY

The Chapter in Review

- The Ice Age ended after 13,000 B.C., ushering in the beginning of the Holocene period.
- Dramatic climatic changes marked the Holocene, including retreating ice sheets, major shifts in vegetational zones, and rises in sea level.
- Many large mammal species became extinct. Hunter-gatherer societies throughout the world developed highly localized adaptations to new, less predictable conditions, with a more intensive exploitation of food resources and, in many areas, a trend toward more permanent settlement, the use of storage technologies, and more complex societies.
- Complexity among hunter-gatherers became widespread after the Ice Age, especially in areas of exceptional resource diversity. Controversy surrounds the issue of complexity, with one school of thought arguing for a connection between resource diversity and abundant, diverse food supplies, and the other considering fishing a strategy of last resort resulting from population pressure and shortage of other foods. Alternatively, it may be due to rapid environmental change.
- This increased social complexity is well documented in the Mesolithic cultures of Scandinavia, where groups exploited maritime resources and birds extensively. Such increases in social complexity were marked by higher population densities, more intensive food exploitation, more long-distance exchange, and greater social ranking, detected in burial ornaments.
- These shifts also appear in the eastern Mediterranean region of Southwest Asia, especially among the Natufian people, who were intensive foragers of wild cereals and nuts, as well as expert gazelle hunters.
- Such intensification of the food quest and greater sedentism preadapted many groups for adopting agriculture and animal domestication.

Key Cultures and Sites

Ahrensburgian
Bromme
Ertebølle culture
Guilá Naquitz
Hoko River
Kebaran culture
Kongemose culture
Maglemose culture
Mesolithic
Natufian culture
Ozette
Star Carr
Swiderian
Vedbaek

Introductory Comments

Chapters 7 and 8 are rather generic, for they deal with worldwide issues, in this case the intensification and greater complexity of hunter-gatherer societies after the Ice Age. The chapter combines a certain amount of general comment and some excursions into theory, but is fundamentally a straightforward narrative, revolving around two basic issues:

- What effect did the dramatic environmental and climatic changes after the Ice Age have on humanity? A fascinatingly contemporary issue: global warming, this time not caused by human acts, and society.
- Why did some hunter-gatherer societies become more culturally, socially, and political complex than others? This is a vigorous debate today, and one that is far from resolved.

Here's how the chapter is organized:

- We begin by defining the Holocene and examining the major environmental and climatic changes, which took hold after the Ice Age, that is to say after about 13,000 B.C.
- Then we look briefly at the strategies which hunter-gatherers use to cope with environmental variation, and review some of the consequences of said environmental change.
- Next, we survey the fascinating Mesolithic cultures of western Europe, which are little known to American archaeologists. The Star Carr Box is especially interesting, because of the long history of research at that site. More complex Mesolithic societies developed in Scandinavia after 7500 B.C., so the description of them leads into a discussion of some of the theories surrounding the growing complexity of hunter-gatherer societies.
- Finally, we describe the Kebaran and Natufian cultures of southwestern Asia, which preceded the appearance of agriculture in that region, societies that were clearly preadapted to growing food rather than foraging for it.

Now Start Reading . . .

The Holocene, Environmental Variation, and the Mesolithic

First, I set the stage, with a brief description of the major climatic changes at the end of the Ice Age. Not only was there rapid global warming during the Bølling-Allerod Interstadial, but then a sudden thousand-year cold snap, the Younger Dryas of about 11,000 B.C., which had major effects on human societies.

It's only in recent years that we have had fine-grained enough evidence for the Younger Dryas, which must have been a traumatic thousand years to live through, especially in areas like southwestern Asia, where intense droughts replaced much wetter conditions and people relied heavily on plant foods.

Here's the real innovation: New ice core research shows how the Holocene atmosphere is almost a third richer in CO_2 than that of any of the preceding 120,000 years. CO_2 is vital to plant growth, thus producing more productive and cold and drought resistant tolerant Holocene plants than those of the late Ice Age. This may be one reason why plant foods of all kinds played such an important role in early Holocene societies, thereby helping preadapt them to agriculture (see Chapter 8).

Table 7.1 simply covers the major cultures in Europe and Southwest Asia described in this chapter and is self-evident. This is purely to give you a chronological perspective on the narrative.

Figure 7.1 chronicles population growth during the Ice Age and afterward, and a situation where the world was filling up—for hunter-gatherers.

TABLE 7.1
Climatic and generalized archaeological sequence in Europe and Southeast Asia after the Ice Age

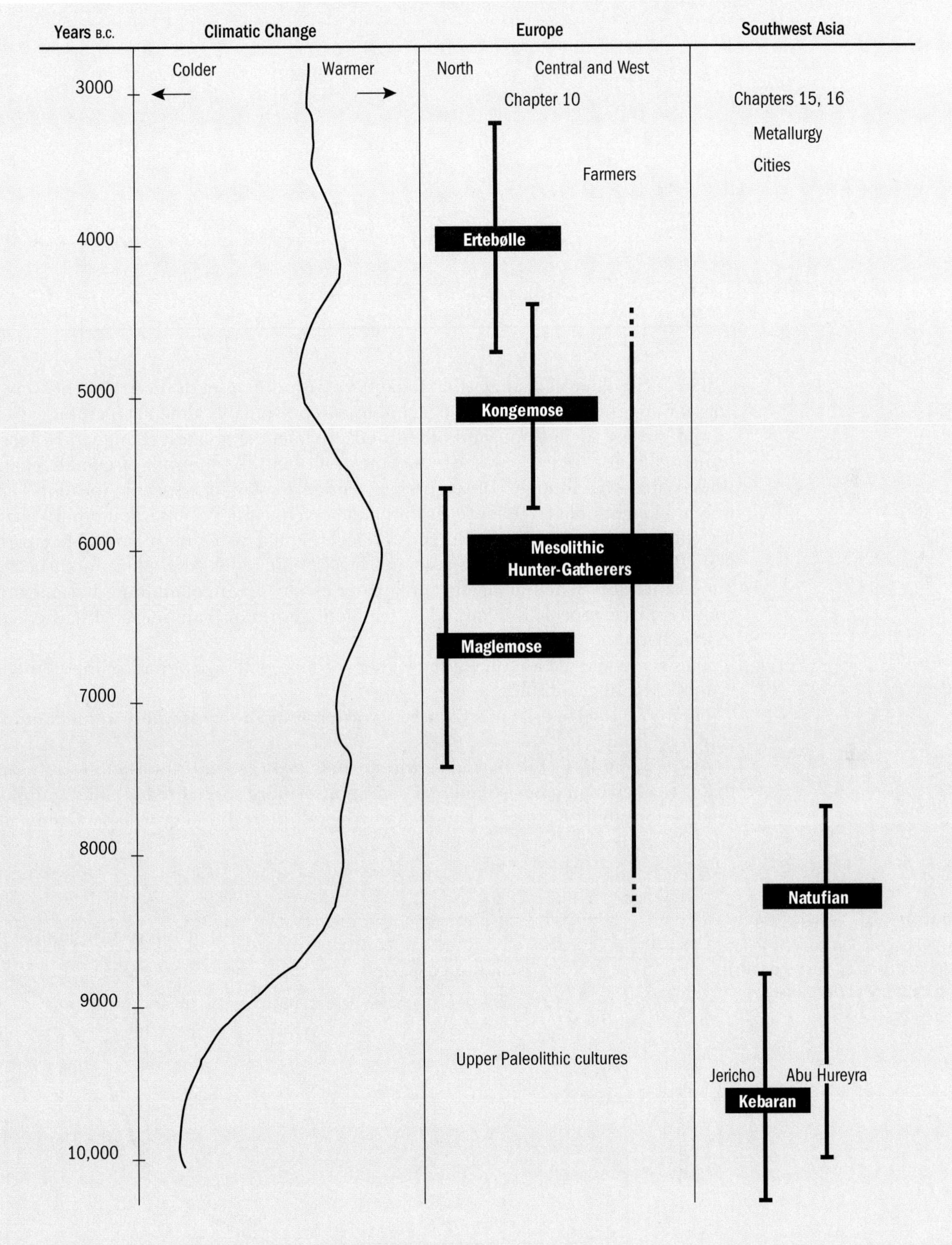

Notes

The technological changes that took place with the onset of the Holocene were all adaptations of earlier late Ice Age technologies, presumably aimed at increasing yields of wild grasses, small game, and other foods. In fact, the greatest change in Holocene hunter-gatherer life ways was a reduction in mobility. As the rate of climate change slowed after the Younger Dryas, people tended to stay in a specific location. They were no longer obliged to move, as they had been in earlier times when rapidly changing climatic conditions caused them to relocate quickly to a more favorable environmental niche. As temperatures rose and local populations rose, plant foods became important. More sedentary living and greater expertise with plant foods became more commonplace, especially in areas like the Baltic shores of Scandinavia, discussed later in the chapter.

This is why the section on coping with environmental variation is so important and is worth reading carefully.

Figure 7.3 is self-explanatory, but it is worth noting the areas where affluent hunter-gatherers lived.

As we mention in the narrative, the greatest technological innovations were ones that reflect changing environmental conditions—more specialized toolkits and much smaller stone tools. Figure 7.6 demonstrates microlithic technology, which was ultimately

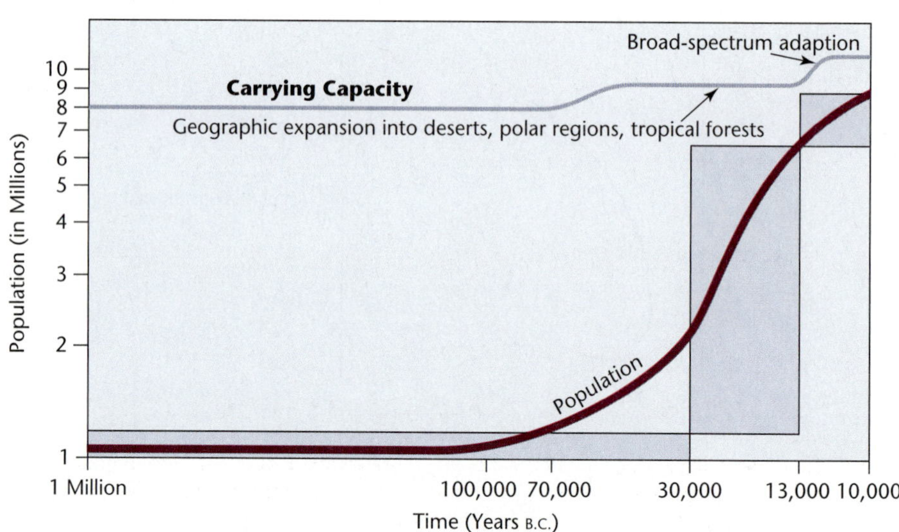

FIGURE 7.1 Increases in world population during the Ice Age matched against the carrying capacity of the globe for humans.

Bering Strait region
Maglemose, Kongemose, Ertebølle
Northwest
Coast
Kebaran and Natufian
Jomon
Western
North America
Midwest and
Southeast
Peruvian
coast

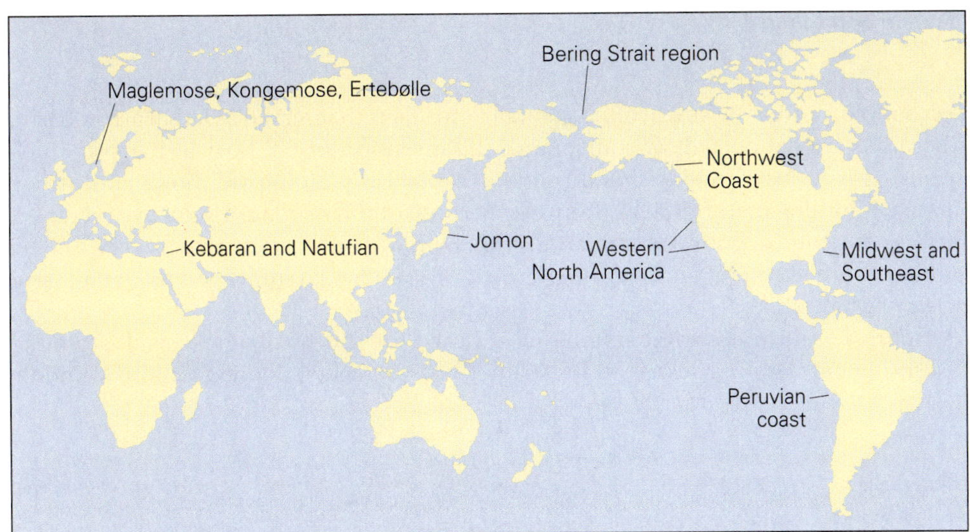

FIGURE 7.3 Map showing general areas where affluent hunter-gatherers mentioned in this book flourished.

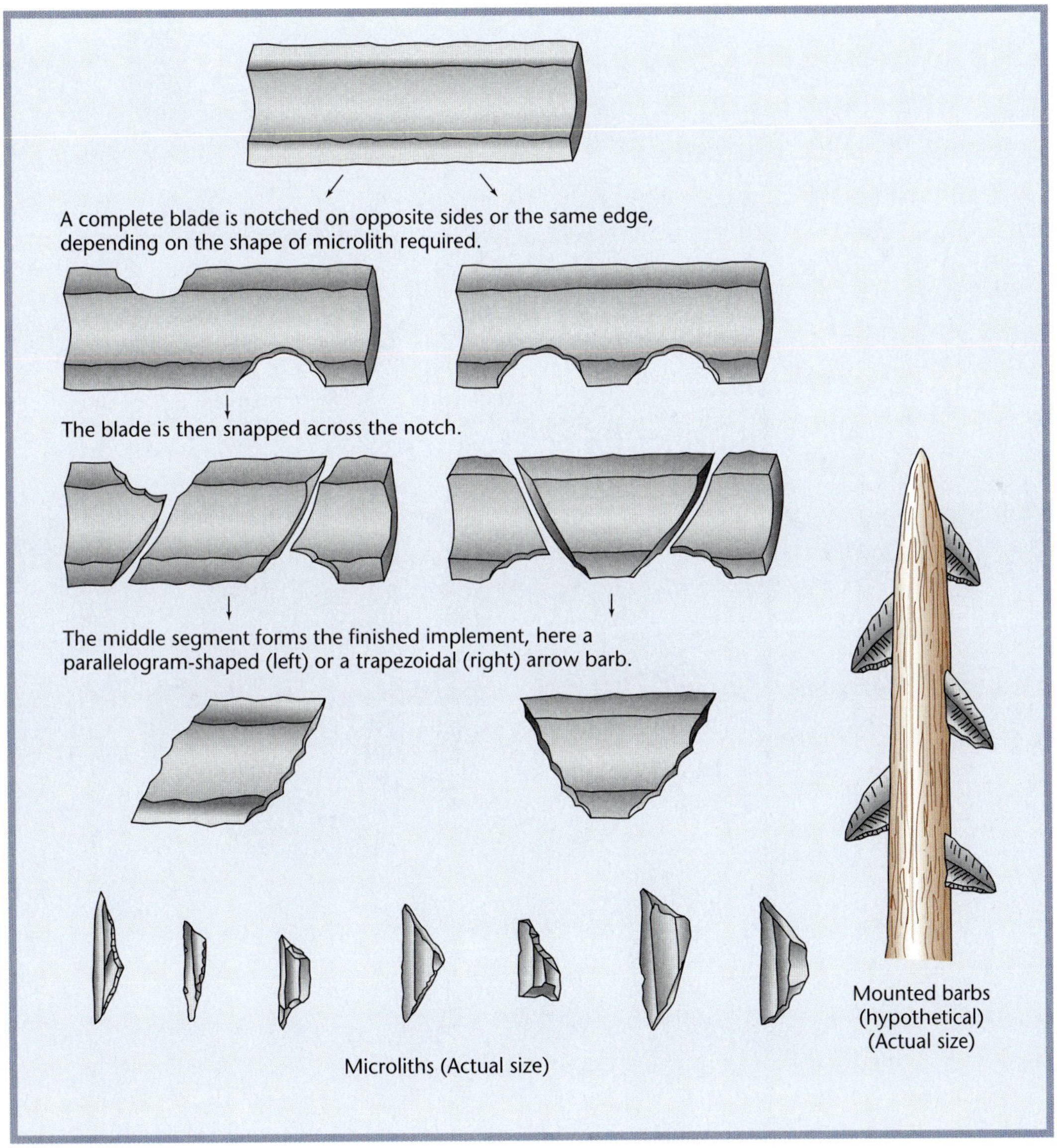

A complete blade is notched on opposite sides or the same edge, depending on the shape of microlith required.
The blade is then snapped across the notch.
The middle segment forms the finished implement, here a parallelogram-shaped (left) or a trapezoidal (right) arrow barb.
Microliths (Actual size)
Mounted barbs
(hypothetical)
(Actual size)

FIGURE 7.6 Microliths. Stages in manufacturing a microlith, a small arrow barb or similar implement made by notching a blade and snapping off its base after the implement is formed.

very simple, producing small, often geometric artifacts that served as lethal arrow barbs. Microliths are connected, of course, with the invention of the bow and arrow, which seems to have been one major invention of the early Holocene. Bows and arrows changed hunting methods, if nothing else because of their superior velocity and range, and also, to some degree, social relationships. Hunting with a spear requires close cooperation between several men; a hunter armed with a bow can hunt even moderate-sized quarry by himself.

Figure 7.7 illustrates some milling stones used for processing grass seeds from the Gwisho site in Zambia, described in Chapter 6. The pecked depression in the middle

FIGURE 7.7 Pounders and grinders used for processing wild vegetable foods from the Gwisho late Stone Age campsite, Zambia, central Africa, c. 1500 B.C. The peck marks served to hold the grains in place.

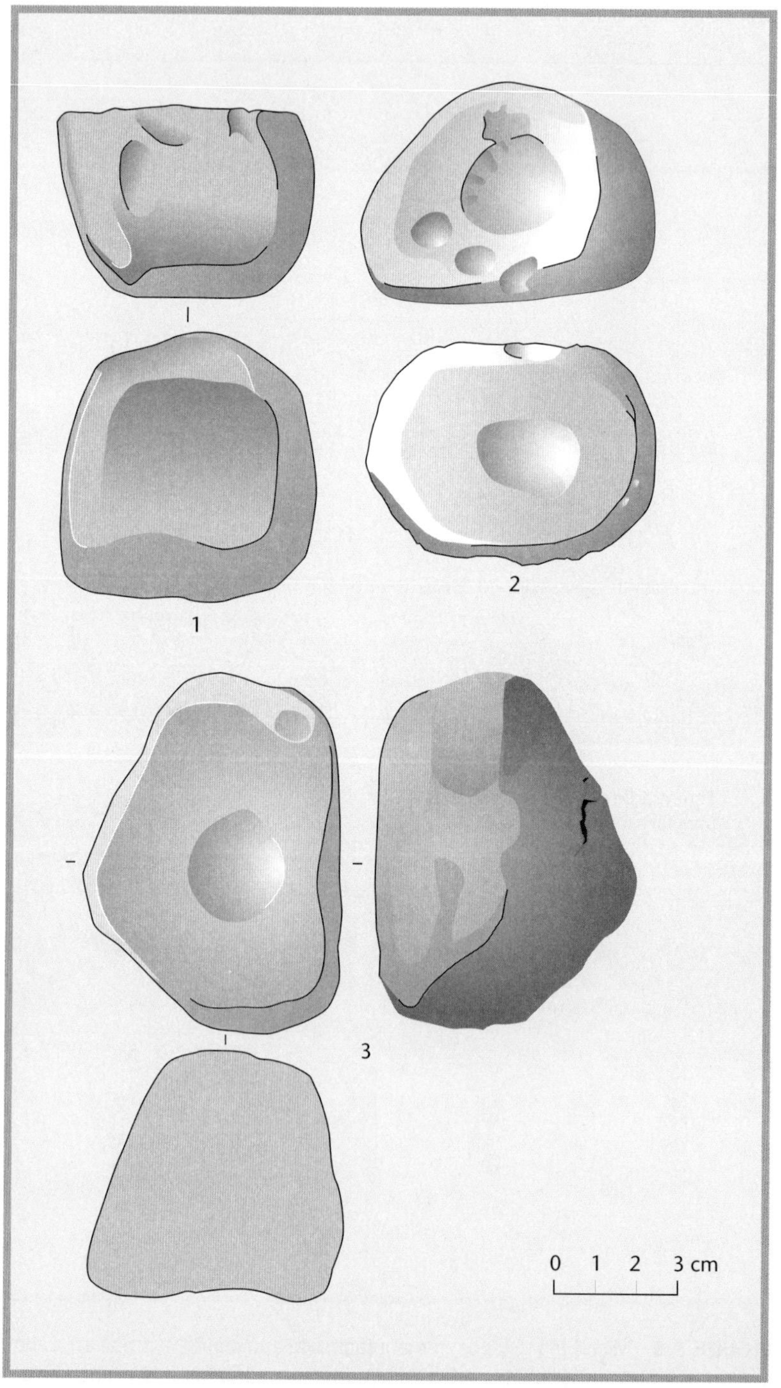

of the stone is characteristic of such artifacts in many parts of the world—another example of a simple, specialized technology.

Star Carr

The Star Carr site in northeastern England rarely figures in any world prehistories, for, in itself, it is merely one of many Mesolithic sites in northern Europe and was a temporary location revisited over many centuries. But the site is almost unique in Britain and is world-famous, simply because of the waterlogged conditions, which provided almost perfect preservation. The site is also internationally known because the excavations were published fully and completely within a few years of the completion of the dig, something that is almost unheard of in today's archaeology. Some Scandinavian waterlogged sites have yielded much more data, but they have never been published in the same widely accessible manner.

The site also owed much to the personality of the Cambridge University archaeologist Grahame Clark, one of the greatest prehistorians of the twentieth century. Clark's early career revolved around the Fenlands of eastern England, a marshy environment where he worked closely with botanists to link layers containing Mesolithic artifacts with well-dated pollen samples from peat levels. In this he was successful, realizing that he needed a waterlogged site to reveal the full range of Mesolithic life in Britain, then only known from scatters of microliths. An amateur archaeologist found Star Carr in 1947. Clark knew this was the place he had been looking for and excavated it over

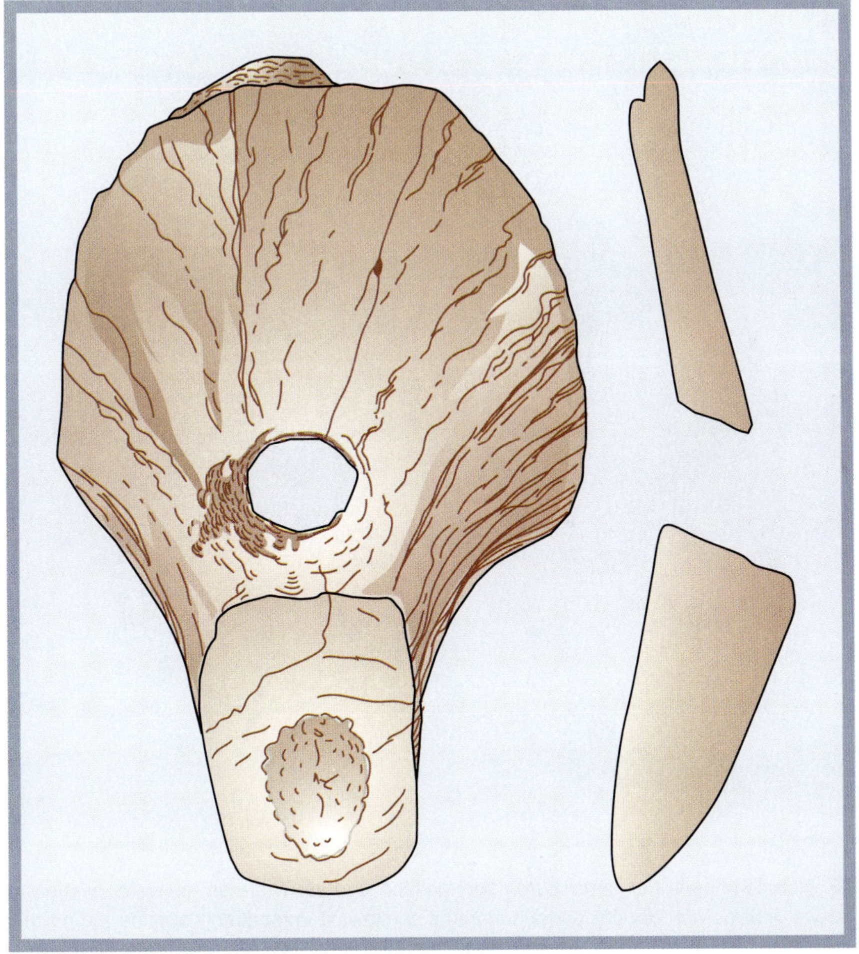

FIGURE 7.9 Elk antler mattock from Star Carr, England (two-thirds actual size).

three seasons with student assistance and on a financial shoe string—far less than the budget of even a small CRM excavation today.

Even today, Clark's *Excavations at Star Carr* (1954) is worth reading as an example of simple, clear archaeological reporting. Forty years of later work have revealed a more elaborate settlement, but shown the fundamental correctness of Clark's interpretation. Few sites have had such a lasting impact on archaeological thinking. The elk antler mattock shown on the previous page is an example of the many perishable artifacts from Star Carr.

FIGURE 7.12 Geometric Kebaran microliths, full size. Such small artifacts were manufactured in large numbers and mounted on wooden shafts as arrowheads or barbs.

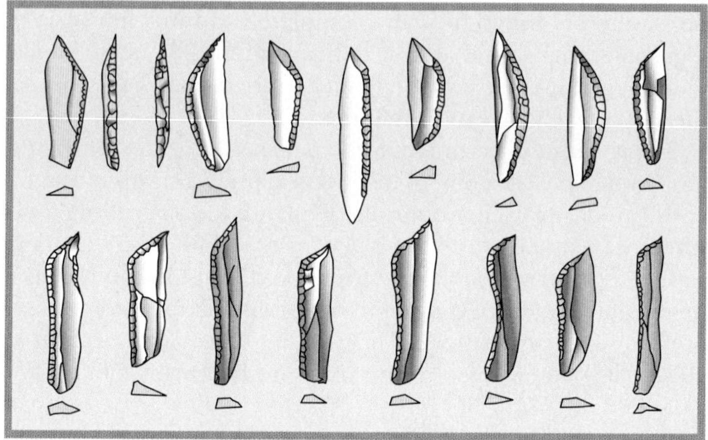

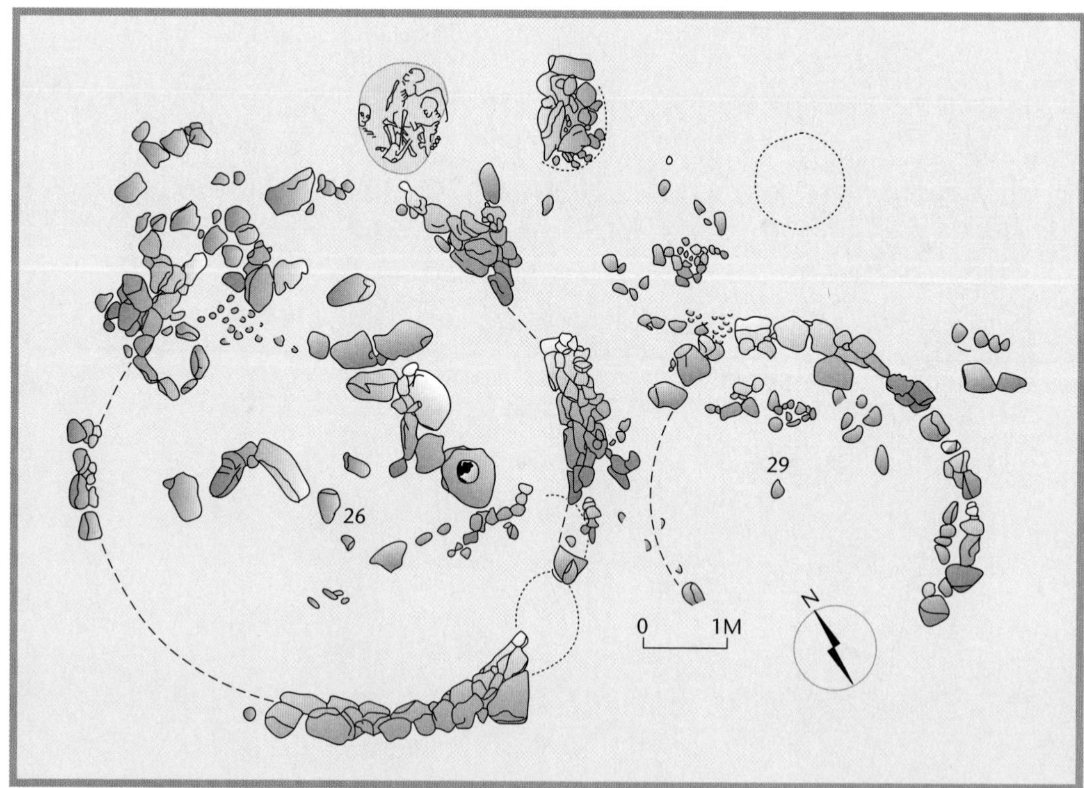

FIGURE 7.13 Natufian house foundations from Ain Mallaha, Jordan. There are mortars, pestles, and storage areas in Structure 26 (left) and a burial in a shallow pit immediately outside the north wall. The smaller hut (right) may have served as a storage area.

The brief description of Mesolithic societies in northern Europe reveals the importance of emerging complexity as an issue in the early Holocene. In recent years, the debate over complexity has focused on strategies used by Holocene hunter-gatherers to acquire food. This is a highly technical debate, which we summarized briefly here, as it is not totally central to our narrative. If you want to explore the whole issue of hunter-gatherer strategies more thoroughly, you have some heavy reading in front of you in Robert L. Bettinger's 2001 article "Holocene Hunter-Gatherers," listed in the Guide to Further Reading for this chapter.

Southwestern Asia

The final section of Chapter 7 describes hunter-gatherer societies in southwestern Asia, and the all-important Natufians, whom we will meet again in Chapter 9. Read this section carefully, as the adaptations made by the people living in this once well watered area that grew drier mirrors those in North America and other areas, where plant foods became major staples.

Figure 7.14 is especially interesting, for it shows serrated sickle blades mounted in a bone handle, said to be tools used for harvesting wild grasses. The blades display the characteristic silica gloss deposited by cutting such stalks. But I sometimes wonder why the edges were serrated. Surely a sharp edge would be more effective. Could these tools have had some other use?

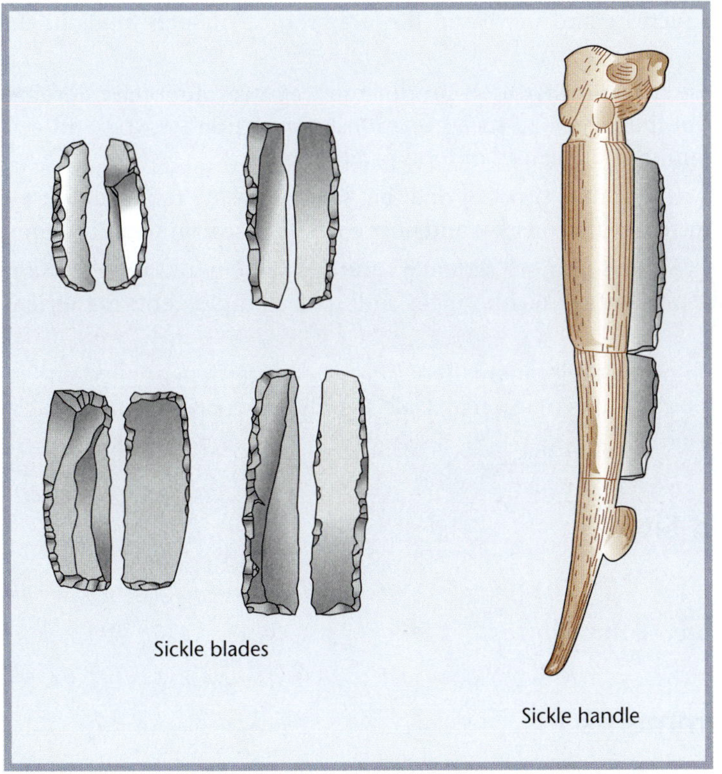

FIGURE 7.14 Natufian bone-handled sickle and flint blades.

chapter

A PLENTEOUS HARVEST: THE ORIGINS

The Chapter in Review

- Many late Ice Age and early Holocene hunter-gatherer societies were preadapted to food production, as they were already exploiting some food resources intensively and living more sedentary life ways.
- Most of these societies were in regions where food resources were diverse and seasonally predictable.
- Higher levels of CO_2 in the atmosphere after the Ice Age resulted in much higher plant productivity and increased the importance of such foods in the human diet.
- In contrast to early theories that food production was a revolutionary development, modern hypotheses invoke social relations, population growth, and ecological factors as multivariate causes of food production.
- Its development was a gradual process, one that saw increasing reliance on food crops, especially in areas with constant and unpredictable environmental change.
- Food production resulted in more sedentary human settlement, more substantial housing, elaborate storage technologies, and special implements for agricultural tasks.
- All these technological developments led to greater interdependence and to more long-distance exchange of raw materials, as well as increasing human social complexity.

Key Cultures and Sites

Guilá Naquitz

For others, see Chapters 9 through 13.

Introductory Comments

With the beginning of Part III, we enter a new chapter of human prehistory, the period when food production replaced hunting and gathering as the dominant life way of humankind. This is how I have organized the discussion:

- Chapter 8 begins with a relatively short summary of the major theories about the origins of food production.

- Then we discuss the consequences of food production, which were much more important than its mere development.
- We examine animal domestication, the changes in plants that result from their cultivation, and the technological innovations that resulted from the new economies.

Please spend a little time on this short chapter, as the ideas in it are of considerable importance in later prehistory.

The reading at the end of this chapter of the *Companion* is especially important (and not found in the text). It describes the basic dynamics of subsistence farming, a critical element in early agricultural societies. It's worth reading carefully.

Now Start Reading . . .

Theories About Origins

The theoretical debate over the origins of food production goes back to the late nineteenth century, with no resolution in sight. Today, compared with a century ago, we know a great deal about the dynamics of hunter-gatherer life, and about those of subsistence agriculture—which means that the debate is sharpened and more informed. Most scientists assume that ever-growing populations and human pressure on food resources were the primary factors driving the changeover. However, a few scholars point to much more subtle influences, such as changes in social and political organization and in day-to-day strategies for survival, as key players. There's a tension between ecological and social approaches, which is bringing new ideas into the arena. Among them are the changing roles of men and women in daily life, which we discuss in connection with the Abu Hureyra site in Syria in Chapter 9, and the role of social inequality and specialist artisans in transforming hitherto egalitarian societies.

It's important to realize that there is no resolution of this debate, for, with every new discovery, with advances in genetics and related fields, the ground changes beneath our feet and research agendas change rapidly. All I can give you here is a summary of some of the current thinking, which evolves significantly with every edition of this book.

Figure 8.2 speaks for itself and documents the surge in human populations on earth since the appearance of food production.

The summary theoretical discussion is relatively straightforward. I suspect, however, that I am downplaying the importance of climate change to a significant degree. It's only in recent years that we have begun to realize just how important the Younger Dryas, with its droughts, was in changing hunter-gatherer life ways in southwestern Asia. Remember that this was an area of now-high plant productivity, where people were very dependent on fall nut harvests and wild grasses. Make no mistake, some of

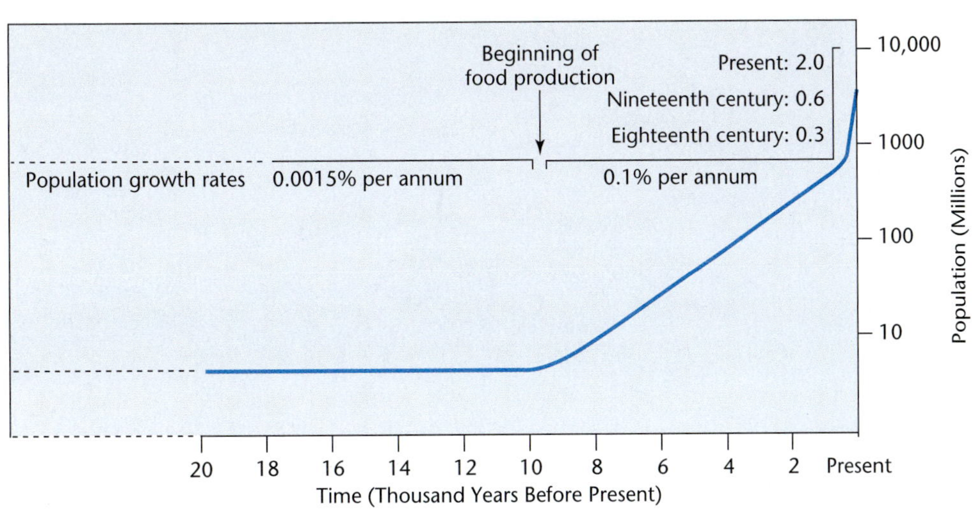

FIGURE 8.2 World population changes since the beginnings of food production. There has been an explosion in human population densities in the past 10,000 years.

these wild grasses were highly productive, so a prolonged drought cycle could have had a devastating effect on society.

Notice that I say "society." This is because we cannot indulge in straight cause-and-effect explanations, to the effect that drought *caused* food production. It did not. It was peoples' decisions when confronted with drought that played a defining role, even if they do not appear in the archaeological record except in terms of their material results.

Guilá Naquitz

Guilá Naquitz is a classic excavation, rather like Star Carr, a case study cited in many courses as a superb example of ecological archaeology and research into ancient subsistence in action. The site itself is remarkable for its unspectacular finds, but is a tribute to the extraordinarily fine-grained information that can be gleaned from a single location visited occasionally by hunter-gatherers becoming increasingly dependent on plant foods. If you want to read an archaeological monograph bristling with technical reports, yet full of common sense discourse on archaeology, theory (and the quirks of archaeologists), you will not go far wrong with the monograph on Guilá Naquitz, edited by Kent Flannery (1986). The box summarizes the main details of an investigation conducted before AMS radiocarbon dating came along. New AMS dates have refined the chronology at the site, but changed few of Flannery's conclusions. Computer simulations, at the time a new feature of archaeological research, played an important role in this investigation. Flannery himself is very much of the "culture as adaptation" side of archaeology, although he has thought deeply about the role of society in culture change.

Accelerator Mass Spectrometry (AMS) radiocarbon dating is the most accurate way of dating much of prehistory, when the dates are calibrated with coral or tree-rings. The method comes into its own with the origins of agriculture, simply because you can date individual seeds rather than merely the levels in which they are found. This means that, within a generation or so, we will have remarkably precise dates for the beginnings of agriculture in different parts of the world based on actual seeds grown by those who experimented with the new economies. These new dated seeds, combined with genetic fingerprinting, will allow us to trace the actual areas of domestication far more accurately than is possibly merely with archaeological sites like Abu Hureyra (see Chapter 9), or the Tehuacán Valley in Mexico (see Chapter 13).

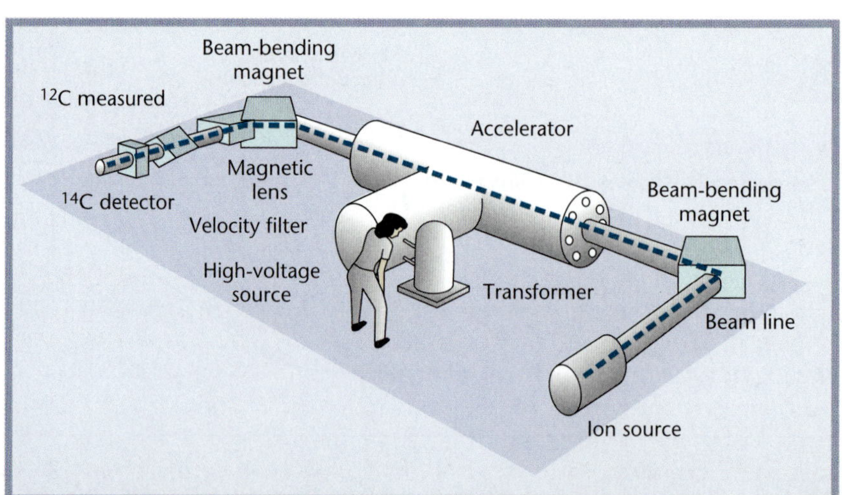

FIGURE 8.3 AMS radiocarbon dating. (Modified from B. Smith, 1998.)

I suspect that the dates for the first domestication of wild grasses in southwest Asia, China, and the Americas will go back deeper into the past than we currently suspect. But they won't go back into the late Ice Age, simply because plants weren't so productive then and people exploited them less intensively.

The Consequences of Food Production

This is an important section, for the consequences of food production were far more important than its invention. As we shall see, the new economies spread rapidly, replacing older hunter-gatherer life ways irrevocably, with momentous consequences for humanity. In some parts of southwestern Asia, for example, only 5,000 years or so passed before village farming societies turned into complex chiefdoms, then civilizations. In Mesoamerica, the same change took hold over a shorter period, perhaps as little as 2,000 years—we cannot be absolutely sure.

This passage of Chapter 8 is straightforward, as are the sections on animal and plant domestication.

I must confess that I debated whether to include these two diagrams, compiled by British archaeobotanist Gordon Hillman. They are complicated, yet of great importance, for they document the all-important change from wild to domesticated crops. Read the caption for Figure 8.7 with special care, as here I encapsulate the essence of Hillman's argument—that the changeover to domesticated grains took hold remarkably quickly, within a few generations. Let's stress once again, however, that the changeover took placed in many areas over a long period. We are not talking about a single epochal event here.

The Dynamics of Subsistence Agriculture (Which Is Not Covered in the Main Text in Any Detail!)

Chapter 8 skirts around a fundamental aspect of early agriculture—that of the dynamics and realities of subsistence farming.

The following account of the dynamics of subsistence agriculture among the Gwembe Tonga of Central Africa serves as background for this simulation exercise. Even if you do not attempt the exercise (which takes about a couple of hours), you will find the following background generally useful.

Agriculture Among the Gwembe Tonga

Surprisingly few archaeologists have ever witnessed subsistence agriculture in action. Many of them are totally unaware of the complex dynamics and realities that drive such farming, still practiced in many parts of Africa and the Americas to this day. During my early career, I (BF) spent considerable time among the Gwembe Tonga of the Middle Zambezi Valley in Central Africa. There, I learned the harsh realities of subsistence farming first hand—the uncertain, capricious rainfall that could water a field adequately, yet leave one two miles away dry. I learned that the dynamics of such farming depend heavily on reciprocity, on kin ties, and on diversifying one's options when planting crops.

Even today, millions of hectares of farming land are tended by shifting cultivators in Africa, Asia, and the Americas. They grow cereals like wheat and barley, also maize, millet, and sorghum. Other groups concentrate on root crops—manioc, yams, taro, potatoes, sweet potatoes, and so on. So varied are the world's environments that there

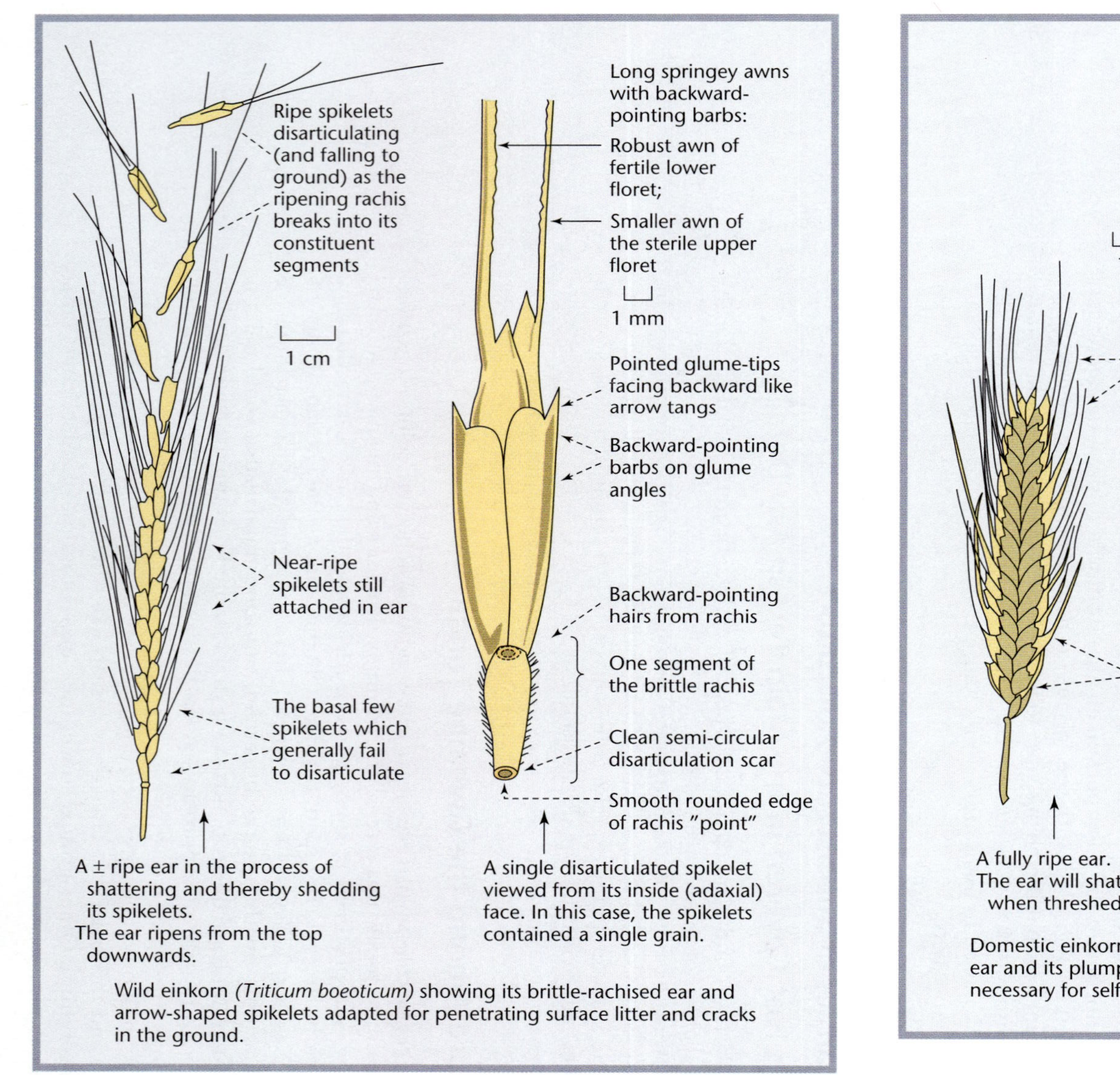

FIGURE 8.6 The features affecting seed dispersal and spikelet implantation in wild and domesticated einkorn wheat.

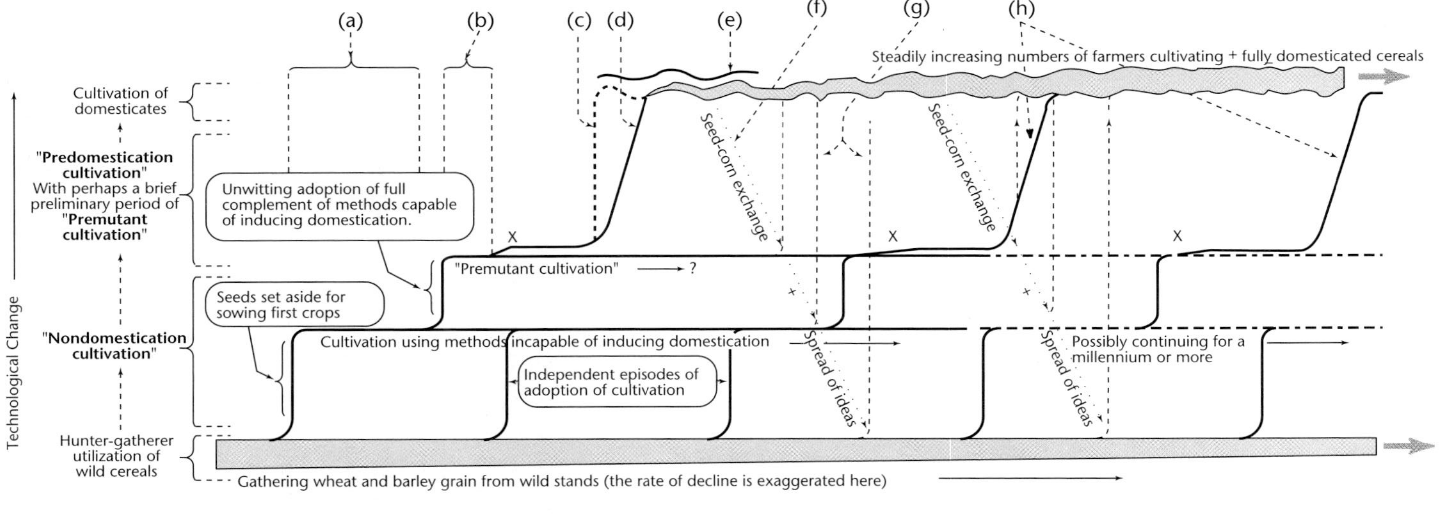

FIGURE 8.7 A summary of the principal events associated with the domestication of wheat and barley. For the sake of argument, this diagram assumes that the domestication of both the wheats and the barleys occurred at several settlements independently. Key to the table: (a) Nonhusbandry domestication. Husbandry (cultivation) methods are incapable of causing domestication. This process may have continued for a long time at some sites but was not universal. (b) A possible temporary period (at some settlements) of premutant cultivation of crops in which domestication-inducing methods were now applied but domestic-type mutants were still absent, so that the start of domestication was delayed even further. (c) Effect of imposing conscious selection midway through the selection process. (d) The primary domestication curve—without conscious selection. (e) Fluctuations in the completeness of domestication due to the incomplete fixation of modifier genes. (f) Transmission of seeded stocks of domesticates to farmers practicing sporadic cultivation and even to hunter-gatherers. Also, transmission of the knowledge of domestication-inducing methods of husbandry to farmers lacking the technology. (g) Abrupt appearance of domesticates in settlements that had just acquired domesticated seed stocks through exchange. (h) Later (independent) domestication of crops at other settlements.

is no such thing as a "typical" shifting cultivator. But all such horticultural societies share a number of common features:

- All use simple technology and labor-intensive methods to clear and cultivate the soil;
- Few of them employ manuring or fertilizer other than ash from burning off cleared brush;
- Their land-use systems depend on an abundance of farming land and relatively low population densities. As long as these two factors remain in balance, their adaptations remain viable and long lasting.

The Gwembe Tonga (sometimes called the Tonga or Valley Tonga) of the low lying, hot Middle Zambezi Valley of central Africa offer an excellent example of how shifting cultivators exploit a mosaic of different soil types. Before they were resettled from their traditional homeland in the 1960s, they lived on the Zambezi floodplain, their lives dictated in part by the great river's annual floods.

The Zambezi River forms the Gwembe Valley as it cuts across southern Africa. The valley forms the boundary between Rhodesia and Zambia. In the late 1950s, a dam was built on the Zambezi, just below the valley, forming Lake Kariba. Due to the permanent flooding of their traditional farmlands, the Gwembe Tonga were relocated. Although their traditional way of life was forever disrupted, the data collected by the anthropologists sent in to assess the impact of the relocation, as well as the causes of endemic famine in the area, forms the basis of the simulation.

The Environment

The environment inhabited by the Valley Tonga is one of extremes. Extremes of heat and cold, extremes of rainfall or the lack, and extremes exhibited by the flow of the river. There are three distinct seasons in the region—the rainy season from November to March, the cold season from April to August, and the hot season from August to November. The seasons in turn are marked by monthly and annual cycles of rainfall and changes in the flow of the Zambezi.

The following pages provide you with some indication of the range of variation in river flow and temperature from year to year and during the year. Study these carefully, because some of this information will guide your planting and harvesting decisions during the simulation. When you read the sections on the economic and agricultural dynamics of the Gwembe Tonga, you may want to refer back to the map that follows. Remember that while a Tonga may have intimate knowledge of the soils, topography and seasonal cycle of rainfall, flood, and dry to guide him in the annual rituals of planting and harvesting, you do not. Your success as a subsistence farmer depends on your ability to absorb this information to guide you in making the right choices as you plant and harvest your crops. While there is certainly an element of common sense in the successful farmer, do not underestimate the importance of specialized knowledge in the quest for survival.

Annual River Level Change

The river level begins to rise in December, and continues rising until March or April. There's a dramatic variability in river flow from year to year. If the flood level is not high enough, the Tonga's floodplain fields do not receive the necessary load of rejuvenating silt, and their productivity is diminished. If the river floods too much, the floodplain and river bank fields are exposed too late for planting, or may be too wet to grow the necessary crops.

Annual Temperatures

The highest temperatures occur from August to October. There is a gradual decline during the rainy season, and then a significant drop in temperatures from April to July—the cold season. The hot season is the period of greatest strain on resources because water and food supplies tend to be in shortest supply then. Survival during these months depends on adequate storage.

Technology

As with many groups of subsistence farmers, the material culture of the Gwembe Tonga is highly functional and fairly restricted, without a great deal of elaboration. This is not to say that they have no arts or crafts, but that they do not have a substantial amount of time to spend on manufacturing goods. Because all of the labor energy involved in food production is human labor (they had no draft animals), there is seldom much time that people have free from agricultural chores to work on other projects. Good descriptions of other aspects of their material culture, such as pottery, weapons, drums, toys, etc., can be found in *The Material Culture of the Gwembe Tonga,* by Barrie Reynolds (1962).

The Tonga had garden shelters built with a low platform. This type of shelter is used to sleep in during the dry season when crops are maturing in the riverbank gardens, away from the village. You would stay here to keep vermin and hippopotamuses from invading your fields at night. They also had a type of mud-plastered granary used to store grains such as millet and sorghum. The peaked, thatched roof helps keep the rains out. The plastering helps to keep rats, birds, and other little thieves out of the food supply. In addition, the Tonga had granaries with walls made of wickerwork and built on elevated platforms of poles and mud plaster.

The Gwembe Tonga practice what is called slash and burn or swidden agriculture. When a new field is cleared, the men lop the lower branches off the taller trees, and cut down the smaller trees. The branches and other refuse are then piled around the taller trees, as in this picture, and allowed to dry out. Then the area is burned. The burning brings down the tall trees, and returns a certain amount of nutrients to the soil. After a few years, the field will have to be abandoned, or fallowed, in order to recover its fertility. Riverbank and floodplain fields do not need to be fallowed, however, because the flooding river deposits new soil each year—automatically rejuvenating the fields. The men use a variety of iron axes in the process of clearing new fields. They have wide blades and short handles. The bulge where the head is hafted on the handle serves both to secure the head and as an added weight to make the axe more efficient.

All planting and weeding is done with the traditional short-handled hoe. They have a knob on the end of the handle to keep it from slipping out of the hand. The hoe, like the axe, is designed with extra weight behind the head so that it does not have to be swung as hard to do the job. The handles are typically less than three feet long. As a result, both planting and weeding require a great deal of stooping over. Think what your back would feel like after eight to twelve hours of weeding with one of these!

It takes about ninety days for millet and sorghum to mature, and thirty to sixty days for the various vegetables produced. After the grain is mature it is harvested by hand using a long knife to cut the stalks. The grain is then stored. When the grain is to be used it must be threshed, winnowed, and then ground or pounded into flour. The threshing is done with a light stick, and serves to crack the husks of the grain. The winnowing is done with a large flat basket and separates the grain from the chaff. Final preparation into flour can either be done by grinding, as this woman is doing, or pounding in a wooden mortar and pestle. All of this work is done by women.

Economic Dynamics

As mentioned earlier, all labor energy involved in Gwembe Tonga agriculture is human labor. There are no mechanized cultivation or processing aids, not even draft animals to drag a plow or grinding wheel. As a result, a good measure of the productive potential of an individual rests on the amount of other people's labor they can count on. Husbands have access to the labor of their wives and children, women have access to the labor of their children.

Tasks that require more labor than that to which a person has direct access require an exchange. Thus, you might ask your brothers and other relatives to help in clearing a new field. In exchange you feed them a meal, perhaps brew some beer for them. In the long run, by helping you they have ensured that you will help them when they need assistance—either with your labor or with food if something should happen to their crops. Regardless of the amount of land an individual may own, if they do not have the labor resources to adequately guard it from predators, or to weed it, or to harvest the crop, they still may not be able to adequately feed themselves and their family. Conversely, someone with plenty of available labor, but insufficient land will have the same problem of not being able to fully take advantage of the available resources.

Among the Gwembe Tonga, each adult generally has ownership of one or more fields. Thus husbands and wives each have their own fields. Wives work in their husband's fields as well as cultivating their own. Their children are available labor for both sets of fields. Both husbands and wives also retain individual ownership of the products of their fields. Both have their own storage facilities. Wives feed their children, their husbands, and themselves from their stores until they run out. When the wife's stores do run out, she must then call on her husband to provide food from his stores to feed the family until the next crop is ready for harvest. The husband in turn can call on other relatives for food if his stores run out—provided that they have sufficient food to share. Thus, although individuals are essentially responsible for producing sufficient food for themselves and their immediate labor pool, there is a simple social safety net in the event of natural calamities such as ruined crops, elephant attacks, etc.

This system does a good job of mitigating the effects of localized calamities. On the other hand, more general catastrophes such as long term droughts affect everyone in the network so that when one person runs out of food and begins depleting other people's food supplies (in an environment where everyone's productivity is now lower) the entire system can become swamped very quickly and general famine ensues. As you will see in the simulation, while things are good everything works fine, but when things get bad, they deteriorate very rapidly and people start dying.

The Agricultural Dynamics

The Gwembe Tonga cultivated three types of fields: 1) Riverbank fields for vegetables and tobacco during the hot dry season, 2) Floodplain fields for sorghum and vegetables in the cold dry season, after the flood waters have receded, and 3) Upland fields for millet and some vegetables in the rainy season. Upland fields must be fallowed after about five years of cultivation in order to recover their fertility. In order to survive the full annual cycle, an individual must have access to upland and floodplain fields, and should have at least one riverbank field to fall back on for vegetables in the hot dry season. Grain is the staple food, and although it is supplemented with meats, vegetables, and wild plant foods, insufficient grain harvests will seriously affect the viability of any family.

The trick to surviving as a subsistence farmer is balancing the food requirements of your labor pool, the amount of productive land available to you, and the labor necessary to take advantage of the productive potential of the land.

chapter 

THE ORIGINS OF FOOD PRODUCTION IN SOUTHWEST ASIA

The Chapter in Review

- Southwest Asia was cool and dry immediately after the Ice Age, with dry steppe over much of the interior. Human populations were sparse and highly mobile as forests spread more widely throughout the region.
- The development and spread of food production took place under conditions of climatic change that favored wild annual cereal grasses. There was a general trend toward more sedentary life ways and a greater emphasis on storage technology and seed grinding after 10,000 B.C. (epitomized by the Natufian culture and related societies in the Levant and Anatolia, groups who foraged intensively for wild cereals).
- Farming began at Abu Hureyra on the Euphrates River in about 10,000 B.C. Sheep and goats replaced gazelle hunting abruptly at the same site and at other settlements after 8000 B.C.
- Abu Hureyra was not unique. Food production began in several regions more or less simultaneously, the Levant being one area, southeastern Anatolia another.
- Herding was well established somewhat earlier in the Zagros highlands, while farming communities linked by long-distance exchange routes handling obsidian and other exotica by at least 8500 B.C inhabited Anatolia.
- Cultural development then proceeded separately in each area of Southwest Asia, but there were increasingly frequent trading connections between each region, which accelerated even more after 3000 B.C.

Key Cultures and Sites

Only major sites mentioned in the chapter are listed here.

Abu Hureyra
'Ain Ghazal
Ali Kosh
Çatalhöyük
Çayönü
Ganj Dareh
Haçilar
Jarmo
Jericho
Netiv Hagud

Introductory Comments

This is the first of five chapters, which describe the origins of food production in different parts of the world. We begin in Southwest Asia, long known as one of the early cradles of agriculture and animal domestication, and the region where the most intensive research has been carried out. A generation ago, I would have said without hesitation that Southwest Asia was where the earliest agriculture began, but no longer. It's becoming clear, as research intensifies, that farming began in China earlier than believed, to the point that the beginning of food production there *may* have been as early as it was in the Levant. We'll have a better idea in a generation or so.

Chapter 9 is a straightforward narrative, which tries to simplify a very complicated story. It's summarized in the "chapter in review section" above. Just how complicated, we are only beginning to discover. Remember how in Chapter 8, we discussed early theories of the origins of agriculture and pointed out that it was pointless to look for the very first place where it all began. The research of the past ten years has shown that the new economies developed in many areas of Southwest Asia at about the same time, probably in at least partial response to the onset of the Younger Dryas, which brought drought to the eastern Mediterranean region.

Here, we tell the story of the first farmers, mainly focusing on the Levant, where the most is known, ending our story with the appearance of new, more sophisticated

FIGURE 9.1 Early farming sites in Southwest Asia, Europe, and the Nile.

farming economies in about 6000 B.C., some 4,000 years after the first farming villages appeared by the Euphrates and Jordan Rivers.

Now Start Reading. . .

The Scenario for the First Farming and the Levant Region

Notice how this section stresses the importance of climate change in the changeover from hunting and gathering to farming. I believe this is the most convincing scenario, given what we know at the moment, but remember what we said in Chapter 8 about Cauvin's theories on the importance of the relationship between humans and nature.

Figure 9.1 is self-evident. It's worth spending a few minutes getting the general geography into your mind, as there are a lot of places and sites in this chapter.

Table 9.1 is useful as a (very) general summary of the major sites and cultures and when they flourished. As research proliferates, so does the technical terminology. This is as simple as I dare make it!

Let's make one important point about this section of the chapter. I stress Abu Hureyra and Jericho here, largely because they are the best-known sites. I keep getting e-mails from people rebuking me for not mentioning other early farming settlements, which are better, bigger, or more relevant. Unfortunately, the sites concerned (which I am normally aware of) are almost invariably inadequately published and excavations are ongoing. Both Abu Hureyra and Jericho are thoroughly documented. Andrew Moore's Abu Hureyra monograph (2000) is a model of what such reports should be. Until we have more to go on, I am sticking to the old familiars, and with good reason.

Take a close look at the photographs of the Jericho plastered skull (Figure 9.4) and the 'Ain Ghazal figures (Figure 9.5). The latter also appear in the chapter opener. Both symbolize the huge surge in ritual activity and, apparently, religious belief after farming became established. I believe much of this was connected with fertility and with the close relationships between living farmers, their ancestors, and their communally owned land.

Abu Hureyra

Abu Hureyra is remarkable for the fine-grained information that Andrew Moore and his colleagues teased from the mound. This box describes one of the most imaginative pieces of research from the site, where biological anthropologist Theya Molleson used the human bones to examine male/female roles.

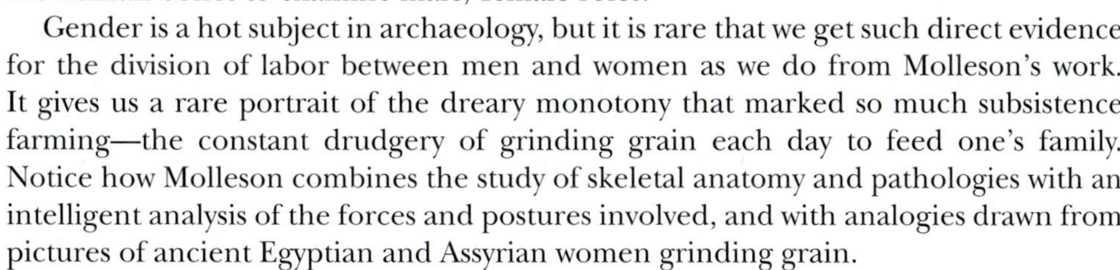

Gender is a hot subject in archaeology, but it is rare that we get such direct evidence for the division of labor between men and women as we do from Molleson's work. It gives us a rare portrait of the dreary monotony that marked so much subsistence farming—the constant drudgery of grinding grain each day to feed one's family. Notice how Molleson combines the study of skeletal anatomy and pathologies with an intelligent analysis of the forces and postures involved, and with analogies drawn from pictures of ancient Egyptian and Assyrian women grinding grain.

This is a lovely piece of research that is elegant in its simplicity and reasoning.

Zagros, Mesopotamia, and Anatolia

Once again, these are straightforward descriptions, which mask a tidal wave of new work, especially in Turkey. The new Anatolian sites are summarized in M. Özdogan and N. Basgelen's edited volume, *Neolithic in Turkey: New Discoveries* (1999), which is well worth consulting if you have a serious interest in this area. Unfortunately, I was unable to locate a copy when revising this edition of *People*. In particular, new discoveries of flamboyant painting and sculpture will put the famous Çatalhöyük paintings in

TABLE 9.1

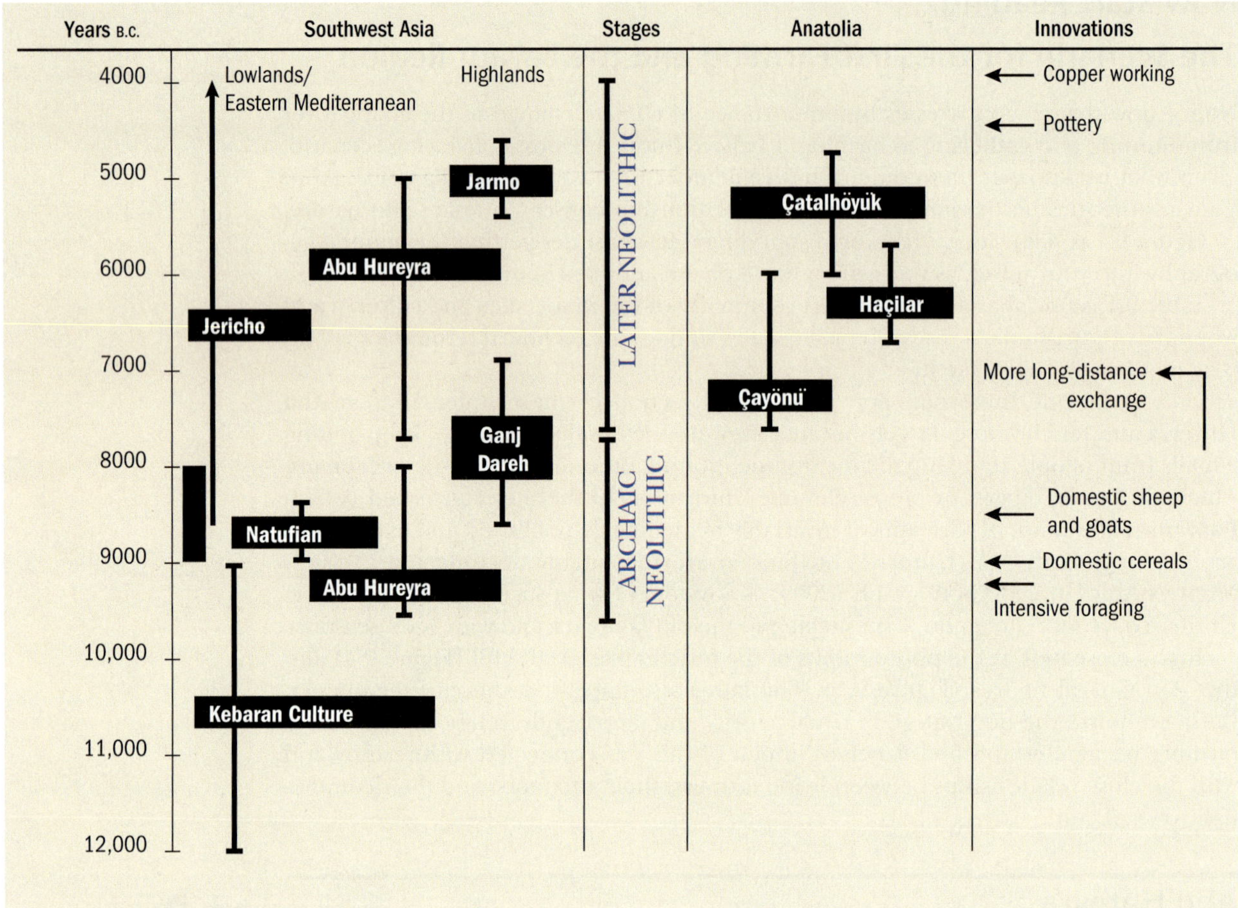

Notes

better historical perspective. No question, there were enormous social changes in human societies in the early millennia of farming.

These two figures illustrate features of Çatalhöyük excavated by Englishman James Mellaart in the 1960s. They show how the town's dwellings clustered together, perhaps for defense, and a reconstruction of one of the shrines. Whether these shrines were separate structures or integral parts of dwellings is the subject of much debate. Much of what we know about Çatalhöyük may change in the next decade or so, as a

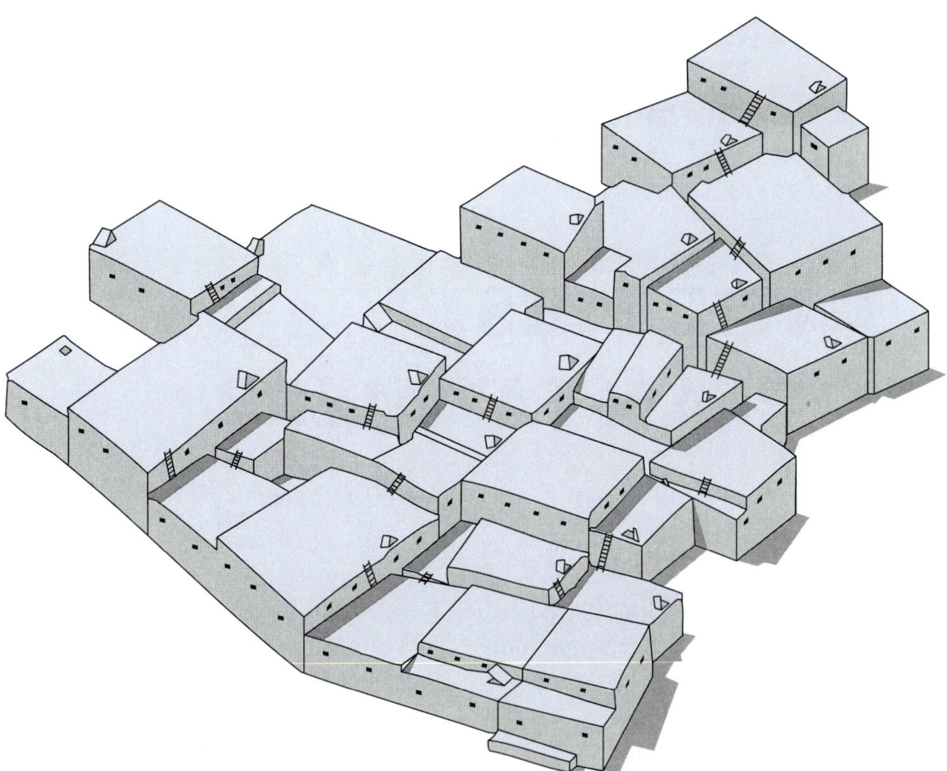

FIGURE 9.7 Schematic reconstruction of houses and shrines from Level VI at Çatalhöyük, Turkey, showing the flat roof architecture and the roof entrance.

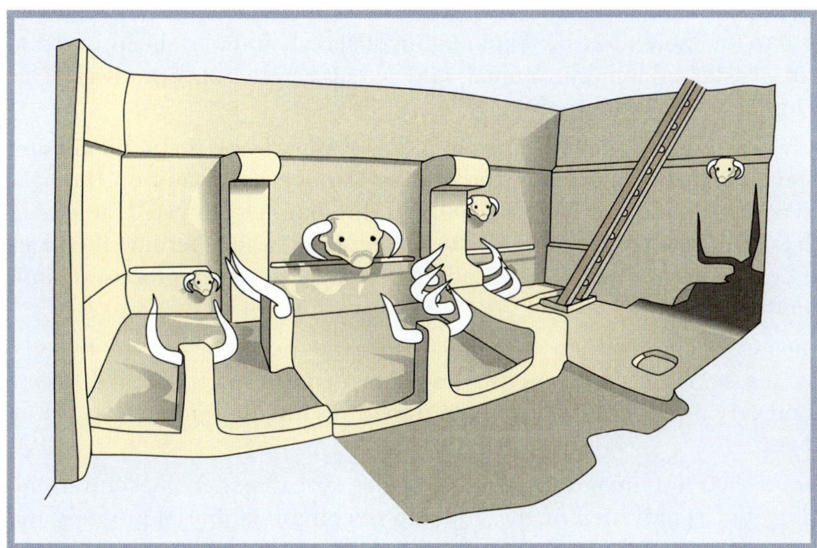

FIGURE 9.9 Reconstruction of the east and south walls of Shrine VI.14 at Çatalhöyük, Turkey, with sculpted ox heads, horns, benches, and relief models of bulls and rams. A ladder at right entered the shrine.

long-term international excavation uncovers more houses and studies every aspect of this extraordinary site.

Çatalhöyük flourished off the obsidian trade, as did many other communities in obsidian-rich Anatolia. Sourcing studies are revolutionizing our understanding of obsidian trade, allowing the linking of specific obsidian outcrops with trade routes in a reliable way. You can find a lot of information about sources in Turkey by typing "obsidian Turkey" into the Google search engine on the Web.

As we said earlier, this chapter carries us from the beginnings of food production up to the appearance of more sophisticated farming societies in about 6000 B.C., at a time of profound economic change which was to culminate, ultimately, in urban civilization in Southwest Asia in about 3100 B.C. (see Chapter 15).

c h a p t e r

THE FIRST EUROPEAN FARMERS

The Chapter in Review

- The European Mesolithic lasted from about 8000 B.C. to the introduction of farming in far northern Europe some 4,000 years later. There were considerable local variations, with a trend toward more permanent settlement in more favored areas.
- By about 6000 B.C., farming was well established in parts of the Aegean area and in southeastern Europe.
- Agriculture and animal husbandry developed in southeastern Europe because of a local shift to the more intensive exploitation of cereals and wild sheep, and also because of a "drift" of domestic animals and cereals across from Southwest Asia, a largely indigenous development.
- The widely distributed Bandkeramik complex documents the first settlement of southeastern European farmers in the Middle Danube Valley and on the light loess soils of central Europe around 5000 B.C. This may be connected, at least in part, with fallout from the flooding of the Euxine Lake, which became the Black Sea. The Euxine disaster could have caused people to move into forested lands away from the lake.
- During the next millennium, food production spread widely throughout Europe, largely in the hands of indigenous Mesolithic peoples, who adopted sheep, pottery, and cereals, which they considered food resources of immediate advantage to them.
- From about 4500 B.C., new religious ideologies spread widely in central and western Europe, as indicated by the building of communal burial mounds and megalithic monuments.
- Some of these new beliefs reflected centuries-old ideologies connected with the longhouses and the communal ethics of the Bandkeramik farmers.
- Others, derived from central and eastern Europe, were beliefs growing out of the appearance of individual power and prestige as a potent factor in local life, power reflected in the growing numbers of exotic artifacts and materials.

Key (Major) Cultures and Sites

Avebury

Bandkeramik complex (or Danubian)

Cardial ware

Easton Down

Franchthi Cave
Grotta dell' Uzzo
Karanovo
Stonehenge
Tripolye

Introductory Comments

From Turkey we move across to Greece, the Aegean area, and the Balkans, as we trace the spread of food production into the western Mediterranean and temperate Europe. In the days of Vere Gordon Childe, back in the 1950s, this was seen as a pretty straightforward process, where "Bandkeramik" or "Danubian" farmers spread rapidly across from the Danube Valley (whence Danubian) northwestward across Europe. Childe's model still holds, at least in broad outline, but, as this chapter points out, things were actually much more complicated, especially as far as adoption of agriculture by indigenous Mesolithic people in Europe is concerned. Then there's another complication, that of the flooding of the Euxine Lake, now the Black Sea, with salt water in about 5500 B.C. That event must have caused serious disruption, as many farming communities were flourishing along the now flooded shores of the lake. I suspect that many of them moved away from the Euxine into the forested regions to the north and west, thereby bringing farming to temperate Europe—but this is a hypothetical scenario.

We know about Europe's past in almost mind-numbing archaeological detail, so I have had to steer a delicate course between the overall picture and more detailed theory and culture history here. Some of the most interesting material in this chapter comes in the second half, when we examine the important social changes which occurred after 3500 B.C. These are reflected both in more tightly packed settlements and also in changes in burial customs, which become an important mirror of social and political changes later on (see Chapter 20). Almost certainly, if you ever visit Britain, you will see either Stonehenge or (if you are wise, for it is more accessible) Avebury. The section on megaliths gives some important background on these, and other such monuments.

Now Start Reading. . . .

First Farming

Table 10.1 is an attempt to lay out the major developments across Europe from the appearance of farming in southwestern Asia to the appearance of agriculture in northwestern Europe. This gives the chronological context for the chapter, and places the major cultures relative to one another, so it's worth a little time.

This section of Chapter 10 is built around hypothetical scenarios, especially Robin Dennell's three phases of food production in southeastern Europe, which coincided with vegetational changes after the Ice Age. It culminated in the founding of permanent agricultural settlements.

Figure 10.1 shows possible routes by which food production spread into southeastern Europe. Figure 10.2 shows the location of sites mentioned in Chapter 10 is a logical follow-on from the previous map.

Agriculture Spreads into Europe

As I mentioned above, this was a complex process, involving constant interplay between newcomers and indigenous Mesolithic hunter-gatherers. Zvelebil and Rowly-Conwy's three-phase transition hypothesis, although basically still to be proven in the field, provides a useful framework for reading this section of the chapter.

TABLE 10.1

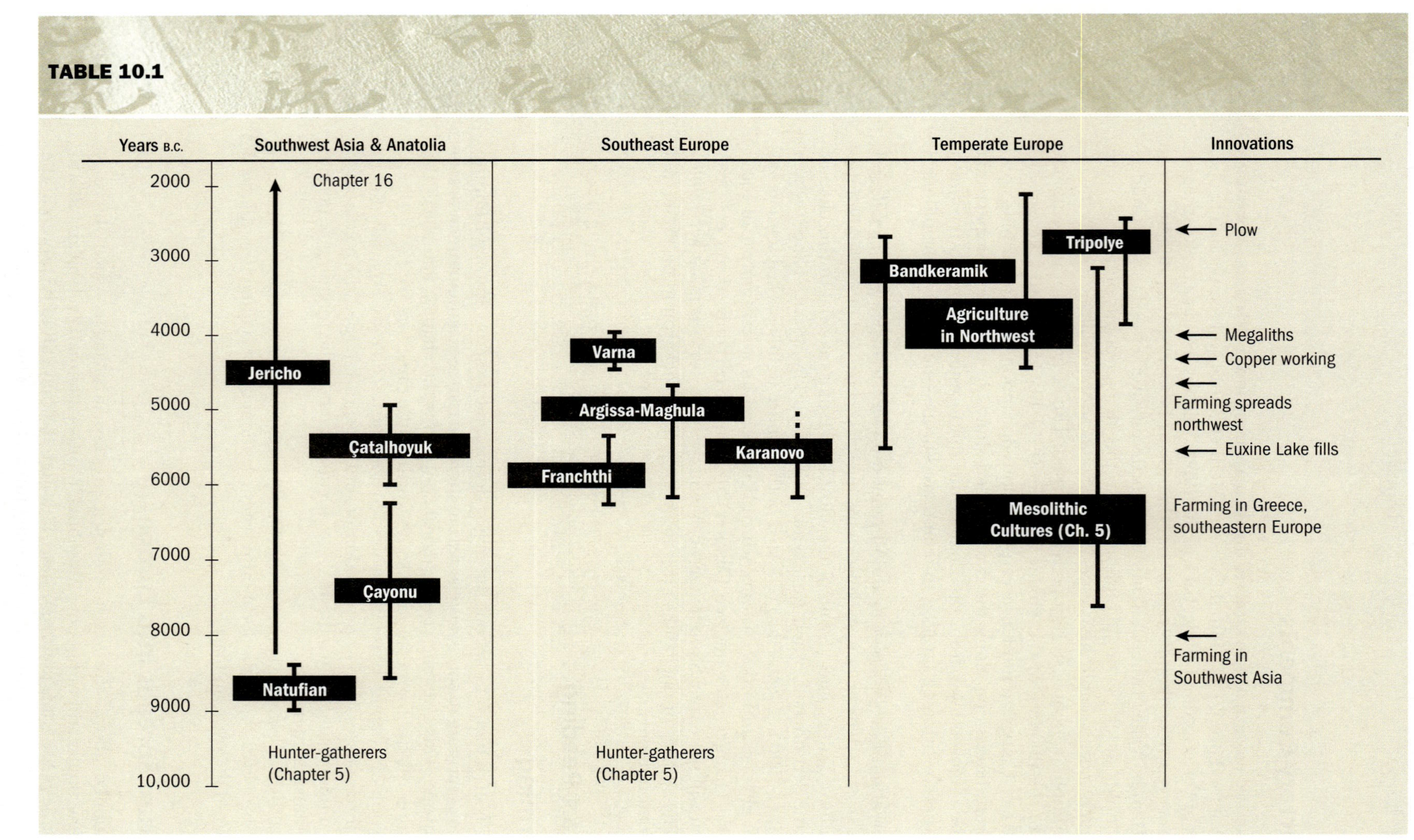
Years B.C.
Southwest Asia & Anatolia
Southeast Europe
Temperate Europe
Innovations
2000
3000
4000
5000
6000
7000
8000
9000
10,000
Chapter 16
Jericho
Çatalhoyuk
Çayonu
Natufian
Hunter-gatherers (Chapter 5)
Varna
Argissa-Maghula
Franchthi
Karanovo
Hunter-gatherers (Chapter 5)
Bandkeramik
Agriculture in Northwest
Tripolye
Mesolithic Cultures (Ch. 5)
Plow
Megaliths
Copper working
Farming spreads northwest
Euxine Lake fills
Farming in Greece, southeastern Europe
Farming in Southwest Asia

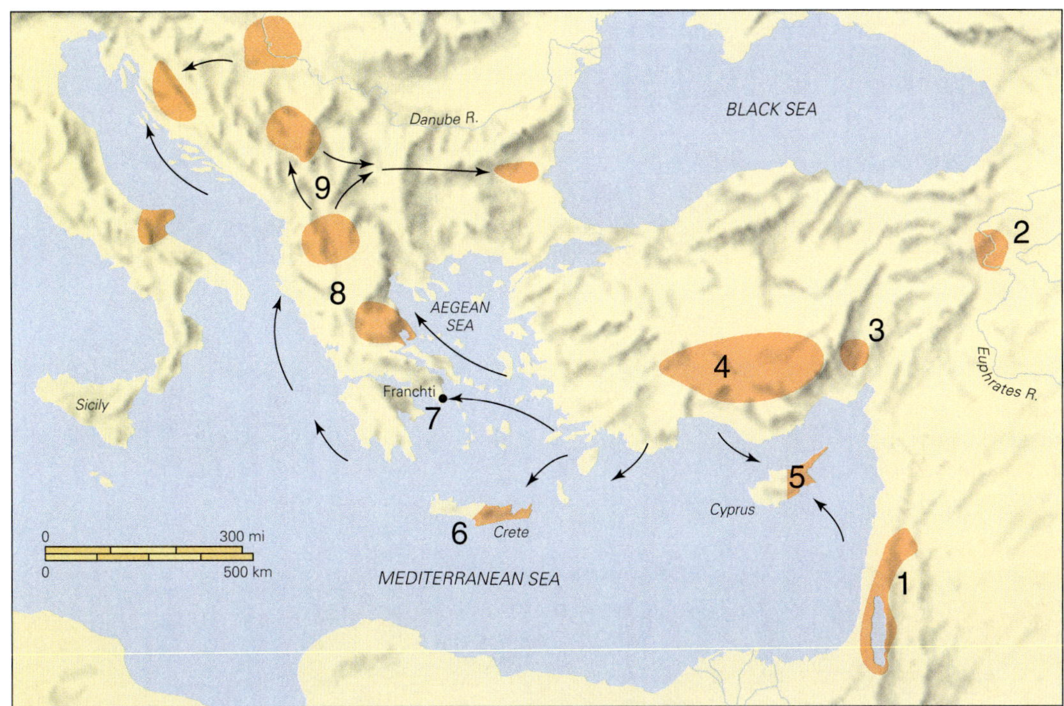

FIGURE 10.1 Map showing early farming areas in Southwest Asia and southeastern Europe. Arrows show possible routes by which the new economies spread. (1) Jordan Valley and the eastern Mediterranean; (2) Çayönü region; (3, 4) Anatolian region, including Çatalhöyük and Haçilar; (5) Cyprus; (6) Crete; (7) Franchthi Cave; (8) Macedonia; (9) Balkans region.

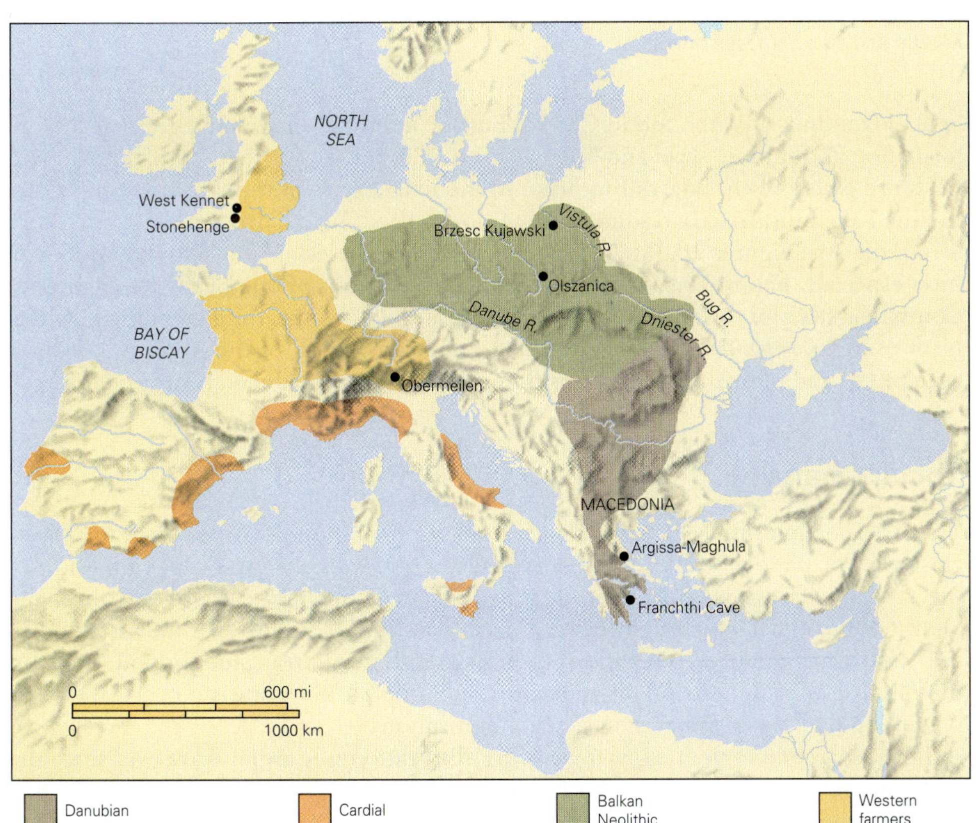

FIGURE 10.2 Archaeological sites in temperate Europe and the distribution of Bandkeramik (Danubian) pottery, Cardial ware, and western Neolithic cultures.

FIGURE 10.3 Linear Bandkeramik pottery (linear-decorated pottery) from Sittard, Holland, with characteristic line decoration (one-fourth actual size).

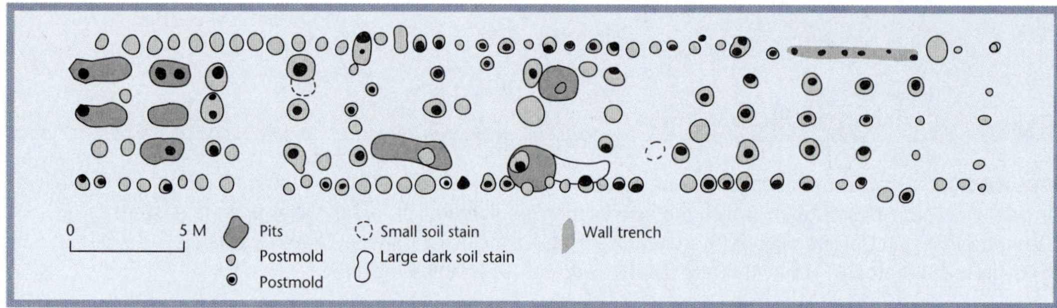

FIGURE 10.4 Plan of a Bandkeramik house from Olszanica, Poland, with wall trenches, postholes, pits, and other features. Such structures housed extended families, perhaps each with its own hearth, and also domestic animals.

Bandkeramik sites abound in Central Europe and have provided a great deal of information about these slash-and-burn farmers. The reason for their spread north and westward is unknown, but, as I indicate in the text, I suspect that the flooding of the Euxine Lake must have had some form of ripple effect, which drove people into more forested areas. Figures 10.3 to 10.5 convey much of the essence of Bandkeramik culture, especially Figure 10.5, which offers a reconstruction of one of their settlements. Combine a study of this with a quick look back at the Gwembe Tonga reading in Chapter 8 of this *Companion,* and you'll have a good sense both of the dynamics of their agriculture and of one of the reasons they spread so rapidly through virgin lands.

Social Changes

This brief section discusses the changes resulting from population growth, the closer clustering of Bandkeramik settlements, and the plow, as well as a quick mention of the spread of food production onto the Russian plains and westward around the Mediterranean. This is straightforward narrative, but I would draw your attention to the "secondary products revolution" theory of Andrew Sherratt, mentioned briefly in the discussion of the plow. This is an intriguing idea. If Sherratt is correct, then this revolution had major impacts on social organization.

I have searched high and low for a better illustration of Cardial Ware ever since the first edition of this book and never found one. If any reader happens to know of one, please let me know!

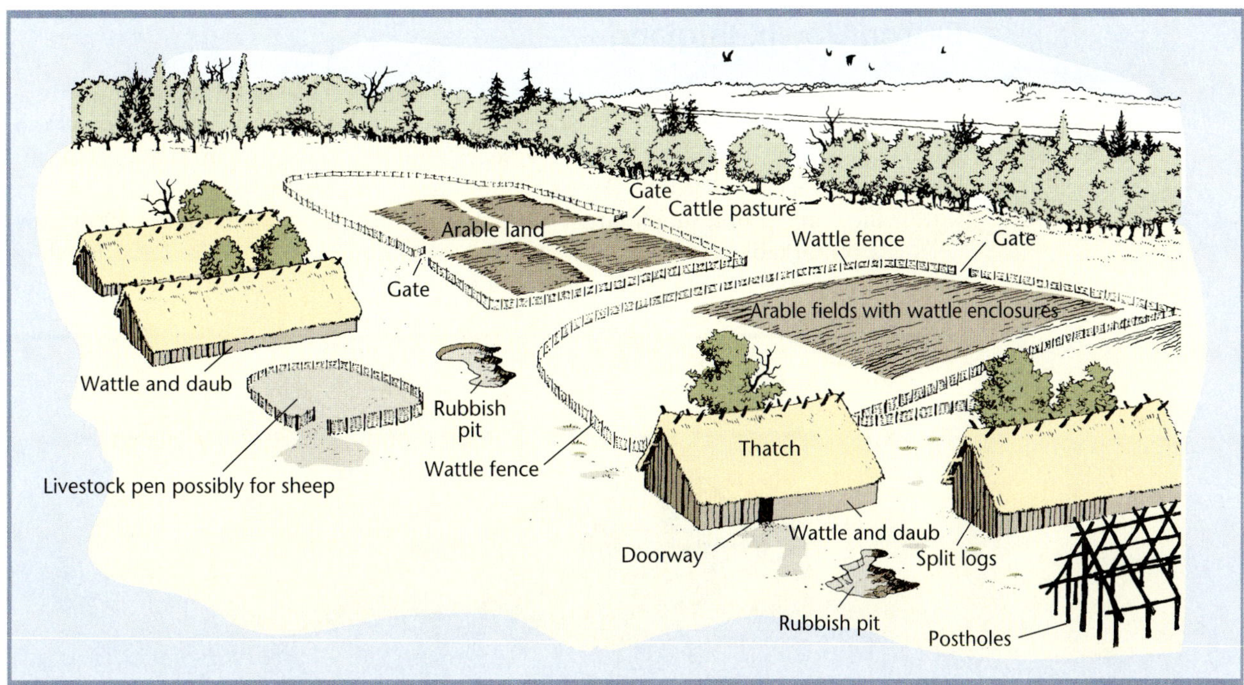

FIGURE 10.5 Reconstruction of a Bandkeramik farming complex, showing longhouses and field boundaries.

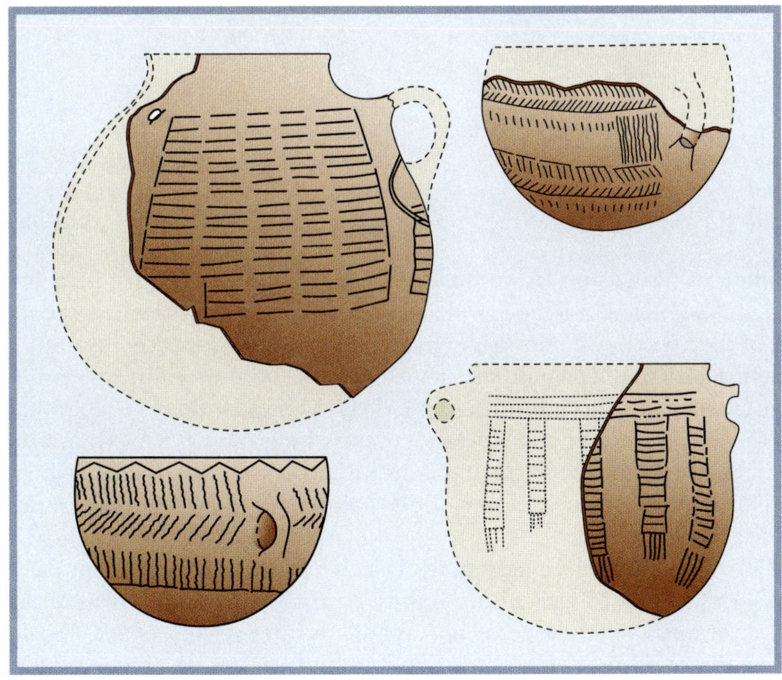

FIGURE 10.6 *Cardium*-shell-impressed pottery from southern France (one-fourth actual size). The *Cardium* shell was widely traded and used for ornamentation.

Megaliths and Burial Customs

Extraordinary monuments, the megaliths, both on account of their great age and because they offer us some of our first insights into the world of the intangible. Some megaliths were communal graves, where fellow kin lay. Others had astrological significance, witness New Grange, Ireland, illustrated in Figure 10.8, or Stonehenge.

Easton Down, England

I chose the Easton Down site as an example not only because of its important cultural and social implications, but also because the excavations are an excellent example of the way in which today's investigators research an important site: minimal site disturbance, very specific research design, a multidisciplinary approach—all carried out within the contact of a much larger issue, in this case the Avebury sacred landscape. This is a remarkable piece of archaeological detective work by any standards, which yielded fine-grained results. It is eloquent testimony of the power of selective, slow-moving excavation.

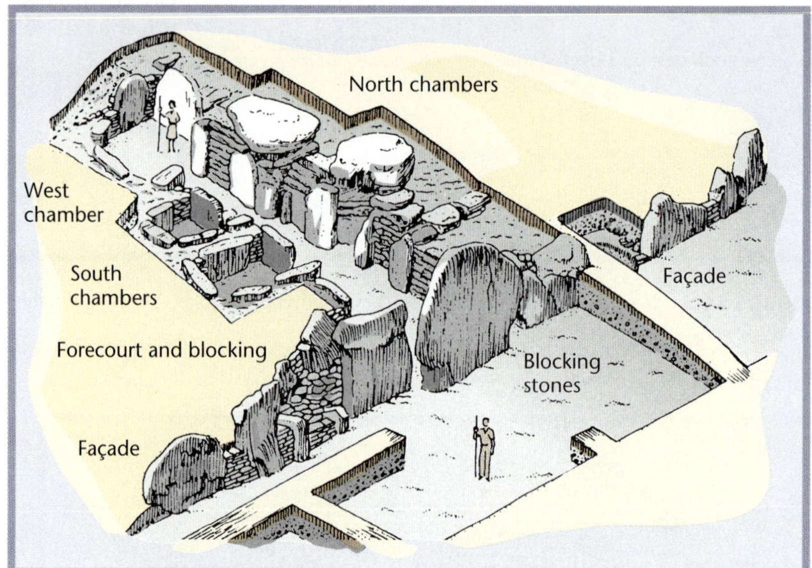

FIGURE 10.9 Interior of a megalithic chamber tomb in West Kennet, near Avebury, England, ^{14}C-dated to approximately 3500 B.C. (After Piggott, 1965.) The West Kennet sepulcher was probably a communal grave, used by a kin group over many generations.

Combine a reading of the Easton Down box, which discusses how science is reconstructing the ancient Avebury landscape, with a close look at Figure 10.9, a reconstruction drawing of the West Kennet long barrow, one of the best preserved examples of such a communal sepulcher. The volume of speculation about megaliths becomes ever larger each year, with a plethora of intriguing ideas like Ian Hodder's theory that they had roots in the ideology surrounding Bandkeramik longhouses. Some may also have been territorial markers, but their connections with ancestors and the land seem unquestionable. This section of the chapter offers a summary of some of the more widely accepted ideas.

Finally, I would stress a summary thought in the last chapter. "Here, as in other parts of the world, one should think of agriculture not as a miracle invention, or in terms of conquest, but as yet another instance of how readily hunter-gatherers adapted to new opportunities and conditions." Herein lies the crux of early food production in Europe.

chapter

FIRST FARMERS IN EGYPT AND TROPICAL AFRICA

The Chapter in Review

- Food production was probably introduced into the Nile Valley at a time of drought, by 6000 B.C. But it is also possible that it was developed independently there.
- The hunter-gatherers of the Nile and of the then-inhabitable Sahara were preadapted to the new economies, which they may have taken up as a means of staving off food shortages in drought years.
- By 4000 B.C., agriculture was well established along the Nile, while cattle were being domesticated and herded in the depths of the Sahara.
- Nile Valley communities soon became dependent on agriculture; they relied on natural flooding to water their gardens until about 3000 B.C.
- As the Sahara dried up after 3000 B.C., pastoralists with cereal crops moved south of the desert, introducing cattle herding as far south as the East African highlands.
- Cereal cultivation, based on shifting agriculture, did not take hold in much of sub-Saharan Africa until the introduction of ironworking south of the desert in the first millennium B.C.

Key Cultures and Sites

Badarian culture
Bir Kiseiba
Fayyum Depression
Merimde Beni Salama
Nabta Playa
Qadan culture
Wadi Kubbaniya

Introductory Remarks and Commentary

Chapter 11 is a short one, a simple narrative account of early agriculture along the Nile, of herding in the Sahara Desert, and of the first farmers and herders in sub-Saharan Africa. There is little comment needed here, so I will be brief.

Study this chronological table carefully, as it provides a framework for the chapter. The details are self-evident.

Here are some important points to note with this chapter.

TABLE 11.1

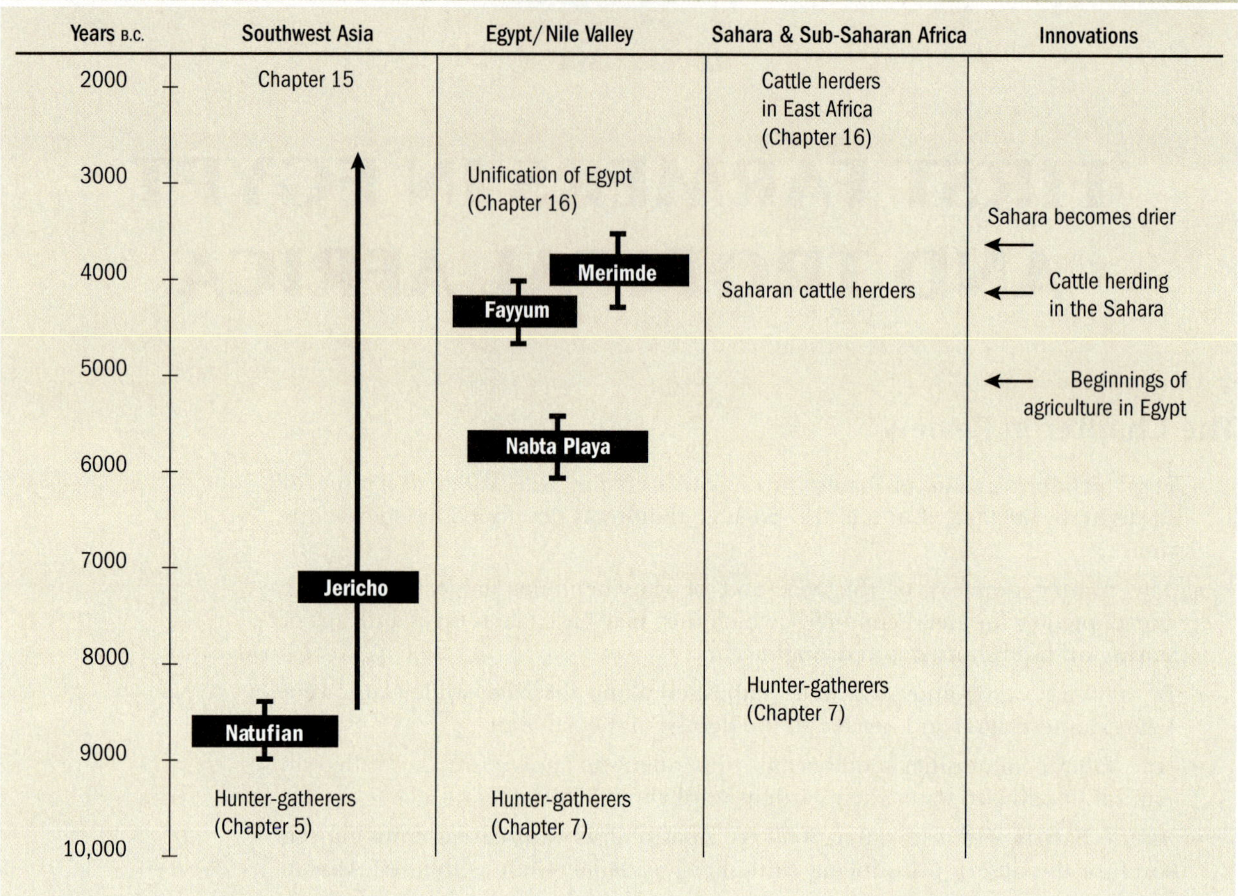

Notes

Egypt

Food production in Egypt seems to have begun considerably later than in the Levant or Anatolia, but this may be an illusion. Any relevant sites in the Nile Valley lie many meters below the modern-day, heavily irrigated floodplain and are effectively inaccessible to us. I would not be the slightest bit surprised if agriculture did not begin along the Nile at least as early as 9500 B.C., but I cannot prove it. Why do I think this? Simply because the Nile was a very fertile environment, and one where wild grasses abounded. In times of growing populations and droughts—and remember that Nile inundations were unpredictable—a logical strategy for averting longer term food shortages is to deliberately cultivate wild grasses to increase the harvest. There is a surprisingly small difference between a good flood and a bad one on the flat river plain, a matter of 2 or 3 meters. So the conditions were there for early agriculture. Furthermore, we know there was competition for resources along the Nile among Qadan bands. One obvious way of reducing conflict is to plant grasses to supplement wild stands—just as they did in the Euphrates Valley.

Was farming introduced or an indigenous development? Current opinion seems to favor a scenario where crops and food production entered from Southwest Asia. Having said this, there are no valid reasons why it could not have been developed indigenously. We may never know, unless some twist of genetic research produces clues.

The Sahara

This is a fascinating area as far as pastoralism is concerned. The rock paintings of cattle and herders from the Central Sahara confirm what the paleoclimatologists tell us. In 6000 B.C., the desert was covered with huge shallow lakes and semi-arid grasslands. The pastoralist population was never large, for the grasslands could not support large numbers of cattle or humans. Each group's herding range must have been enormous, while remaining anchored to permanent water.

I find Andrew Smith's scenario for the domestication of *Bos primigenius* compelling, for it fits with what we know of large herd animal behavior in modern-day Africa. (I have myself walked in full sight of buffalo and they were unconcerned.) As we say in the text, archaeologist and demographer Fekri Hassan believes that some desert pastoral groups extended their ranges into the fertile Nile Valley, movements which would have brought them in touch with sedentary farmers. These contacts must have assumed great importance when the desert dried up after 6000 B.C.

You may remember in Chapter 3 how we referred to the Sahara as a giant pump, which sucked people in during wetter times and pushed them out during droughts. This is exactly the effect that took place with the desert pastoralists. And, as we will see in Chapter 16, the values and particularly ideas of cattle chiefs may have come to the Nile Valley and been an important factor in the emergence of powerful Egyptian chiefs, then rulers of small states, which culminated in a unified Egyptian state.

But we are getting ahead of ourselves, for this comes into play in Chapter 16.

Sub-Saharan Africa

An interesting question arises here. Why did food production, and the domestication of animals, come to sub-Saharan Africa so late? One reason may be the great richness of game populations in many parts of Africa, especially those parts unaffected by tsetse fly, which is fatal to cattle. Another one may be the prevalence of hardwoods in African woodland, which are extremely hard to fell with stone technology. When farming did come to the region, it spread first, as it did in Europe, on easily cultivable soils, so soil selection was all-important. Indeed, one of the reasons for such a rapid spread of the new economies may have been the relatively limited areas where simple slash-and-burn cultivation was possible and where cattle could be grazed safely. In all probability, cattle herding reached the southern tip of Africa long before agriculture, simply because cattle require large tracts of grazing land and distances between reliable water supplies are often quite long. And the introduction of agriculture to many parts of Africa required the domestication of tropical grasses (probably on the fringes of the Sahara) as well as the tougher working edges of iron technology.

Again, the dynamics of subsistence agriculture raised in the Gwembe Tonga reading in Chapter 8 are relevant here.

chapter

ASIA AND THE PACIFIC: RICE, ROOTS, AND OCEAN VOYAGES

The Chapter in Review

- As in Southwest Asia, food production began in Asia during the early Holocene, perhaps as early as 10,000 B.C., but became fully established in a cold interval that followed initial warming, around 6500 B.C.
- In southern China, some rice was perhaps cultivated as early as 9000 B.C. Rice agriculture was widespread by 6500 B.C.
- The staple in the Haunghe Valley of northern China was millet, cultivated at least as early as 6500 B.C., perhaps much earlier.
- The Yangshao culture flourished over much of the Haunghe Basin, a society of self-contained villages, replaced by more elaborate Longshanoid cultures by 3000 B.C.
- In Southeast Asia, the staple crop was rice, probably first cultivated along low-lying, swampy coasts. The new economies soon spread inland during the third millennium B.C., bringing village life to much of the region.
- Hunters and foragers settled island Southeast Asia at least as early as 35,000 B.C., and simple root horticulture had been established in highland New Guinea by 6000 B.C.
- The people of the Lapita cultural complex traded widely through the south-western Pacific after 1600 B.C.
- It was not until the past 2000 years that offshore canoes settled Micronesia and Polynesia, and New Zealand was colonized between A.D. 1000 and 1200.

Key (Major) Cultures and Sites

Banpo
Dopenkeng culture
Hemudu
Jomon tradition
Khok Phanom Di
Kuk
Lapita complex
Longshan (Longshanoid)
Peiligang
Pengtoushan
Spirit Cave
Xianrendong
Yangshao
Yayoi period

Introductory Remarks

Chapter 12 covers an enormous area of the world, where archaeology is still at an early stage of development. Nevertheless, recent discoveries are beginning to tell a fascinating story. The narrative in this chapter is in three parts:

- The origins of agriculture in China, which includes that all-important crop, rice;
- The beginnings of food production in Southeast Asia, again intimately tied to rice;
- The settlement of the offshore Pacific Islands, a development which had to wait for agriculture (easily storable foods), effective navigational methods for passage-making out of sight of land, and the double-hulled canoe.

For all the complexity of this chapter, there is a chronological gradient through it, starting with the origins of farming in China, somewhere between 10,000 and 6500 B.C., and ending with the settlement of New Zealand in the early second millennium A.D.

With Chapter 11, the great diaspora of *Homo sapiens sapiens* ends, with the settlement of the biologically impoverished offshore islands of the Pacific. This diaspora had begun over 100,000 years ago, in tropical Africa.

Now Start Reading . . .

Table 12.1 lays out the chronology of major cultures from China to the Pacific, laid out against Southwest Asia, in the left column. Like the other chronological tables, this is

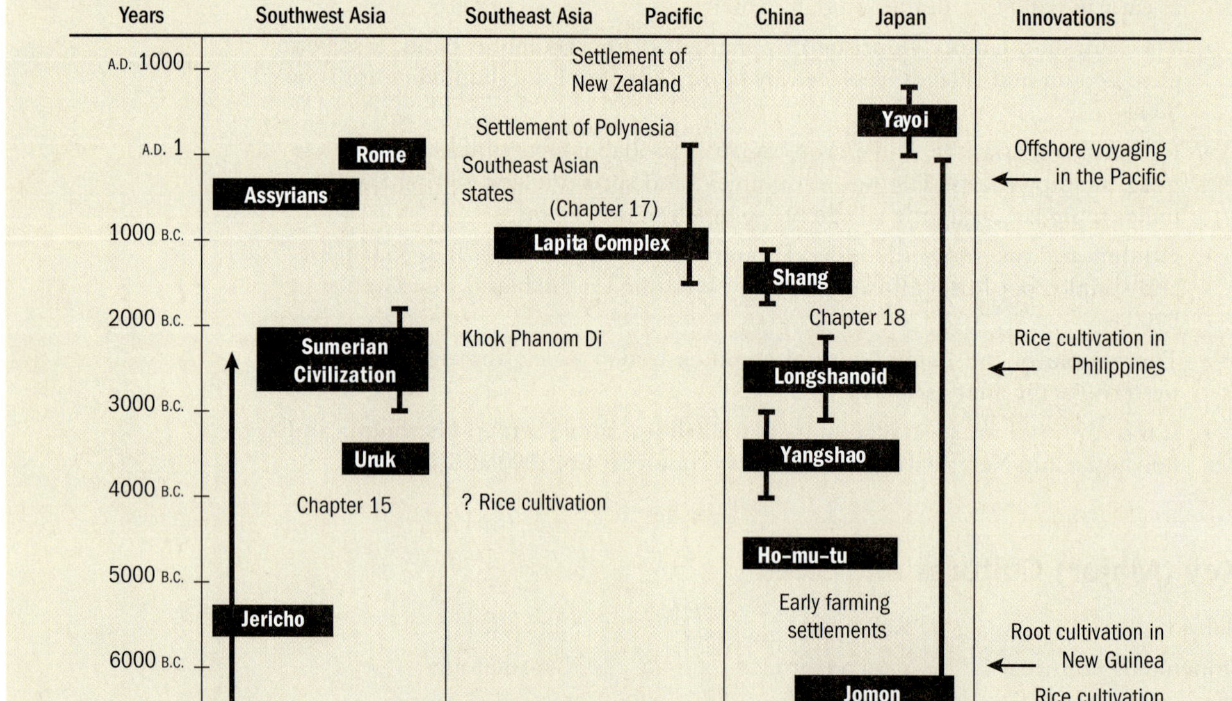

designed to give you an overall chronological perspective on the chapter and is self-evident.

Early Food Production in East Asia

China

This is the great mystery. How old is food production in China? I predict that within a generation we will find out that it is as early, if not earlier, than in southwestern Asia. Why? Because the conditions for its appearance were, in many respects, identical to those in the west—growing populations, drought from the Younger Dryas, intensive use of plant foods, and a simple, and logical step to cultivating wild grasses to supplement wild stands.

Figure 12.1 shows the general areas of early Chinese farming.

The big question mark is rice, which is, of course, one of the world's major crops. Yet we know almost nothing about its origins. At present the earliest evidence comes from the Yangze River Valley, although I would not be the slightest bit surprised if it turned up very early indeed outside this particular valley. Then there is South Asia, where almost nothing is known about the early archaeology of the Ganges River valley. But there we have the same problem as we do in Egypt: deep layers of silt that have buried early farming sites deep below modern ground level.

Just as in southwestern Asia, rice agriculture spread rapidly once it became well established. How long a period of experimentation there was with cultivating wild rice before fully domesticated forms appeared is a matter for discussion. Judging from Gordon Hillman's experiments, discussed in Chapter 8, it may have been a short time, despite claims to the contrary from Chinese sources.

The earliest farming technology was very simple, witness this reconstruction of a Hemudu "shovel" made from a water buffalo shoulder blade. However, in both

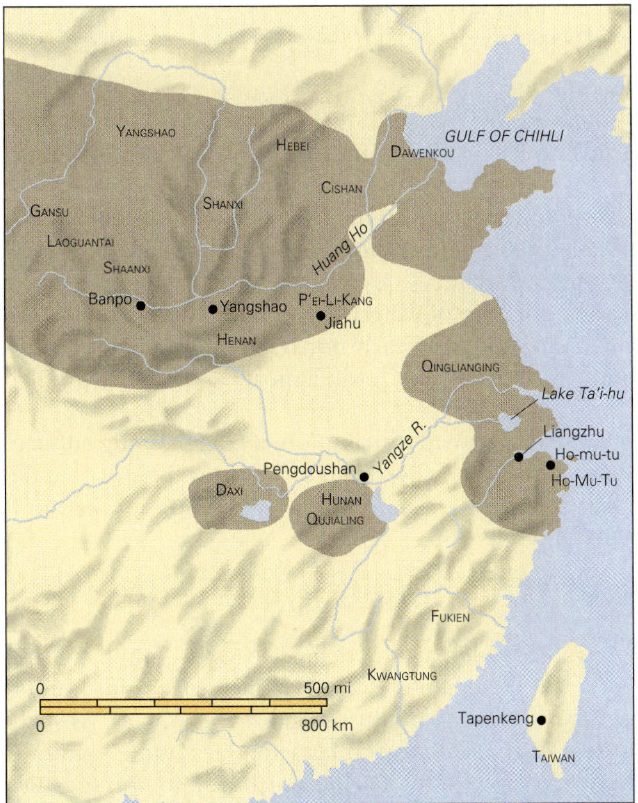

FIGURE 12.1 Early Chinese farming cultures, with names of some major local variants. Yangshao sites occur both within the northern shaded area and outside it. Southern sites of corded pottery are found in the Kwangtung, Fukien, and Taiwan areas.

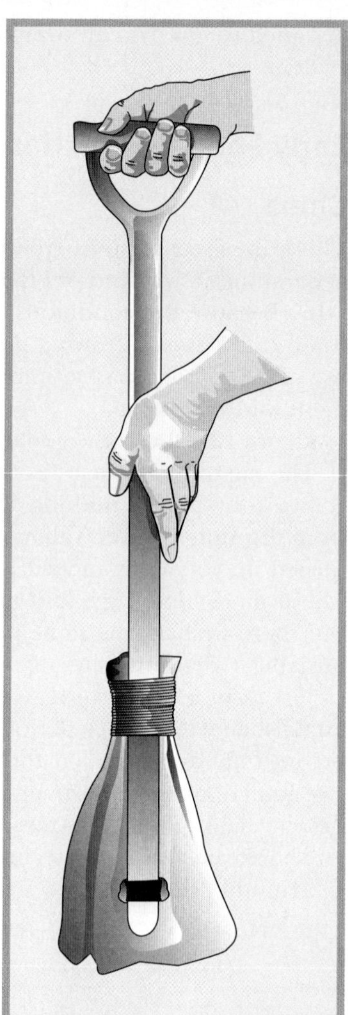

FIGURE 12.2 Artist's reconstruction of a Hemudu culture shovel-like agricultural implement, based on well-preserved examples of such artifacts at the site. The blade was formed from a shoulder blade of a water buffalo.

southern and northern China, it's noticeable how quickly substantial farming settlements became established and how rapidly society became more sophisticated, with signs of social ranking. At the same time, early farming societies soon developed distinctively Chinese traits, identifiable in the pottery, much of which was used for cooking in the Chinese style, even at this early date.

Figures 12.3 and 12.4 show the elaboration of Yangshao dwellings and pottery in the north. The Yangshao was the most widespread of early northern Chinese farming cultures, but so little is known about many areas that it will almost certainly prove to be one of many such societies.

Figure 12.5 on page 108 shows the widespread distribution of later farming cultures with many common features, but there were major local differences. Figure 12.6 depicts some distinctive cooking wares from Longshanoid sites and amplifies the point we made about Chinese-ness above.

Japan

Again, this is a straightforward narrative, which cannot do justice to the Jomon culture. This is a fascinating, long-lived series of societies that developed elaborate hunter-gatherer societies with a strong basis in fishing, mollusks, and sea mammals. As such, it has the potential to throw a great deal of light on other sedentary hunter-gatherer societies and their elaboration, such as those of the Pacific Northwest. Jomon sites also

FIGURE 12.3 Reconstruction of Yangshao houses from Banpo, China.

FIGURE 12.4 (a) Yangshao pottery from Banpo, China (approximately one-fourth actual size). (b) The fish motifs often used to decorate Yangshao vessels can be clearly seen (other motifs are drawn separately).

have the potential to chronicle a gradual changeover from hunting and gathering to farming, something still little documented in Japan.

Southeast Asia

There are two issues here, the first revolving around the domestication of indigenous plants like yams, the other around the first appearance of rice farming.

Almost certainly there was some indigenous experimentation with native crops among the broad spectrum of hunter-gatherers who inhabited the area at the end of

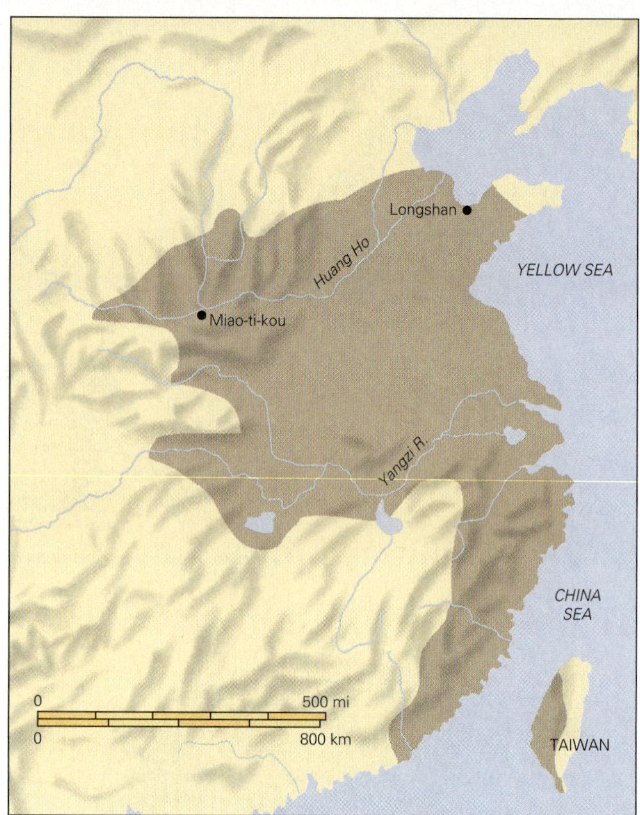

FIGURE 12.5 Approximate distribution of later farming cultures in China (dark shaded area).

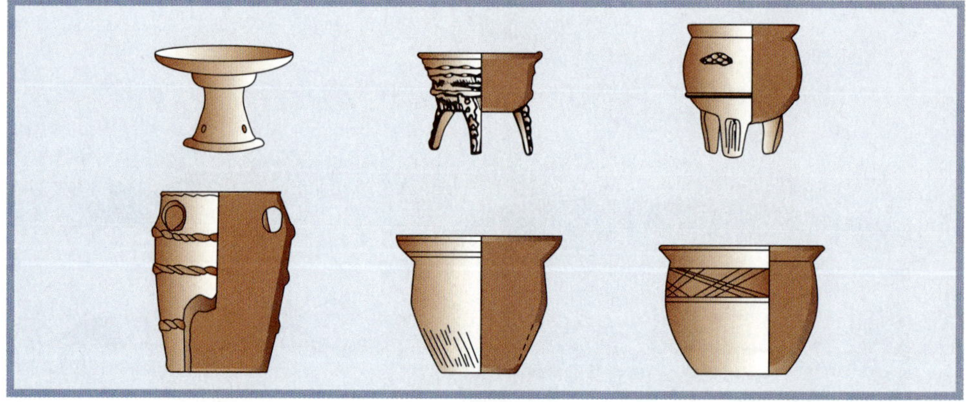

FIGURE 12.6 Some typical Longshanoid vessels used for cooking and other purposes from Miao-ti-Rai, China (scale not recorded). From the earliest times, Chinese ceramics reflected the distinctive Chinese cuisine based on steaming and stir-frying.

the Ice Age. Here, once again, we encounter the phenomenon known as "vegeculture," which we mentioned in the previous chapter, where people simply chop off the top of a plant and place it in the ground. This kind of cultivation may have been practiced for thousands of years in forest clearings, long before anyone thought of farming, simply as a way of fostering wild plant growth. So we will probably never know when the first plant domestication began in mainland Southeast Asia—perhaps earlier than we suspect.

Clearly, the flooding of the low-lying mainland coast after the Ice Age played a considerable role in the adoption of farming. Certainly, root cultivation seems to have begun on the offshore islands like New Guinea quite early.

Current thinking has rice being domesticated in China, then spread southward into Southeast Asia. The crop certainly seems to have arrived late in the region, around 2,500 B.C., compared with China. And, if Higham and Thoserat's work at Khok Phanom Di is to be believed, it also spread irregularly, especially near the coast.

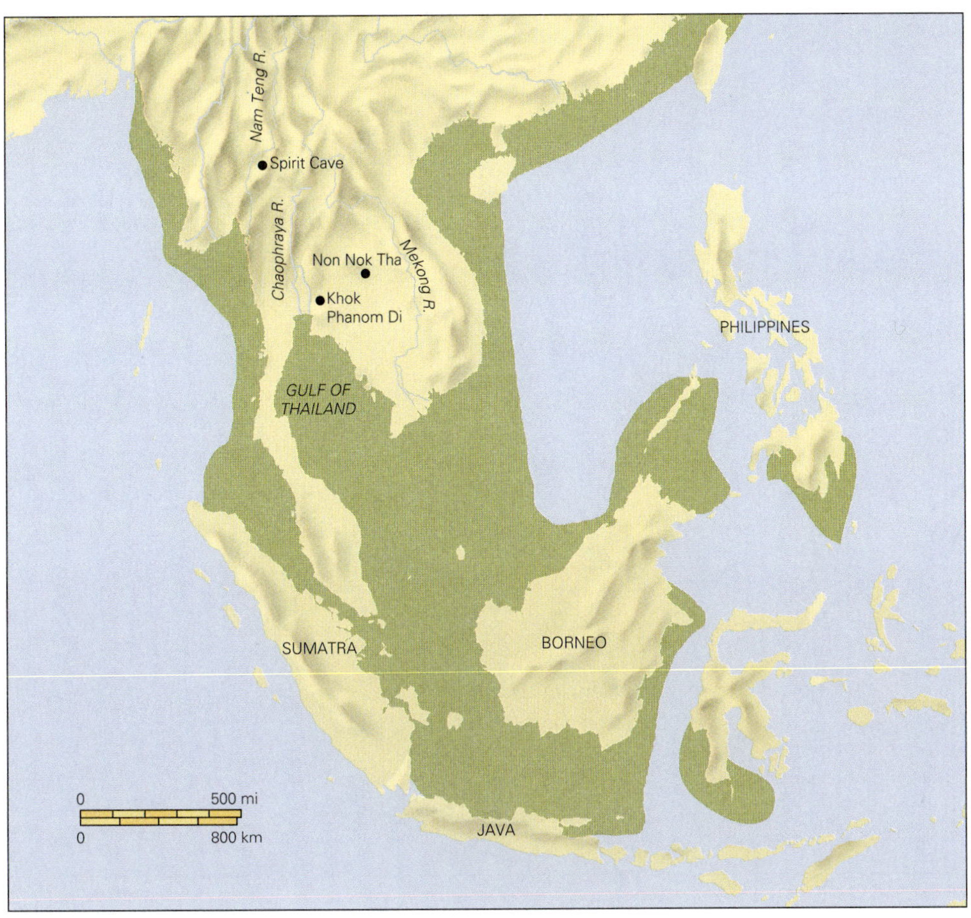

FIGURE 12.8 Southeast Asian sites mentioned in this chapter. Shaded areas show the extent of low sea levels during the last glaciation.

Khok Phanom Di

Khok Phanom Di is one of those sites which, when excavated, transforms our knowledge of an entire region's history. The cemetery at the site provided unrivaled information on not only between seventeen and twenty generations of expert potters, but on an emerging social complexity in a community which traded its wares widely. The Princess's burial documents not only social status, but the connection between such status and her expertise as a potter through the burnishing stones found by her feet and the vessels covering her body. When studied, the skeletons from Khok Phanom Di may provide unique information on the pathologies caused by the hard work and repetitive movement associated with pot making.

Island Southeast Asia and the Pacific

This section describes the appearance of farming on the offshore islands of Southeast Asia, especially the appearance of water control at Kuk on New Guinea as early as 7000 B.C. Within two thousand years or so, forest clearance for yams and taro was apparently well under way. All of this may seem unimportant to the broader themes of world prehistory, but it is not, for the rest of this chapter shows how farming helped the colonization of the far offshore islands of Micronesia and Polynesia.

The Lapita complex is one of the most important cultural traditions in Southeast Asia and the southwestern Pacific, and, unfortunately, one of the least known. This was the society, or most likely numerous societies, which developed the double-hulled canoe and founded trade networks that extended from mainland Southeast Asia deep

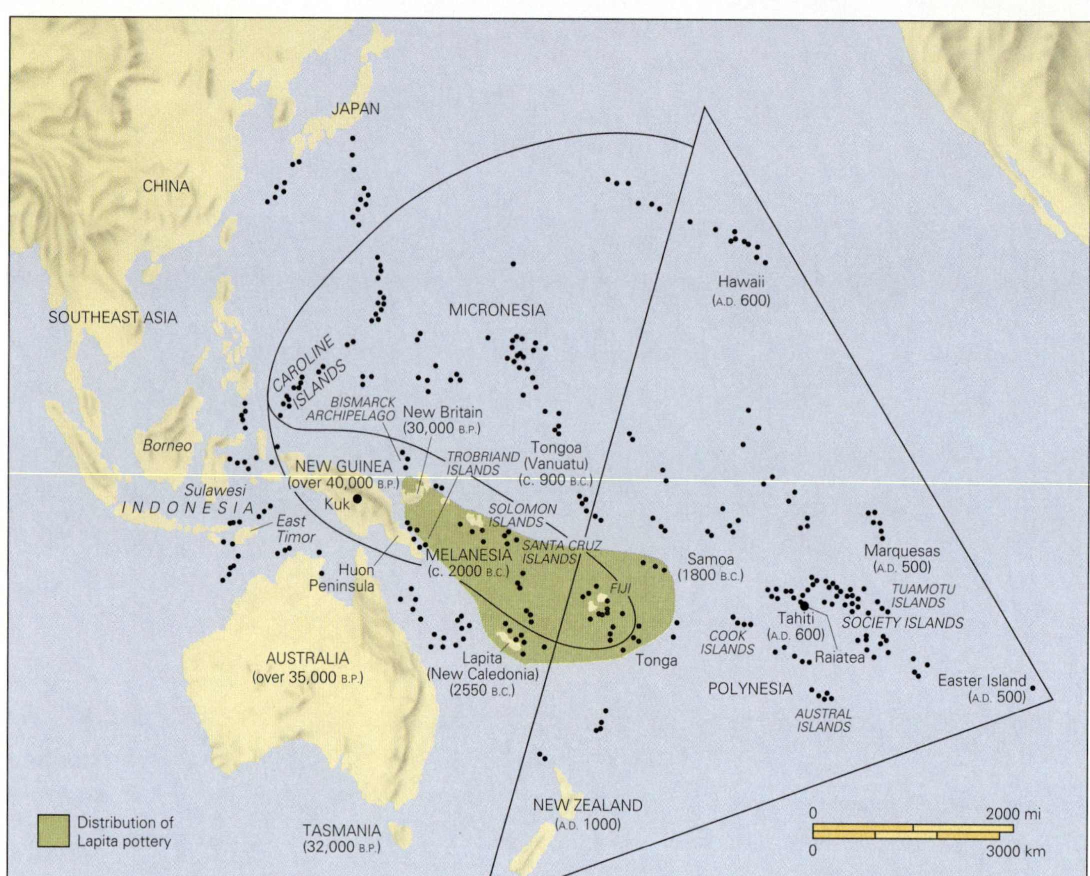

FIGURE 12.10 Map of Pacific sites. Dark shading shows the distribution of the Lapita cultural complex. Lines delineate Melanesia, Micronesia, and Polynesia. Dates are for first settlement.

into the Pacific. Lapita groups were also responsible for the deep water navigational methods described in the "Indigenous Pacific Navigation" box. How do we know it was so important? Simply because distinctive shell-decorated Lapita pottery has been found over an enormous area, as far out into the Pacific as Fiji. Lapita canoes carried obsidian, which can be sourced all the way from the Bismarck Archipelago to Fiji.

For generations, scientists debated the settlement of Polynesia in somewhat apocalyptic terms. They speculated about canoes blown offshore by accident, "accidental drifts," as the way the islands were settled rather than by deliberate voyaging—this despite Captain Cook's obvious reference to indigenous navigation, quoted at the beginning of the chapter. The breakthrough came in the 1960s, when yachtsman David Lewis and others came across the last indigenous navigators and apprenticed themselves to them. In fact, the art had never vanished, as scholars believed, and thrived in remote Micronesian archipelagos. In recent years, resurgence in canoe building and voyaging has proven the effectiveness of the traditional methods far from land. No question, both Micronesia and Polynesia were settled by deliberate voyaging, some of it to extremely deserted parts of the Pacific, and as far afield as Easter Island.

The chapter ends with the settlement of New Zealand, whose prehistory offers a fascinating example of what happened on overpopulated, isolated land masses, where there was intense competition for agricultural land.

c h a p t e r

THE STORY OF MAIZE: EARLY FARMERS IN THE AMERICAS

The Chapter in Review

- Native American agriculture was based on quite different crops from those in the Old World, among them root crops like potatoes and sweet potatoes. Maize was the most important cereal.
- Since there were many fewer potential domesticates than in the Old World, domesticated animals were limited to few species—for example, the llama, the turkey, and the guinea fowl.
- The earliest cultivation may have begun in the humid tropical lowlands, for traces of cultivation are said to date to as early as 7000 B.C. in Panama. In drier, more open country, agriculture developed in hunter-gatherer societies that were coping with constant environmental change and unpredictable population shifts.
- At locations like Guilá Naquitz, Mexico, wet-year subsistence strategies involving deliberate planting eventually became permanent shifts in subsistence activities.
- Among the staples of Native American agriculture were beans and maize, probably domesticated from a Central American native grass named teosinte as early as 4000 B.C.
- Maize agriculture spread from southern Mexico and Guatemala thousands of miles to the north and south. There were farmers in the highland Andes and in coastal Peru by 3000 B.C., but maize and cotton did not become vital cultivated staples until about a thousand years later.
- Maize agriculture reached the North American Southwest by about 1500 to 2000 B.C. By 300 B.C., sedentary villages and a much greater dependence on farming were characteristic of the Southwest, leading to the emergence of the Hohokam, Mogollon, and Ancestral Pueblo cultural traditions, among which the ultimate ancestry of modern southwestern peoples lie.
- Many groups in eastern North America turned to the deliberate cultivation of native plants as food supplements after 2000 B.C., but maize and bean agriculture did not arrive from the Southwest until the first millennium B.C.
- After 1000 B.C., a series of powerful chiefdoms arose in the Southeast and the Midwest, peoples among whom elaborate burial customs and the building of burial mounds and earthworks were commonplace.

- The Adena tradition appeared in about 700 B.C. and was overlapped by the Hopewell in approximately A.D. 100.
- About A.D. 800, the focus of economic, religious, and political power shifted to the Mississippi Valley and the Southeast with the rise of the Mississippian tradition. This tradition, with its powerful religious and secular leaders, survived in a modified form until European contact in the sixteenth century A.D.

Key Cultures and Sites

Adena
Ancestral Pueblo
Asana
Cahokia
Casas Grandes
Cerro Juanaqueña
Chaco Phenomenon
Chilca
Cliff Palace, Mesa Verde
Cochise
Coxcatlán
El Paraíso
Guilá Naquitz
Hohokam
Hopewell
Huaca Prieta
Mississippian
Mogollon
Mound City
Moundville
Newark
Paloma
Panaulauca
Playa Culebras
Poverty Point
Pueblo Bonito
San Marcos
Snaketown

Introductory Comments

Food production in the Americas involved plants and agriculture more than domesticated animals. As you know, the megafauna became extinct at the end of the Ice Age, leaving few potential domesticates (see Chapter 5). By the time Columbus reached the New World, the native Americans had developed a remarkable expertise with domesticated plants of all kinds, notably maize, beans, and potatoes, as well as other cereal and root crops. Since the European *entrada,* many native American staples have become vital crops in many parts of the world—plants like the chili pepper, maize, potatoes, and the tomato, to mention only a few.

Chapter 13 takes us on a journey through the world of native American cultivators and is divided into two broad parts.

The first part of the chapter covers the origins of maize, and the beginnings of food production in Mesoamerica and the Andean region.

The second part, the larger one, focuses on early farmers in North America, concentrating on two major culture areas—the Southwest and eastern United States.

Once again, this is a straightforward narrative, where I have tried to keep site and culture names to the minimum, while focusing on the big issues—the origins of major crops, their spread, and the impact of said crops on local societies.

Now Start Reading. . .

Before we begin the story of farming, please spend a few moments getting the basics of Table 13.1 into your mind. Like other chronological tables, it's organized by area, with a section at the right showing equivalent developments elsewhere, as well as innovations. Notice that cereal cultivation began comparatively late in the Americas compared with the Old World, and also that once it started, more complex societies soon developed in Mesoamerica and the Andes.

The Origins of Food Production

Carl Sauer was a famous Berkeley cultural geographer, who pointed to humid, low-lying tropical zones as the most likely places for the earliest agriculture. If phytolith

TABLE 13.1

Years	North America: East	North America: West	Mesoamerica	Andes	Developments Elsewhere	Innovations
A.D. 1500	Mississippian	Anasazi			Age of Discovery	← European contact
A.D. 1000		Hohokam	Mesoamerican states (Chapter 21)	Andean states (Chapter 22)		
A.D. 1	Hopewell, Adena	Mogollon			Rome	← Maize in eastern North America
1000 B.C.	Poverty Point	Early farming				
2000 B.C.				Huaca Prieta	Shang civilization; Sumerians	← Maize in southwestern North America; ← Maize in coastal Peru
3000 B.C.			Village farming	Chilca	Ancient Egyptians	← Native plants cultivated in eastern North America; maize cultivation in Mesoamerica(?)
4000 B.C.						
5000 B.C.	Koster	Cochise	Tehuácan	Paloma		← Llama domesticated in Andes
6000 B.C.			Guilá Naquitz		Village farming in Southwest Asia/China	
7000 B.C.				Plant-tending in the Andes		

FIGURE 13.1 The stages through which teosinte passed on its way to becoming domesticated maize, with (a) showing the earliest teosinte form. (b to d) The harvesting process increased the shrinking of the teosinte branches and led to the husks becoming the enclosures for corn ears. (e) Shows the stabilized maize phenotype. (After Galinat, 1985.)

analysis is to be trusted, then the earliest maize farming began in hot areas like Panama. Unfortunately, archaeological preservation is poor in such regions, so we lack little more than phytolith samples to document such early cultivation.

We summarize what is known, and show how some crops were grown before maize was domesticated from the wild grass, teosinte. It is with the story of maize that the real archaeological action begins.

Figure 13.1 documents the stages in the transformation of teosinte into domesticated maize. It is self explanatory.

A generation ago, there were great controversies over the origins of maize, as botanists searched for the wild ancestor of domesticated corn. This was resolved in favor of teosinte, rather than a wild form of maize, by the 1970s. The big developments since then have been AMS radiocarbon dating and genetic fingerprinting. The former allows one to date tiny specimens such as individual seeds, while fingerprinting points to an early domestication of corn in southwestern Mexico.

AMS is still in its early days, but enough samples have been processed to show that maize cultivation may have begun somewhat later than the 5000 B.C. date which was commonplace until now. But there is absolutely no reason why we should not discover earlier maize cobs in areas close to the hypothesized source area, river valleys relatively close to the Tehuacán Valley.

Figure 13.2 shows the archaeological sites covered in Chapter 13 and is self explanatory.

The Tehuacán research is nearly half-a-century old, but still offers the best evidence for early maize agriculture. MacNeish's excavation methods were crude by today's

FIGURE 13.2 Archaeological sites and culture areas mentioned in this chapter.

standards, and did not use flotation techniques, which are routine on dry sites today. Had he used them, we might be in possession of much more complete botanical evidence, such as was the case at Abu Hureyra in Syria (see Chapter 9), where flotation was used intensively. But one cannot blame MacNeish, as he worked before flotation was developed.

I suspect that the highland Andes was a major center of plant domestication, especially of potatoes and other root crops, simply because so many varieties of such crops are known from there. Potatoes were certainly domesticated long before the earliest known dated tubers of 2000 B.C. or so.

The coast saw thousands of years of intensive fishing, shellfish gathering, and plant foraging before agriculture began. And when it did, it was only in the river valleys that dissect the arid coastal plain. Here, as elsewhere, plant cultivation began as a supplement to foraging. Irrigation and water control generally were the keys to larger scale agriculture of plants other than squashes in coastal river valleys. As we will see in Chapter 22, intensive irrigation agriculture as well as rich coastal fisheries supported elaborate states along Peru's North Coast.

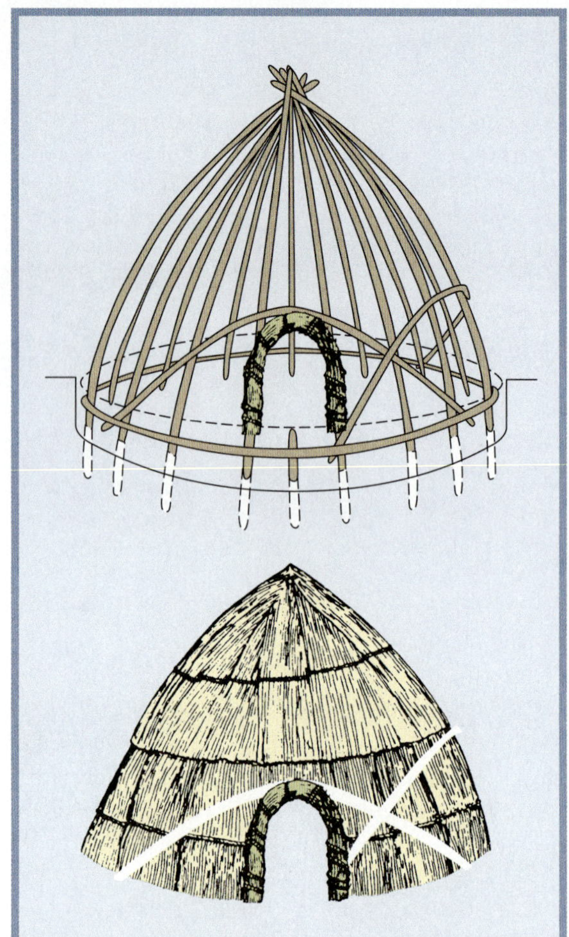

FIGURE 13.6 Reconstruction of a Chilca house. A circular structure, it had a domelike frame of canes bound with rope and covered with bundles of grass; the interior was braced with bones from stranded whales. Seven burials had been deposited in the house before it was intentionally collapsed on top of them. The skeletons were wrapped in mats and all buried at the same time, perhaps because of an epidemic. (After Willey, 1971.)

North America: The Southwest

(Site map is Figure 13.2)

This section is but a cursory summary of the archaeology of the Southwest, one of the most intensively studied culture areas in the world. The narrative zeroes in on two main topics: the spread of maize and other crops into the Southwest from Mexico, a development that was the catalyst for the eventual development of Pueblo cultures; and the three great traditions of Pueblo culture, which developed in the first millennium A.D. The Southwest is unusually well dated, thanks to dendrochronology. There are now so many tree-ring samples from the region that dendrochronologists can now trace the progress of multi-year droughts across the Southwest on a year-by-year basis.

This is a straightforward account, which needs little added to it here. But it's worth making the point that the notion of mobility is a central part of Pueblo Indian tradition. Such mobility was the most effective response to major droughts or drought cycles, and may account for the abandonment of Chaco Canyon in the twelfth century A.D., and of Mesa Verde a century later.

Chaco Canyon

Chaco Canyon is one of the most spectacular historic places in North America. Somewhat off the beaten track, it is well worth the journey, for the pueblos and kivas are exceptionally well preserved and the setting is magnificent. Despite more than a century often intensive research, there are still many mysteries about the site and its landscape. The site box gives a brief summary of what is known about Chaco and its outliers, also of the mysterious "roads" which fanned out from the Canyon. Early investigators focused on the archaeological sites, their contents, and their architecture. It's only in the last twenty or thirty years that the experts have turned to the environmental setting—ever since the "roads" came to light on aerial photographs and infrared images. The meaning of the roads is still much debated, and we still lack sustained native American input into the symbolic meaning of the trackways. The Canyon and its environs are eloquent testimony to the importance of landscape in ancient societies, for the Ancestral Pueblo were well aware of a much wider landscape than their own pueblos, one with important symbolic meaning. It is these symbolic meanings that today's archaeology is concerned with, not only at Chaco, but at other important sites like Avebury and Stonehenge in England and the city of Teotihuacán in Mexico, whose layout replicated the symbolic world (see Chapter 21).

Eastern North America

(Site map at Figure 13.2)

This section surveys the extraordinary hunter-gatherer and farming societies that developed in eastern North America over the past 4,000 years.

We begin with Poverty Point, a site and culture of the first and second millennia B.C., which still defies explanation, beyond a general conclusion that it was a place of major ritual and economic importance. From there, we trace the development of the so-called Moundbuilder cultures—Adena and Hopewell—remarkable for their elaborate burial customs and preoccupation with the ancestors. We stress that these were more ceremonial complexes than specific cultures, communities, and chiefdoms linked by exchange networks and ritual beliefs, and probably ceremonial gift giving. The notion of "peer-polities" is especially useful, as it stresses the point that these societies were made up of hundreds of communities that depended on one another in times of scarcity. Ties of reciprocal obligation that balanced out food shortages in bad years linked them.

Both Adena and Hopewell relied heavily on hunting and gathering, but horticulture became more and more important as the centuries passed. If William Dancey is correct, both food production and ceremonialism flourished during the closing centuries of Hopewell in the early first millennium A.D. until the need for such ritual activity ceased.

The Mississippian section begins by stressing two cultural developments of the early first millennium A.D.—the elaboration of mortuary customs and the first appearance of more important individuals. Widespread political and religious changes ensued, as maize and bean cultivation spread across the Plains into the southeastern United States. Pay careful attention to the discussion of why Mississippian tradition was so distinctive. This is couched in terms of pervasive ritual beliefs and ceremonialism. If this definition is correct, then the Mississippian tradition was driven more by political and social changes, and by factionalism and competition, than by economic developments. The Mississippian was a dynamic and constantly changing tradition, the product of a society driven by factionalism and inter-community squabbling.

It's worth noting that maize and bean cultivation requires forest clearance and much intensive modification of the landscape than just growing native plants. The result—major changes in settlement patterns from earlier times, more intensive cultivation, and a need for communal labor to clear and plant land.

The Mississippian was never a unified state, but a series of small, constantly changing chiefdoms, some of which were centered on major towns, like Cahokia or Moundville. These chiefdoms were the most elaborate societies in ancient America, but they never achieved the complexity and elaboration of the Mesoamerican and Andean states described in Chapters 21 and 22.

chapter

THE DEVELOPMENT OF CIVILIZATION

The Chapter in Review

- Chapter 14 contrasts the historical and anthropological approaches to the origins of states and summarizes the six main theories developed by archaeologists.
- Gordon Childe's "Urban Revolution" theory centered on the development of the city.
- Another group of theories involved the intensification of agriculture and irrigation. Exchange networks and warfare have also been espoused as potential causes of civilization.
- Many modern theories revolve around systems-evolutionary hypotheses and explanations involving environmental change.
- A new generation of social approaches, on the other hand, argues that religious and informational factors, epitomized by centralized authority, have been key elements in the regulation of environmental and economic variables in early civilization.
- Such theories also stress that the social structure of a society ultimately determined its transformation, so the search for the causes of civilization focuses on ecological variables and the opportunities they present to individuals pursuing political goals in different societies. In other words, how is ecological opportunity or necessity translated into political change?
- Recent researches are now focusing on the dynamics of how ancient civilizations functioned—on factionalism, ideology, and gender as promising areas of inquiry.
- The record of early civilizations can be written in cyclical terms. Their collapse may be closely connected to diminishing returns from social complexity, as well as normal political processes such as succession disputes.

Key Cultures and Sites

None—see later chapters

Introductory Comments

Chapter 14 serves as general background for the remaining chapters of the book and is concerned with the various theories that seek to explain the origins of state-organized societies. The chapter has three broad parts. First, we define some of the salient features of cities and civilizations. Then we describe the six classic theories of

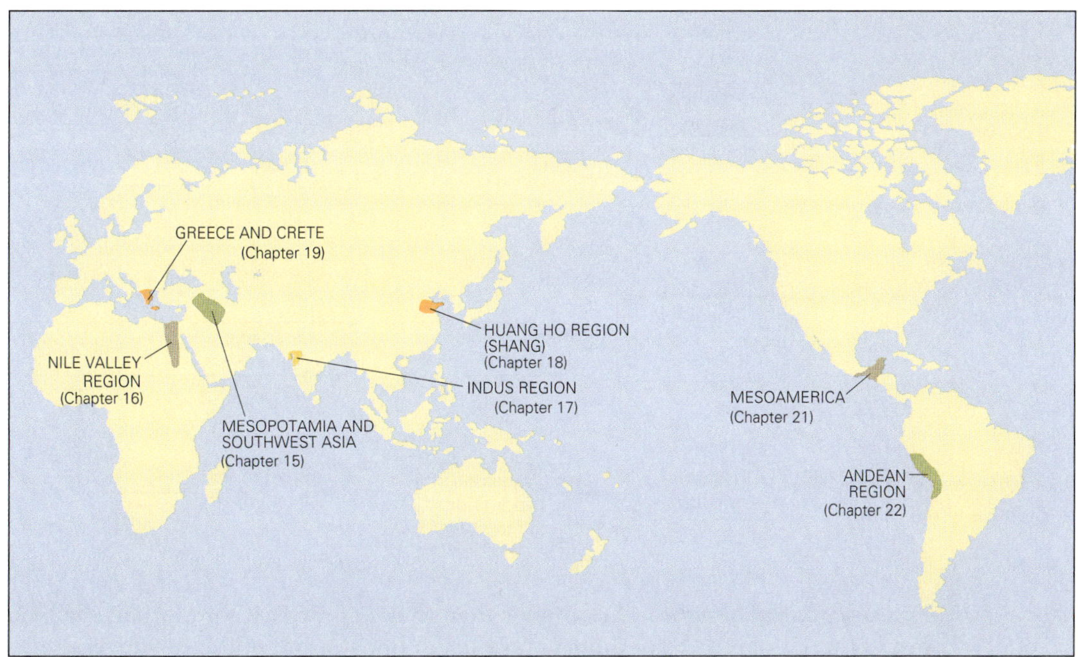

FIGURE 14.1 Locations of major preindustrial states described in this book.

the emergence of state societies. Finally, we survey contemporary theoretical approaches to the origins of civilization. This is very much a general overview, which is worth thorough reading, as we will assume that you have these basics in your head later in the book.

Now Start Reading . . .

It's worth taking a few moments to look at this map (Figure 14.1), so that you are clear in your mind where the earliest state-organized civilizations flourished. Each of them is covered in a specific chapter in the book.

Civilization and Cities

A reminder—we use the terms "civilization" and "state-organized society" interchangeably in this book.

These short sections are very important, for they lay out some of the common features of all pre-industrial civilizations and of cities. They also give you brief definitions of "civilization" and "city," which are useful for working purposes. The ultimate issue is complexity, a degree of organizational complication both in cities and civilizations that is generally unimaginable in simpler societies. Another important facet of both is centralization, epitomized by the flow of authority, power, and wealth to the center, for the benefit of a supreme ruler and a tiny number of other people.

Favorite exam questions haunt these sections—they are well worth close study!

The Six Classic Theories

More ink has been spilled over the origins of states than over almost any other topic in world prehistory, and with good reason. The subject is of great importance. In this section, we take you through the major theories that dominated the debate at a time

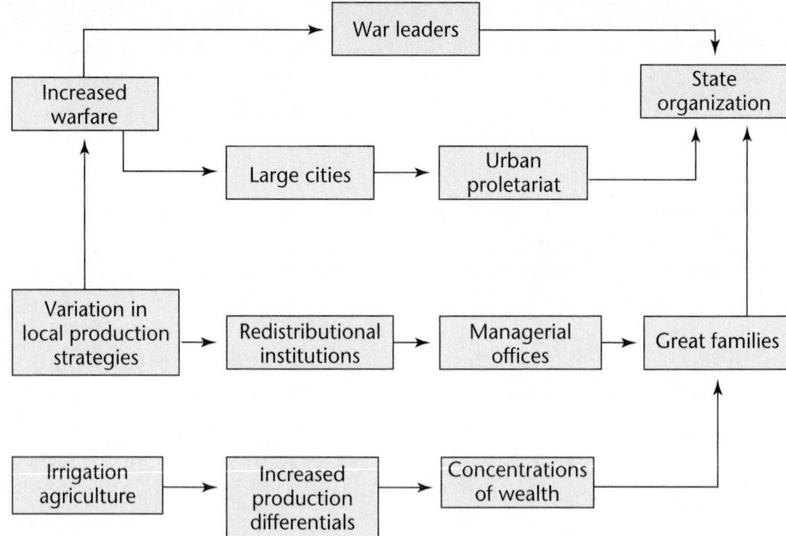

FIGURE 14.6 Hypothetical model of the state's beginnings. (Compiled from R. M. Adams, 1966.)

when causes were thought to be simpler than they were. But it's important that you have a grasp of them, as all of them contribute in one way or another to current theorizing on the subject.

Gordon Childe's "Urban Revolution" has been an especially pervasive hypothesis, largely because he published it in popular books, and also because it was adopted with enthusiasm by world historians like Arnold Toynbee a half century ago. They were looking for simple, easy frameworks for their broad visions. Critiques of it are numerous—but the wisest comment is that of Robert Adams at the end of the discussion about land ownership and social organization.

As we point out, the early ecological theories built on three components of the Childe hypothesis—large food surpluses, diversified food economies, and irrigation agriculture. These are still considered major factors in all early states.

Technology, trade, and warfare are very much secondary factors in the development of states, as we discuss. Today, we have a great deal more data on early states than we did even a generation ago: new technologies such as remote sensing, as well as settlement archaeology and ethnohistory, are providing us with portraits not only of the layout of cities, but of the relationships between them and their hinterlands. So we now know that the rise of states was a complex process, with no one factor in particular being the proverbial smoking gun.

This realization lies behind the systems models, which were popular in the 1960s and 1970s. These were closely tied to processual archaeology, to the study of processes of cultural change and to the cultural ecology that lies behind them. Such theories also highlight the importance of environmental change. In a new generation of much more precise climatological studies, environment may turn out to be much more important than we once suspected.

The Adams model, illustrated in Figure 14.6, shows the potential complexity of systems models.

Social Theories

Systems-ecological theories, with their reliance on anonymous processes, are now seen to be too mechanistic, too anonymous. So, in recent years, the focus has turned to people and groups, to the ways in which ancient civilizations functioned on a day-to-day basis. We summarize some of the major theoretical approaches here, especially the importance of power when defined in economic, social, and ideological terms. The bottom line: if a ruler could impose authority by administrative and military means, he could maintain his position. But it would be a mistake to underestimate the power held by kin leaders in a society who handled such vital issues as land ownership and inheritance. As Norman Yoffee says in the "Power in Three Dimensions" section, there were many paths toward social complexity, many of them regulated by constraints such as storage. Chiefdoms were one path for social evolution, states another.

The Lord of Sicán

The Lord of Sicán ruled over a kingdom on Peru's North Coast after the Moche state had collapsed. His spectacular burial is somewhat overshadowed by the Lords of Sipán finds of half a millennium earlier. The Lord's golden funerary mask with mucus dripping from its nostrils gives us a firm link between shamanistic rituals and the use of hallucinogenic drugs to induce trance and ancient Andean leadership. Such practices are still commonplace in South American Indian society to this day, and are also depicted on the walls of the Chavín de Huantar temple of the first millennium B.C. Much of what we know about the most able rulers of ancient times comes from their burials. Sicán is no exception.

"Chiefly cycling" emphasizes the constant fluidity of state formation, the dynamic processes that could take hold, and the importance of dynamic, very able individuals who were the agents of change, not merely part of the process of change. Combine very able individuals, competitive and military advantage, and emerging conditions of social inequality, and you have all the ingredients for the emergence of the state.

The Collapse of Civilizations

This is an oft-neglected subject, partly because it's more sexy to be concerned with the development of states rather than their demise. But in recent years, some people have begun thinking seriously about collapse. The most famous collapse of all is that of the Maya civilization of the southern lowlands of Mesoamerica, which has been debated at length for three quarters of a century. It seems that a combination of climatic, environmental, economic, social, and political factors came into play (see Chapter 21). This short section summarizes some of the issues, and concludes that declining returns from social complexity may have been one of the major villains—quite apart from the normal political processes such as factionalism.

chapter

EARLY CIVILIZATIONS IN SOUTHWEST ASIA

The Chapter in Review

- By 7000 B.C., highland peoples had settled in northern Mesopotamia in areas where agriculture was possible through the use of seasonal rainfall. These Hassuna people lived in close contact with other societies downstream that developed irrigation agriculture.
- In about 6500 B.C., Halafian painted wares appeared over a wide area of upland northern Mesopotamia and Anatolia; they are thought to coincide with the emergence of chiefdoms in this area.
- The delta lowlands may have supported farmers before 6500 B.C., but the first traces of them appear in the 'Ubaid culture of the sixth millennium. They practiced small-scale irrigation and lived in groups of communities linked by trade networks.
- In time, some villages, like Eridu, became ceremonial centers and towns. A rapid evolution to urban life ensued—marked by fast population growth, the congregation of people in small cities, and the development of long-distance trade.
- This new urban society was organized in distinctive stratified social classes.
- Copper metallurgy developed at about the same time in the highlands and soon came into widespread use.
- By 2900 B.C., Sumerian civilization was in full swing and was part of what we call a nascent world system, which linked polities as far afield as the Iranian Plateau and the Indus in the east and the Mediterranean and the Nile Valley in the west.
- Mesopotamia never achieved political unification under the Sumerians. Rather, dozens of city-states vied for political and economic supremacy and competed with other societies in northern Mesopotamia and close to the Zagros Mountains.
- Sumerian civilization flourished until about 2000 B.C., when it was eclipsed by Akkadian and then Babylonian power.
- In the late second millennium B.C., the city of Assur in the north nurtured the Assyrian Empire, which was extended by vigorous and despotic kings during the first half of the succeeding millennium. At one time, the Assyrian Empire stretched from the Mediterranean to the Persian Gulf.
- The Assyrian Empire fell in 612 B.C., and the power vacuum was filled by the Babylonians under the rule of Nebuchadnezzar. Babylon fell to Cyrus the Great of Persia in 539 B.C., and Mesopotamia became part of the Persian Empire.

Key Cultures and Sites

Akkadian state	Elamites	Kish	Tell al 'Ouelli
Assur	Erech	Shari-i-Shokhta	Tepe Yahya
Assyrian empire	Eridu	Sumerian civilization	'Ubaid
Babylon	Halafian	Susa	Uruk
Choga Mami	Hassuna		

Introductory Comments

Chapters 15 through 20 describe developments in the Old World after the first appearance of urban civilization in Mesopotamia, surveyed in this chapter, and along the Nile (see Chapter 16). Each chapter unfolds chronologically, so that you journey through time, starting with the earliest developments, ending on the threshold of written history or beyond.

Chapter 15 divides into three parts:

- First, we describe the origins of Mesopotamian civilization and the development of the first cities in the lowlands.
- Then we survey Sumerian civilization and its basic institutions.
- Lastly, we examine the later history of Mesopotamian civilization, where we rely more on historical than archaeological evidence.

This is a reasonably easy-to-follow journey, so much so that it masks much more complex developments. Space prevents us from describing a great deal of what was going on in this enormous region between 4000 and 1000 B.C. The point is that what happened in southern Mesopotamia was not unique. Larger, more complex towns turned into cities elsewhere as well as in the flat delta lands. States formed in many areas, especially close to key trade routes and along the always-strategic eastern Mediterranean shore at about the same time as they first appeared in Mesopotamia. So just don't think of the Sumerians—they are the best known early state but were far from unique as city dwellers, even as early as 2500 B.C.

The Mesopotamians of the fourth millennium B.C. lived in an increasingly wider world, no longer circumscribed by the narrow confines of their own city or town, or city state. For the first time, we witness the appearance of the first glimmerings of more global economies. Some scholars call this a "world economic system," but this has been criticized as an inappropriate term.

Chapter 14 covers the beginnings of this more complicated world, which teemed with big-state rivalries in later centuries, described in Chapter 19.

Now Start Reading . . .

The Beginnings of Civilization

This chapter builds on the developments described in Chapter 9, where we chronicled the increasing complexity and sophistication of farming life.

Figure 15.1 shows the overall geography and locations of major sites mentioned in the chapter.

Talk about an interconnected world! This chronological table is a sea of arrows, which epitomize the new world of increasingly interconnected states after 3000 B.C. The table ranges from south Asia to the Nile, from Europe to the Aegean and Mesopotamia. I placed it here to give you background on the relationships between

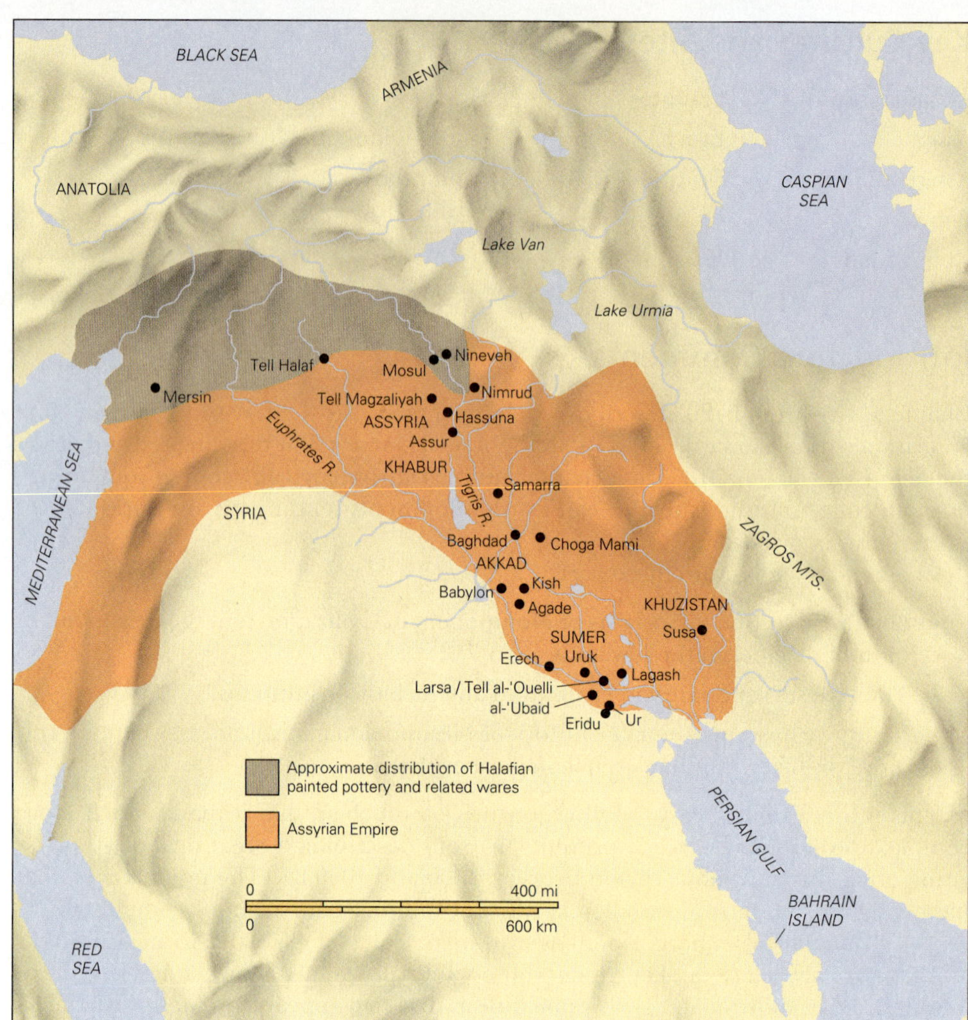

FIGURE 15.1 Sites and cultural distributions mentioned in this chapter. (Tepe Yahya and Shari-i-Shokhta lie to the east of the map.)

the different societies described in Chapters 15 to 20. It's worth spending a little time going over it to get the basic relationships and connections in your mind—for technical terms, turn to the relevant chapter.

This section of the chapter covers developments after the establishment of full-fledged agriculture and animal herding over southwestern Asia. First, we describe the village farming cultures marked by Hassunan and Halafian pottery. Here, as elsewhere, distinctive clay vessels provide clues as to the distribution of different societies. Halafian pottery is sufficiently different to the point that it can be identified over large areas—much desired by outsiders, it was exchanged with many distant communities.

Hassunan and Halafian clay vessels are very colorful and unmistakable. But when you move into the south, 'Ubaid pottery is quite different. Apart from the black painted decoration, the clay sometimes has an almost greenish hue, which is unique in my experience. The lowland settlement section places 'Ubaid in an environmental context. We often forget just how much the Mesopotamian environment changed as the Persian Gulf rose to modern levels. The circumscription caused by environmental change and rising sea levels may have been a major catalyst for the development of irrigation agriculture and cities.

Erech and Uruk epitomize the early city. The focus of these new, much more elaborate communities was the temple, rebuilt again and again at the same sites over many centuries. The Eridu ziggurat in particular has yielded a mine of information on how these structures developed.

TABLE 15.1
Major early civilizations of Southwest Asia and their interconnectedness

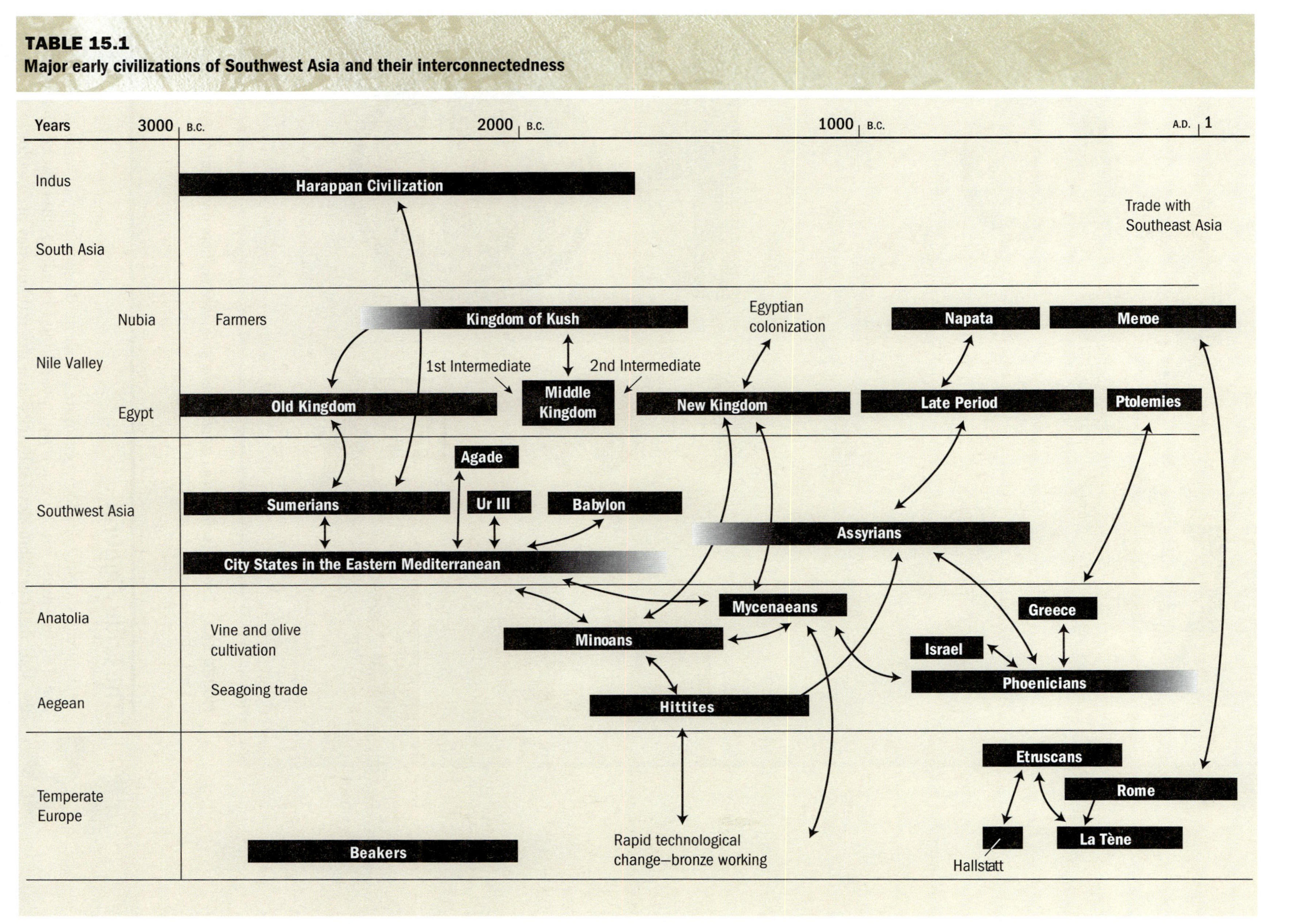

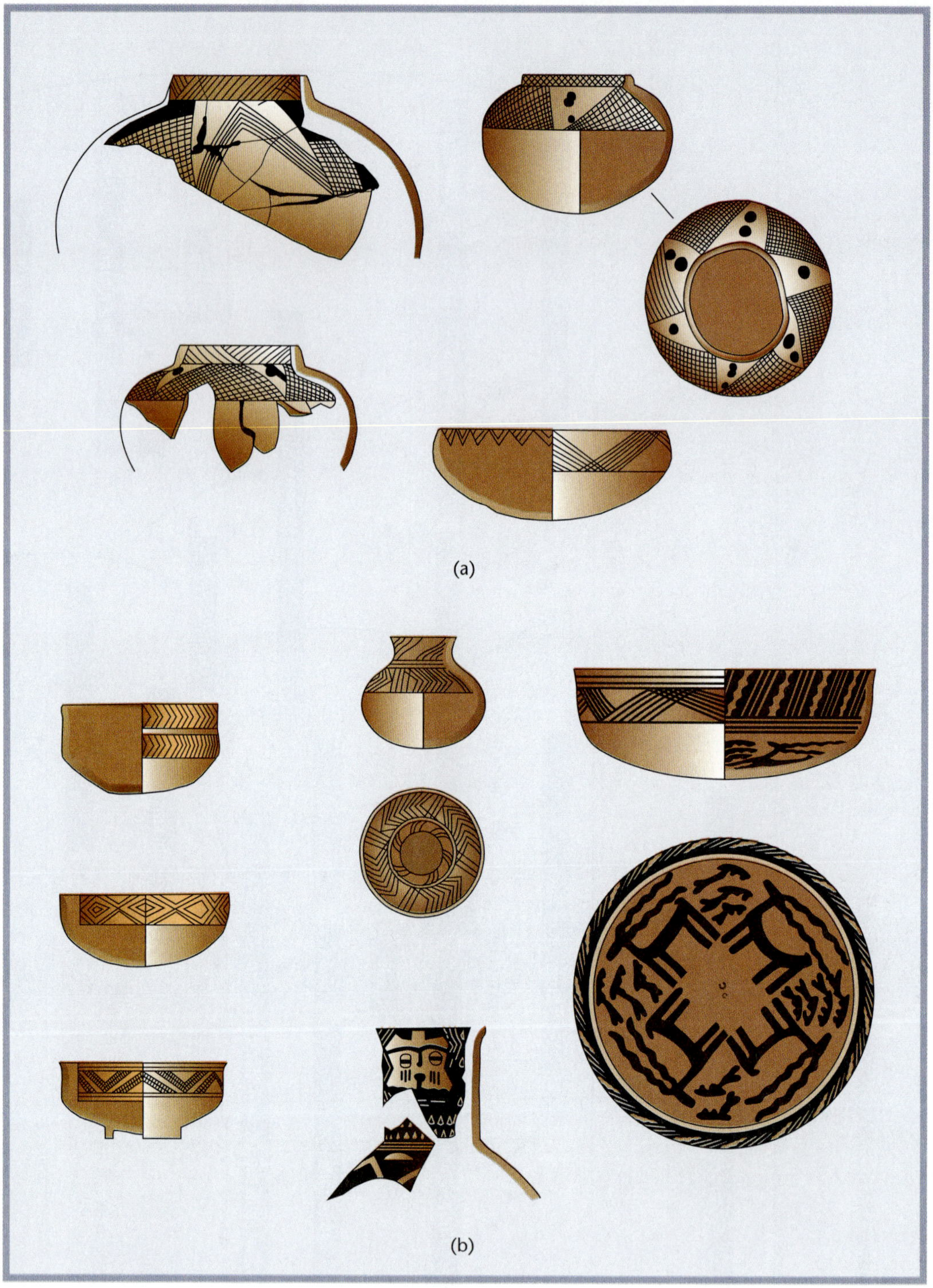

(a)

(b)

FIGURE 15.2 Early Mesopotamian painted pottery: (a) vessels from Hassuna; (b) Samarra-type vessels from Hassuna. (All one-eighth full size.)

The Eridu Ziggurat

Ancient cities are never easy to excavate, let alone those of the Sumerians, which were made of sun dried brick. As a result, abandoned buildings literally melted back into the soil, making them devilishly hard for the modern-day archaeologist to recover. Victorian archaeologists were baffled by mud brick architecture. German archaeologist

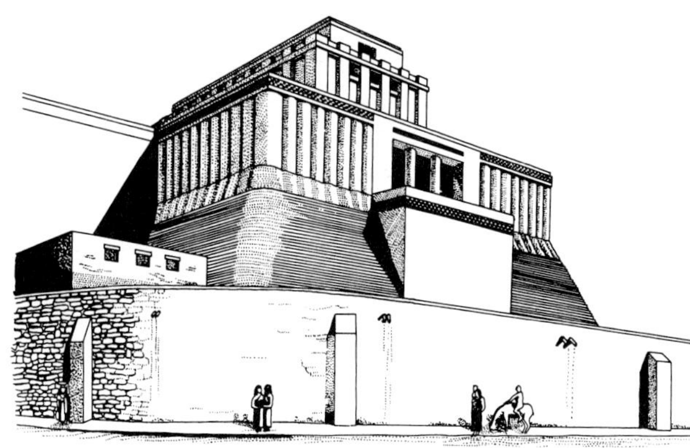

FIGURE 15.4 Artist's reconstruction of an Uruk culture temple at Eridu. Notice the great platform supporting the temple and the drainage pipes in the walls.

Robert Koldeway was the first excavator to master a technique for tracing mud brick walls. He trained teams of workers who learned the different consistencies of the soil, and the subtle but distinctive sounds let out by virtually invisible mud brick walls. Since Koldway's day, compressed air has become the tool of choice, while remote sensing devices like subsurface radar have promise for the future. The Eridu ziggurat is a classic example of a ziggurat excavation conducted with patience and the assistance of large teams of workers. They revealed a shrine and mud brick platform rebuilt again and again in the same place. Figure 15.4 represents the culmination of this architectural evolution, a sophisticated building by any standards, excavated to a considerable degree with compressed air. It's interesting to note the power of intensely sacred places. When Mexican archaeologist Eduardo Matos Moctezuma excavated the Templo Major in the heart of the Aztec capital, Tenochtitlán, he found a similar pattern of constant rebuilding—in the same place.

The earliest cities were probably agglomerations of villages, which became the city's crowded neighborhoods, organized by kin affiliation, and, perhaps, craft specialty.

The description of Uruk in these pages ranges widely over the increasing complexity of emerging civilization in the fourth millennium B.C. This is reflected in the development of cuneiform script, shown in Figure 15.6.

Sumerian Civilization

Living in Sumerian society can never have been easy, for economic, political, and social life were always changing. There was no monolithic Sumerian state, merely a patchwork of small city-states, which negotiated, fought, and engaged in a constant game of intricate diplomatic Monopoly. The larger political entities that developed were the result of the increasing interconnectedness of the Mesopotamian world, stemming in considerable part from the lack of timber and metal ores in what is now southern Iraq. Sumerian society was a crucible of technological innovation—metallurgy, river vessels, and plows, to mention only a few.

The Sumerian world was one of harsh extremes—great heat and winter cold, but one blessed with fertile soils, when irrigated. The Sumerians lived in a world where they seemed to be at the mercy of the gods and the forces of nature. They were one of the first societies to develop their own literature, which comes down to us on cuneiform tablets. Modern-day experts on their cuneiform are even compiling a Sumerian dictionary, such is the wealth of material.

As we say at the end of this section, increasingly, small city-states became interdependent, small cogs in a larger world. And it was these webs of interconnectedness that led to the volatile, much larger states of later times, described in the last part of the chapter.

Earliest pictographs (3000 B.C.)	Denotation of pictographs	Pictographs in rotated position	Cuneiform signs c. 1900 B.C.	Basic logographic values	
				Reading	Meaning
	Head and body of man			lu	Man
	Head with mouth indicated			ka	Mouth
	Bowl of food			ninda	Food, bread
	Mouth + food			kú	To eat
	Stream of water			a	Water
	Mouth + water			nag	To drink
	Fish			kua	Fish
	Bird			mušen	Bird
	Head of an ass			anše	Ass
	Ear of barley			še	Barley

FIGURE 15.6 Development of Sumerian writing, from a pictographic script to a cuneiform script and then to a phonetic system. The word *cuneiform* is derived from the Latin *cuneus,* meaning "a wedge," after the characteristic impression of the script.

Exchange and the Widening of Political Authority

The final part of the chapter covers a much wider area of southwestern Asia, beginning with a description of the trade in raw materials on the Iranian Plateau, which fueled urban growth in Mesopotamia and also had connections with the Harappan civilization of Chapter 17. Tepe Yahya and Shari-I-Shokhta were important centers in this trade, but whether the commerce was in the hands of foreign merchants or indigenous entrepreneurs is a matter for discussion.

From the Iranian Plateau, we move into a discussion of wider political authority, where several dynamics had parts to play: rising populations, increased interdependence and competition, and the constant tensions between desert nomads and sedentary people farming the land. In times of drought, for example, nomads and their flocks encroach on settled lands and river floodplains. When rainfall is plentiful, they move out on the desert. This dynamic is as old as farming itself. But at the core of expanding civilizations and empires was one all-important catalyst—that of charismatic, competent leadership in a world where secular rulers were becoming all-powerful. This was the story of the Ur dynasties, of the Akkadians and Babylon. And the Assyrian monarchs were successful because of their military abilities and absolute despotism.

With the Assyrians, we enter a much wider diplomatic, military, and political world, which we summarize later on, in Chapter 19.

chapter

EGYPT, NUBIA, AND AFRICA

The Chapter in Review

- Ancient Egyptian civilization arose out of complex processes of forced and voluntary integration along the Nile Valley. Increasing trade contacts with Southwest Asia, culminating in the emergence of the ancient Egyptian state in about 3100 B.C, accelerated this process.
- Egyptologists conventionally subdivide ancient Egyptian civilization into four main periods: the Archaic and Old Kingdom, Middle Kingdom, New Kingdom, and the Late period, the first three of which were separated by brief intermediate periods of political chaos.
- The Old Kingdom was notable for its despotic pharaohs and its frenzy of pyramid construction, an activity that may be connected with pragmatic notions of fostering national unity.
- The Middle Kingdom saw a shift of political and religious power to Thebes and Upper Egypt. New Kingdom pharaohs made Egypt an imperial power with strong interests in Asia and Nubia.
- Ancient Egyptian civilization began to decline after 1000 B.C., and Egypt fell under Roman rule in 30 B.C.
- Nubia, upstream of the First Cataract, was exploited by the Egyptians for centuries, but it came into its own as the pharaohs' power declined. Nubian kings from Kush actually ruled over Egypt in the eighth century B.C., but they were forced to retreat to Meroe, far upstream, two centuries later.
- Meroe became a center for the Red Sea and Indian Ocean trade, ruled by kings and queens who preserved Egyptian customs. It prospered until the fourth century A.D., when it was conquered and finally eclipsed by the kingdom of Aksum in the Ethiopian highlands.
- The camel opened up the Sahara to regular gold and salt trade, fostering the development of powerful West African states such as Ghana, Mali, and Songhay.
- At the same time, expanding Indian Ocean trade nurtured a network of trading towns on the East African coast.
- During the fourteenth and fifteenth centuries A.D., Great Zimbabwe in southern Africa controlled much of the gold and ivory trade in southeastern Africa.

Key Cultures and Terms

Abydos
Adulis
Aksum
Archaic Egypt
El-Amarna
First Intermediate Period
Ghana
Giza
Great Zimbabwe
Jenne-Jeno
Kahun
Karnak
Kerma
Kilwa Island
Kush

Late Period
Luxor
Maadi
Mali
Meroe
Middle Kingdom
Naqada
Nekhen
New Kingdom
Saqqara
Second Intermediate Period
Songhay

Introductory Comments

Chapter 16 covers a great deal of ground, far more than just ancient Egyptian civilization. It's tempting, of course, to spend an entire chapter on Egypt, but this remarkable civilization is part of a much larger African world, even if most of its dealings were with eastern Mediterranean states. *People* is unique in offering coverage of Africa as a whole, so you can envisage Ancient Egypt in a broader historical context.

This chapter has three parts, but they run in chronological order, beginning along the Nile, ending in Southern Africa:

- First, we cover the beginnings of Egyptian civilization and describe the salient features of Ancient Egypt.
- Second, we move southward into Nubia, which interacted with Egypt throughout its history. In the end Nubians became pharaohs, before founding Meroe deep in the Sudan. This part ends with a description of the Aksum state in Ethiopia.
- Lastly, we briefly survey the kingdoms of tropical Africa, which flourished during the past 2,000 years.

Once again, this chapter builds on developments in an earlier chapter, Chapter 11, where we described the late arrival of cattle herding and farming south of the Sahara Desert.

Now Start Reading . . .

Figure 16.1 is a simple map, showing the major sites mentioned in the text.

Table 16.1 teems with arrows and interconnections! Please examine this in tandem with Table 15.1 to get the full significance of the increasingly interconnected world of Egypt. Whether along the Nile or south of the Sahara, connections with a wider world played a decisive role in the course of history, and this table reflects them. In particular, please note the ties between Africa, northeast Africa, and India, and through there to Southeast Asia and China. You may not know that Chinese ships visited the East Africa coast in the seventh century A.D. There is even a picture of an African giraffe being paraded at the Chinese court!

You might want to Post-it this table and Table 15.1, as you may need to refer to them again soon.

Origins of Ancient Egypt

This section is fascinating, if nothing else because of the meld of archaeology and Egyptian ideology, also myth, which makes up our knowledge of unification.

The story of unification revolves around a series of fiercely competing kingdoms, among them Naqada, Nekhen, and This. Figure 16.2, developed by Egyptologist Barry Kemp, encapsulates the intricate game of what he calls Monopoly that unfolded along the Nile before 3000 B.C. Study this carefully to get the general dynamics in your mind.

Figure 16.3 gives the extents of the Upper Egyptian kingdoms.

Of the actual process of unification, we know little, but the Egyptians symbolized it in the linking of the gods Horus and Seth. This notion of harmony and unification, of order as opposed to chaos, was the essence of Egyptian civilization. Disorder was

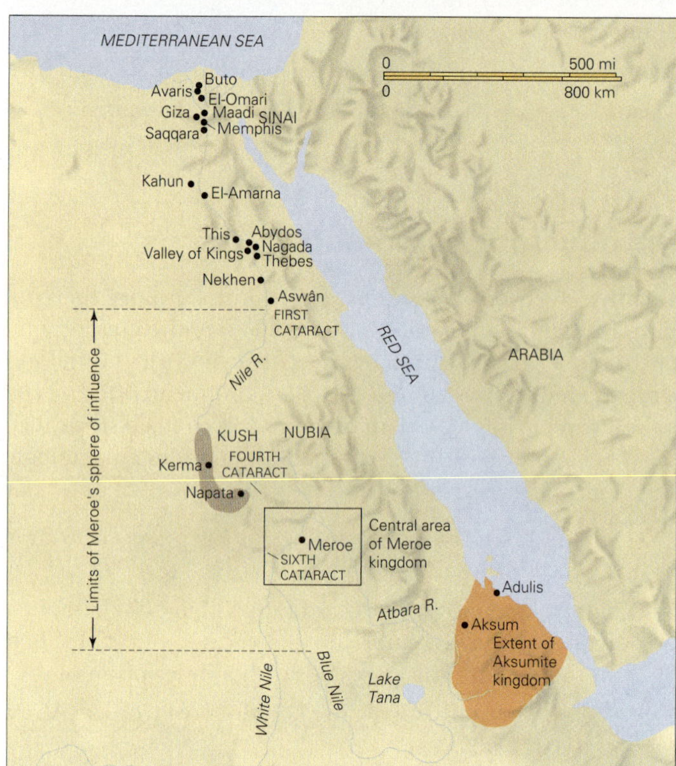

FIGURE 16.1 Ancient Egypt, Ethiopia, and Nubia.

prevented by the rule of kings and by the benign force of the sun. Read the "Scenario" section carefully, for it is fundamental to understanding Ancient Egypt.

Archaic and Old Kingdom Egypt

Table 16.2 is a quick reference check on the major developments in ancient Egyptian civilization, provided purely for convenience. The chronology can vary from one Egyptologist to another, but this is a widely used version.

With the Old Kingdom, we are on firmer historical ground, made the more so by some remarkable fieldwork at Abydos in recent years, which has centered on some of the earliest royal graves and the identity of the first pharaohs. The first ruler, who moved the royal capital to Memphis near the modern city of Cairo (a Medieval city), was named Horus-Aha. His grave yielded merchandise labels, which show that he traded with eastern Mediterranean kingdoms, including a large traffic in wine.

This section is important because it gives you general background on Egyptian kingship, the notion of the "Great Culture." There's also some background on the orgy of pyramid building orchestrated by the pharaohs after 2600 B.C. We pay close attention to the Step Pyramid at Saqqara.

The Step Pyramid at Saqqara

Nearly everyone tends to look at an Egyptian pyramid, exclaim "Wow!", and move on. This is a great mistake, as the Step Pyramid demonstrates. All the Egyptian pyramids were burial places for pharaohs, but the pyramid itself was only one component in an elaborate mortuary complex. Saqqara is one of the best preserved, complete with its symbolic palaces and the central plaza, which was designed as a setting for one of the most important ancient Egyptian rituals—the *Sed* ceremony. *Sed* was performed after a 30-year reign, or more frequently in a time when life expectancies were short. At

TABLE 16.1

The web of relationships between Asia, Africa, and other regions after 500 B.C.

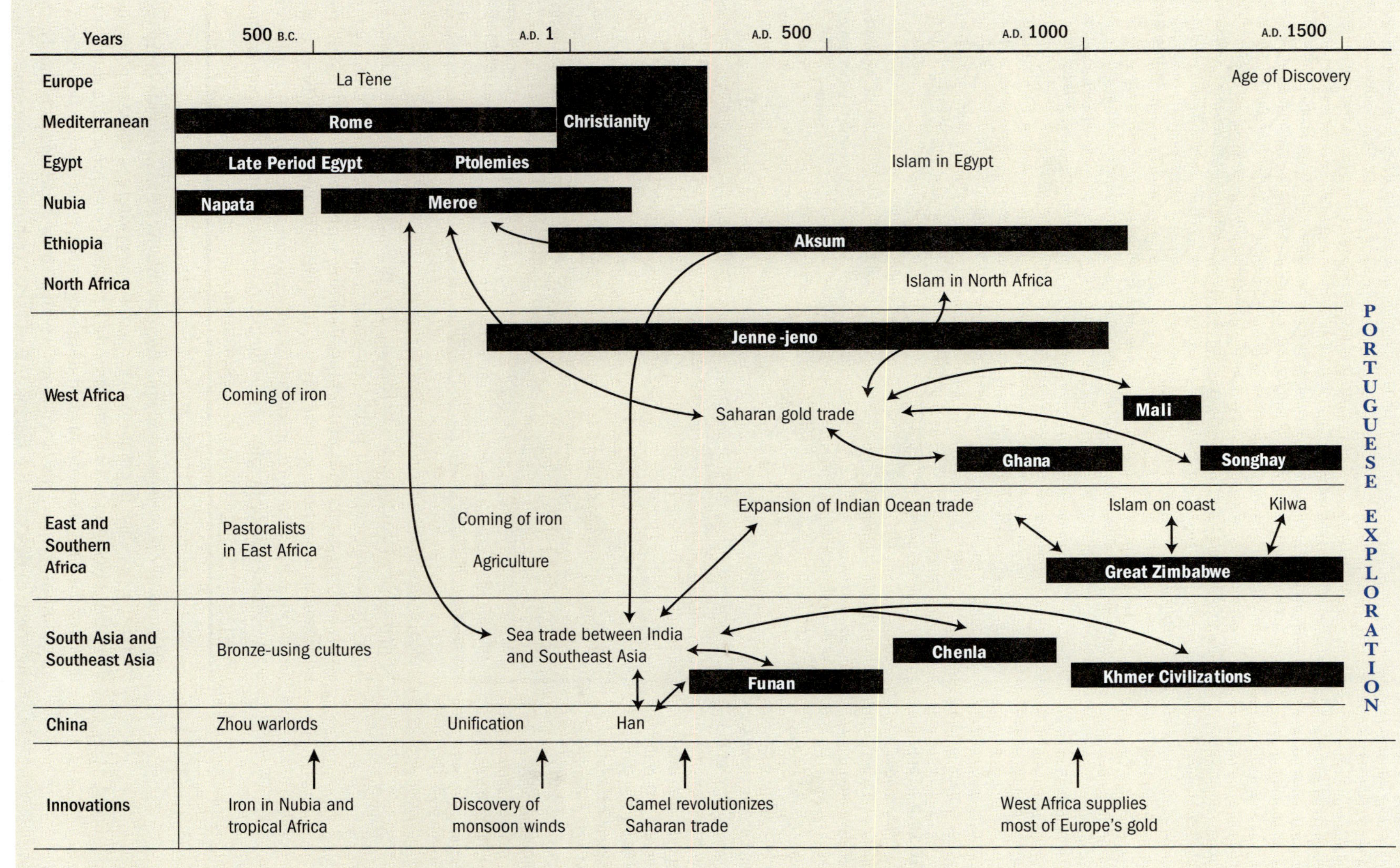

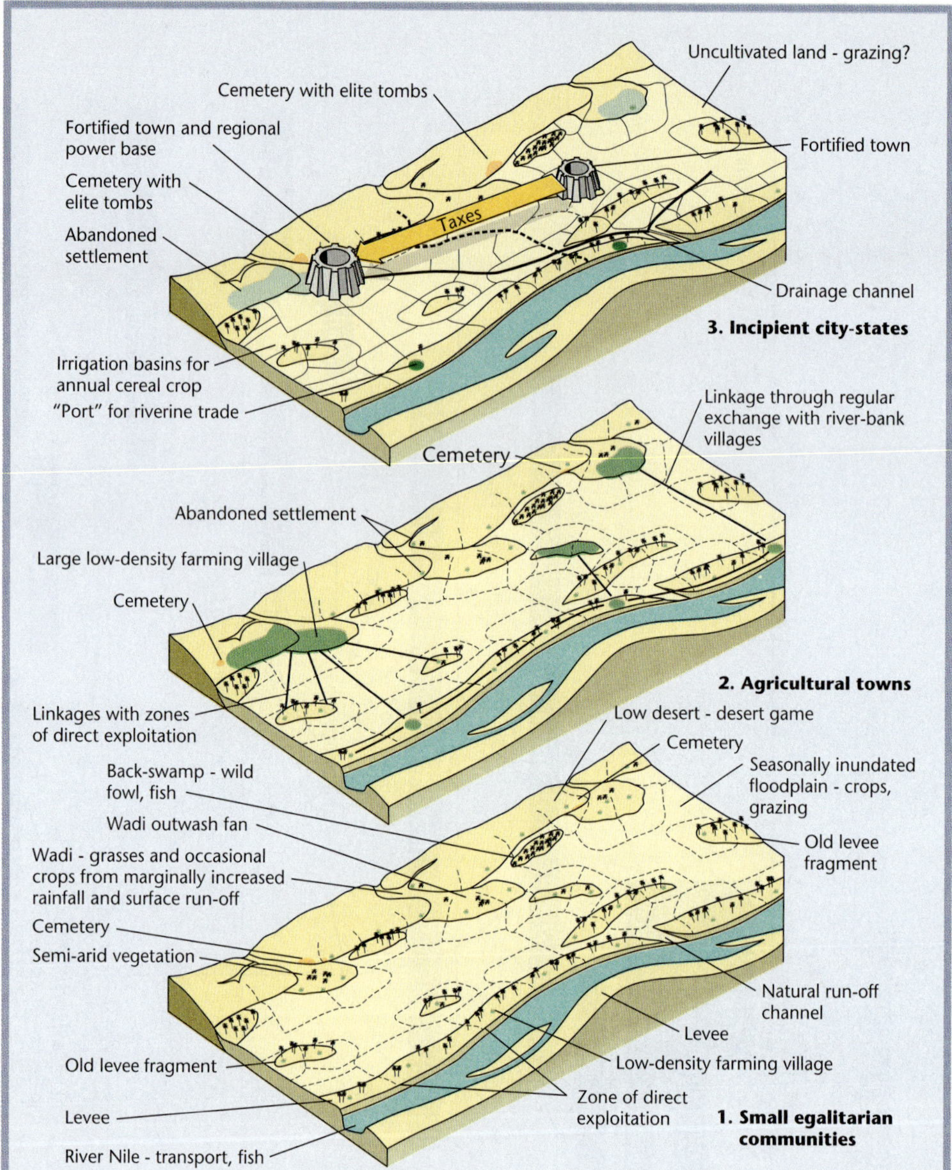

FIGURE 16.2 Early Egyptian "Monopoly." (1) Small egalitarian agricultural communities exploited the diverse floodplain environments of the Nile. (2) The small villages became agricultural towns, often at the edge of the valley, maintaining links with one another and with trade routes along the river. (3) Incipient city-states formed with a strong tax base of subordinate communities. Major towns were fortified, and the elite were buried in cemeteries.

Saqqara, the setting appears before us. The thrones of Upper and Lower Egypt where King Djoser appeared in public (in itself a rare and carefully choreographed occasion), and the arena with markers symbolizing Upper and Lower Egypt, round which he strode in a symbolic gesture. At *Sed,* the pharaoh claimed the Two Lands, as a territorial claimant, in a ceremony that commemorated harmony and unification, two of the fundamental principles of the Egyptian Great Culture. Saqqara is one of the few places where we see this set in architecture.

Writers of every persuasion spill liters of ink over the pyramids every year, for they exercise a peculiar fascination over people everywhere. I must confess that I do not share this fascination, for Giza and other pyramid complexes are more interesting in terms of their settings and surrounding structures, as well as the beliefs and rituals that surrounded them. This is what we try and stress here. Unfortunately, there is not the space to describe the fascinating workers' cemeteries and entire town devoted to those who labored at Giza, built outside the pyramid precincts—the focus of recent

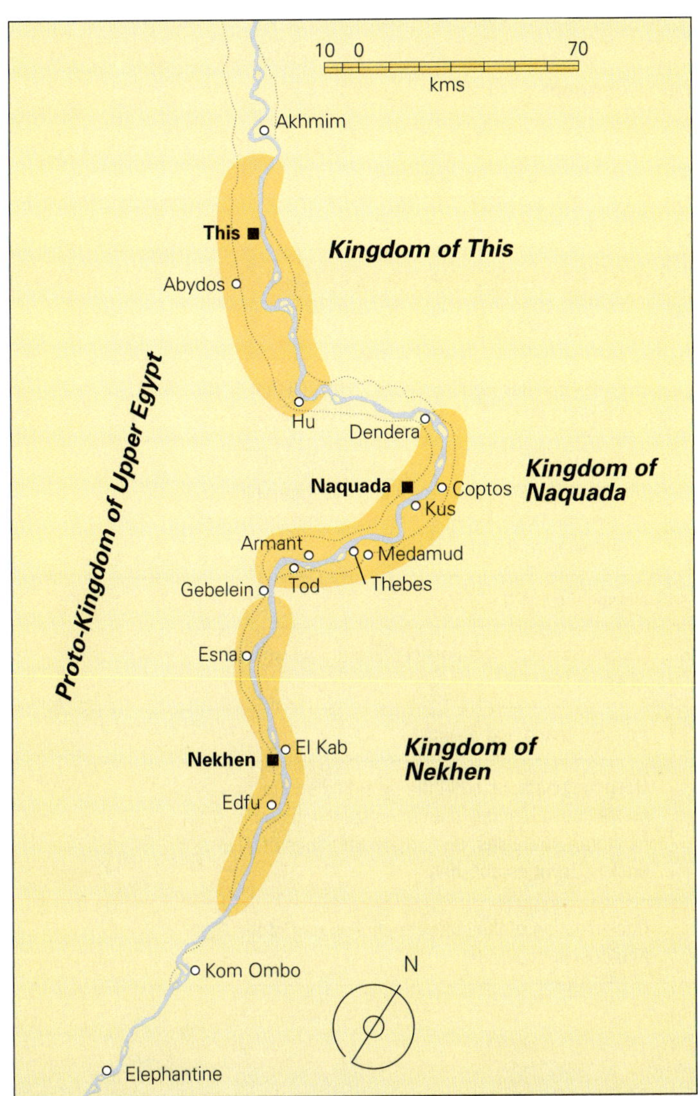

FIGURE 16.3 The spread of the Upper Egyptian proto-kingdom through the Nile Valley, c. 3300 B.C. This is a gross simplification of a very complex, and ever-changing, political situation.

research. Suffice it to say that there were large facilities for baking bread and drying fish, two essential components of the rations handed out each week to those who worked on the pyramids or maintained the shrines.

Egypt after the Old Kingdom

I cannot possibly do justice to the richness of Egyptian civilization here, but there are plenty of good books that go into much more detail if you want more—see the Guide to Further Reading. I give a simple narrative description here. Some basic points are worth emphasizing:

- It's a myth to say that Egyptian civilization was unchanging, monolithic. It was not. Although many elements were conservative, there was constant change dictated by growing population, external and internal politics, droughts, and all manner of other factors.
- During the New Kingdom, Egypt became an imperial power and far more outward looking and militaristic than in earlier times. But it is a myth to think of it as an isolated land. Old Kingdom pharaohs obtained timber from the eastern Mediterranean coast (the famed "cedars of Lebanon").

TABLE 16.2
Major subdivisions and developments of ancient Egyptian civilizations

Years B.C.	Period	Characteristics
30	Roman occupation	Egypt becomes an imperial province of Rome.
332 to 30	Ptolemaic period	The Ptolemies bring Greek influence to Egypt, beginning with the conquest of Egypt by Alexander the Great in 332 B.C.
1070 to 332	Late period	Gradual decline in pharaonic authority, culminating in Persian rule (525 to 404 and 343 to 332 B.C.).
1530 to 1070	New Kingdom	Great imperial period of Egyptian history, with pharaohs buried in the Valley of Kings; pharaohs include Rameses II, Seti I, and Tutankhamun, as well as Akhenaten, the heretic ruler.
1640 to 1530	Second Intermediate period	Hyksos rules in the delta.
2040 to 1640	Middle Kingdom	Thebes achieves prominence, also the priesthood of Amun.
2180 to 2040	First Intermediate period	Political chaos and disunity.
2575 to 2180	Old Kingdom	Despotic pharaohs build the pyramids and favor conspicuous funerary monuments; institutions, economic strategies, and artistic traditions of ancient Egypt established.
3100 to 2575	Archaic period	Consolidation of the state (treated as part of the Old Kingdom in this book).
c. 3150	Unification of Egypt under Narmer (Menes)	

• The nature of kingship was all-important, as was the concept of *Ma'at.* The right order grounded Egyptian civilization.

• Above all, a great deal depended on the abilities of the king. A strong, long-lived ruler like Rameses II exercised remarkable power. But if a king was weak, or someone died suddenly (a commonplace event in a world with short life expectancy), then the state could slide into a period of political unrest, even civil war. Remember what we said about individuals of exceptional ability in Chapter 14. In this connection, it would be interesting to know more about the political fallout from Akhenaten, with the heretic pharaoh's excursion into evangelical sun worship!

Nubia

Many people who are fascinated by Egypt never give a thought to Nubia, the "Land of the Bowmen," as the Egyptians called it. This was because many Nubians served as mercenaries in the pharaoh's armies, especially as deadly bowmen. I think Nubia is fascinating, especially in its changing relationship with the land of the pharaohs that culminated in Nubians ruling Egypt. This section is a simple narrative, which takes us from Kerma to Meroe, and then into the emerging desert caravan trade.

The camel is a fascinating beast, and I wish we had more time to spend on it here. It is not the camel that was the catalyst for desert trade, although, obviously, it was important. It was the *saddle* worn by the camel—for rising, load carrying, or fighting. Load-carrying saddles were what allowed caravans to venture deep into the desert and, eventually, to cross the Sahara. By Medieval times, thousands of people lived their entire lives in caravans, congregating at cities that became cross-roads where long distance routes converged. Cairo was one, and Meroe was one of the earliest of them.

We end this section on the Ethiopian highlands, with the little known kingdom of Aksum, which enjoyed extensive trading relationships with Indian Ocean routes. The royal tombs are unique and the subject of recent research.

Tropical Africa

For years, many archaeologists and most world historians thought of tropical Africa as a backwater, where little happened after the evolution of the first humans and *Homo sapiens sapiens*. How wrong they were! The remainder of Chapter 16 chronicles some of the major developments that took hold after the introduction of agriculture and domesticated animals some 3,000 years ago. Specifically, we describe the origin of states in West Africa, three of the major kingdoms which followed, and the so-called "Stone Towns" of the East African coast, connected to the Indian Ocean trade.

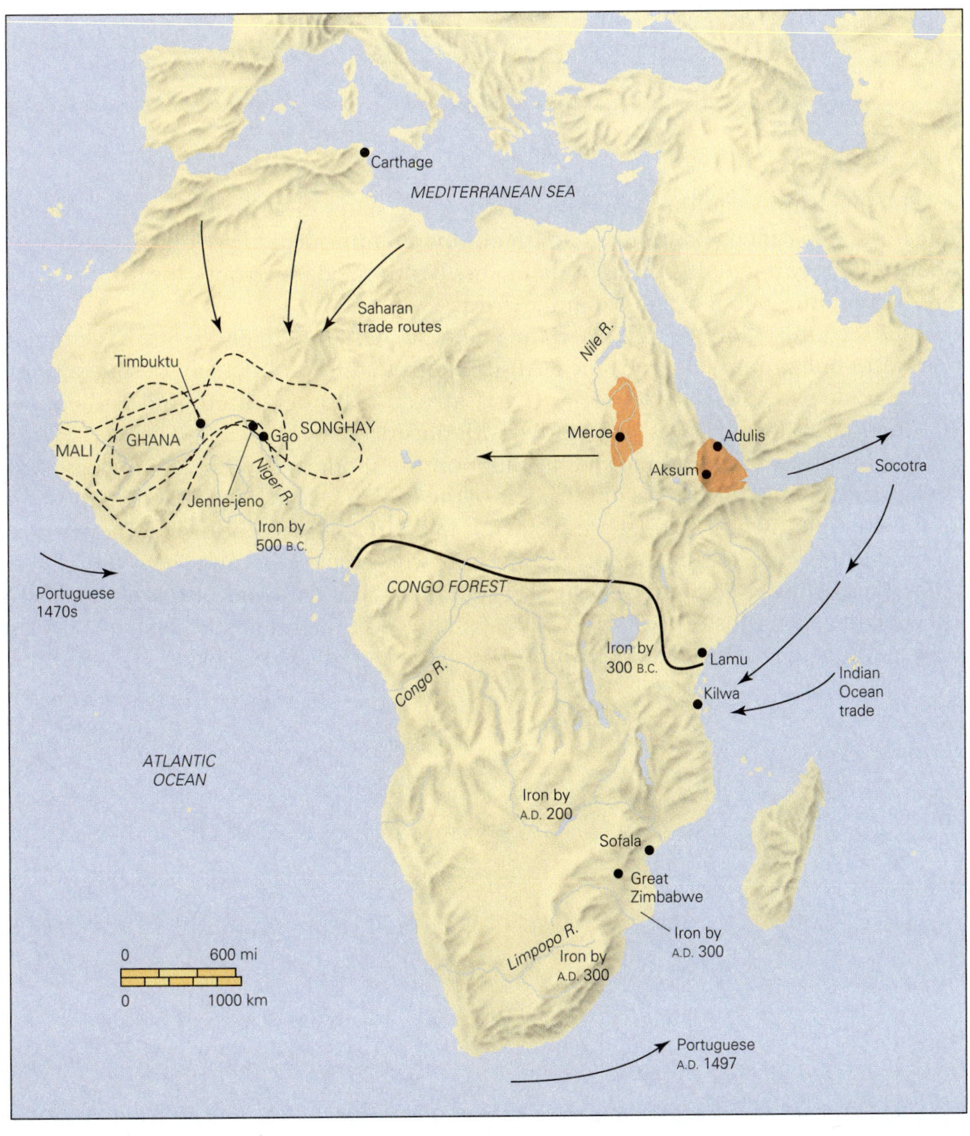

FIGURE 16.16 Map showing the extent of Bantu Africa and the indigenous states mentioned in the text.

FIGURE 16.18 Architect Peter Garlake's reconstruction of the Sultan's Palace at Kilwa, on the East African coast.

The map shows you the general location of the states described here, and also delineates the so-called "Bantu line," south of which Bantu-speaking peoples settled after about 2,000 years ago. It's thought that many Bantu-speaking groups introduced food production into much of sub-Saharan Africa.

This section is more descriptive than analytical, designed to give you a basic framework. But one point is clear: tropical Africa controlled its own destiny, despite a flourishing trade with the outside world. It was Africans who organized gold and copper production, collected slaves, and traded with outsiders.

The historic palace and mosque at Kilwa on the modern-day Tanzanian coast symbolizes the toehold that the Islamic traders of the Indian Ocean maintained on the edge of the continent. Until very late in history, it was Africans who controlled the interior, were aggressive in seizing opportunities, and whose states became increasingly entwined in the wider economic world of recent times. But the roots of this engagement go back deep into history, with the Nubians, the Aksumites, and the Malians of West Africa, who, after all, supplied two-thirds of Europe's gold in A.D. 1492.

chapter

EARLY STATES IN SOUTH AND SOUTHEAST ASIA

The Chapter in Review

- State-organized societies on the Indian subcontinent developed from indigenous roots in about 2600 B.C.
- The Harappan civilization of the lowland Indus Valley developed as the result of a major shift in Sumerian long-distance trade patterns and long-term interactions between the Harappan culture of the lowlands and the Kulli Complex of the Baluchistan highlands.
- Harappan civilization flourished along the Indus for about a thousand years. It was an urban society with many smaller satellite settlements, carefully planned and ruled by priest-kings who controlled both religious and economic life.
- After 1700 B.C., the major cities went into decline, but Harappan society flourished in rural settings for a considerable time. The center of economic and political gravity moved eastward to the Ganges River valley, culminating in the Mauryan Empire of the first millennium B.C.
- Southeast Asian peoples had developed bronze working by at least 1500 B.C. The process of forming local states (*mandalas*) began around the same time, but the first historical records of complex states date to the third century A.D. Many such states developed in and around the central Mekong Valley, and later the central Cambodian basin.
- There, after A.D. 802, flourished the flamboyant Khmer civilization, a society based on divine kingship and strong notions of conformity. After six centuries of spectacular development, the Khmer civilization came in contact with expanding Islamic trade networks and new religious doctrines, which caused its partial demise.

Introductory Comments

Chapter 17 travels far away from the familiar landscape of the Mediterranean world, to areas where archaeology is still in its infancy. Again, we tell a chronological story, the chapter dividing into two broad parts:

- The beginnings of civilization along the Indus River and the rise of the Harappan civilization, its eventual demise, and the shift of civilization to the Ganges in the east, culminating in the Mauryan civilization.
- The growth of trade between Mauryans and Southeast Asians, the origins of states in that region, and the spectacular Khmer civilization that resulted.

No question, the roots of South Asian civilization, even of Hinduism, lie in the Harappan. But here's the major question: was this an indigenous civilization or one that gained its inspiration from outside? In the case of Southeast Asia, we can be sure that the states were indigenous, even if their rulers were strongly influenced by beliefs and ideas from outside.

Key Cultures and Sites

Angkor Borei
Angkor Thom
Angkor Wat
Ben Na Di
Co Loa
Dong Son culture
Harappa
Harappan civilization
Khmer civilization
Kulli Complex
Mauryan Empire
Mehrgarh
Mohenjodaro
Nindowari
Noen U-Loke
Oc Eo
Sembiran

Now Begin Reading . . .

South Asia

The map shows the location of major Harappan sites.

There is little doubt in my mind that Harappan civilization was an indigenous development in the Indus and Saraswati River Valleys. I have little more than a hunch to support this idea, but there are some noteworthy hints:

- Harappan civilization is distinctively local in its art and architecture. In particular, some of the seal inscriptions have motifs that recall much later Hindu beliefs.
- There are clear signs of larger communities, rapidly growing trade with the highlands, and of towns preceding the appearance of the Harappan cities. This strongly suggests indigenous origins.

From the beginning, Harappan civilization covered, or influenced, an enormous area, with relatively few large urban centers. This was very much a dispersed, rural civilization, which developed infrastructures and administrative hierarchies enabling the control of larger areas. Gregory Possehl's shrewd comparison with Upper and Lower Egypt—different regional differences within a single state—hits the nail on the head. The Harappan was an urban civilization, but one with a dispersed settlement pattern

FIGURE 17.1 The Harappan civilization, showing sites mentioned in this chapter.

and strong rural roots. So when the cities collapsed, the cultural system endured in the countryside for a considerable time.

Harappan civilization never achieved the full maturity of Mesopotamian states and is a somewhat frustrating society to study. So far, efforts to decipher Harappan script have failed. We do not know the names of individual rulers, or anything about their ideology and beliefs. All we can note are the striking similarities to later beliefs, a symbolism that may have been remarkably similar to that of modern Hinduism.

The reasons for the collapse of Harappan cities are still unknown, but may be connected with shifts in trade, changes in river regimens, and even climatic change. The drying up of the Saraswati River as a result of earthquake activity may have been a major cause of disruption. The centuries after 1500 B.C. were ones of profound change, the time of the *Rigveda* hymns described in the text. Rice cultivation, iron metallurgy, and other innovations caused civilization to flourish along the Ganges River to the east.

The Mauryan civilization was of great importance in south Asian history, yet we know very little about it archaeologically. If ever I were given the choice of an early civilization to investigate, I think that it would be the Mauryan, simply because of the incredibly rich archaeological record, which remains largely unexplored. Historically, the Mauryan was of enormous significance, simply because of the expansion of trade across the Bay of Bengal into Southeast Asia, which brought new ideas to a region already undergoing considerable social and political change.

Southeast Asia

Now we move across the Bay of Bengal into a region that only now is being explored archaeologically in any detail.

Rice, trade, and iron technology were important catalysts here, as were ideas from South Asia and China, which percolated along maritime and land trade routes. I think that the Noen U-Loke site in northeastern Thailand is a key site in documenting the changes. Archaeologist Charles Higham (who also played rugby for Cambridge

FIGURE 17.9 Southeast Asia, showing sites mentioned in the text.

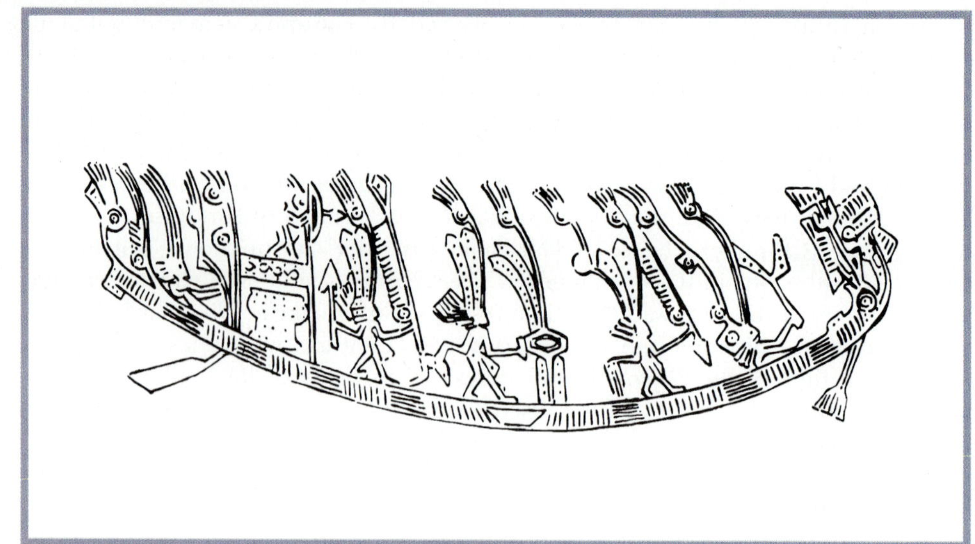

FIGURE 17.10 A Dong Son boat that formed part of the decoration on a bronze drum. A war prisoner and well-armed warriors ride in the craft, which carries a drum stored in a cabin with an archer perched on the roof.

University) and Thai colleagues have chronicled the remarkable changes in burial customs and the rise of social complexity in the cemeteries at the site. Noen U-Loke provides strong evidence for indigenous development of states, as local rulers arose, like those of the Dong Son culture of Vietnam's Red River Valley.

Right from the beginning, powerful leaders surrounded themselves with all the regalia of prestige, including the drums from which the Dong Son drawing comes.

States may have been indigenous developments, but ideas from outside played a very important role. As I point out, this is because of Southeast Asia's strategic position between South Asia and China, especially the sheltered waters of what the Chinese called Funan, the Mekong Delta.

The last section of the chapter describes the remarkable Khmer civilization, which arose as a result of new doctrines of divine kingship. The important things to look out for here:

- The notion of the *mandala,* the concertina-like effect of small kingdoms that expand and contract at the edges.
- The strong correlation between Divine Kingship, and the almost manic centralization of Khmer civilization. Everything revolved around, and came to, the center.
- The powerful influence of Hindu doctrine, which caused great palace/temples like Angkor Wat to be constructed as symbolic representations of the Hindu cosmos—think Maya cities in Mesoamerica, where you have the same phenomenon.

Angkor Wat

The great Khmer sites are staggering creations, which dwarf the pyramids, the Maya city of Tikal, or the Temple of the Sun God Amun at Karnak. They make Stonehenge look like a country shrine. I was overwhelmed by the sheer size and intricacy of Angkor Wat, by the truly beautiful friezes of elephants and armies, sinuous dancing girls, and kings in all their state. I was amazed by the stupendous effort that went into building them, only possibly because of the easy transport of heavy materials by water. Just like the Egyptian pyramids, where most building activity took place during the Nile floods, so the temples at Angkor were built using loads of stone and wood transported by canoe.

If there is one series of archaeological sites you must visit, it is the temples of Angkor. A smaller site, Ta Proehm, is perhaps the most vivid of all, for the ruins lie entangled in dense forest, with the roots of trees growing out of the walls, and slowly strangling them. The shattered buildings and walls are silent, a shadow of their former glory. Then, suddenly, you turn a corner and encounter a smiling dancing girl cavorting timelessly in a sheltered niche, as fresh as when she was first carved on the wall. The effect is overwhelming, for the past is around you and engulfs you. There may be tourists around, but it is easy to be alone, to let the extraordinary effect of the Angkor sites flow over you. And such enjoyment of the past is what archaeology is all about.

chapter

EARLY CHINESE CIVILIZATION

The Chapter in Review

- Early Chinese civilization emerged independently of state-organized societies in the West.
- By 4000 B.C., population densities were rising in farming communities throughout China, and there are signs of social differentiation in village cemeteries.
- Exchange networks already linked thousands of small communities by 4000 B.C., spurring social and technological changes that included copper metallurgy and the widespread use of earthen fortifications.
- A new cosmology based on animals and the use of divination to communicate with the dead came into widespread use.
- The Shang civilization of the Huanghe Valley is the best-known early Chinese state, flourishing from 1766 to 1122 B.C. It was probably the dominant state among several throughout northern China.
- Shang society was organized along class lines, with the rulers and nobles living in segregated precincts, whereas the mass of the people were scattered in townships and villages in the surrounding countryside.
- Shang civilization ended with the overthrow of the Shang Dynasty by Zhou rulers, who reigned over a wide area of northern China from 1122 to 221 B.C.

China was unified under the Emperor Zheng (Shihuangdi) in that year.

Key Cultures and Sites

Anyang
Ao
Liangzhu culture
Longshan cultures
Shang Civilization
Xia
Xiao-tun
Zhou

Introductory Comments

Chapter 18 surveys the origins of civilization in China, ending with the unification of the country under the Emperor Shihuangdi in 221 B.C. This is a straightforward linear narrative that attempts to reconcile legend with archaeological fact.

TABLE 18.1

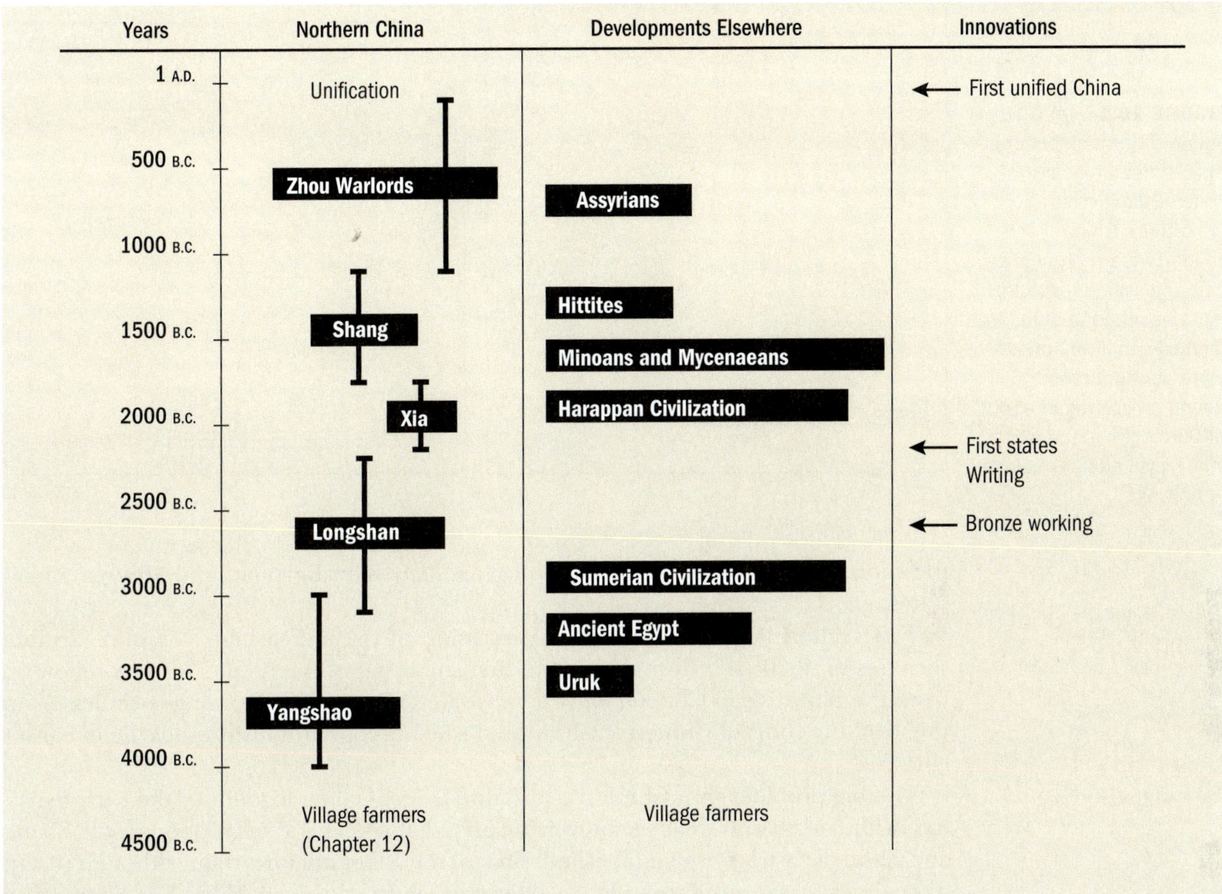

Notes

Now Start Reading . . .

Origins of Chinese Civilization

This simple chronological table places the Chinese sequence discussed in this chapter in the context of developments elsewhere. Chinese states developed completely independently of the west, emerging at about the same time as Harappan civilization along

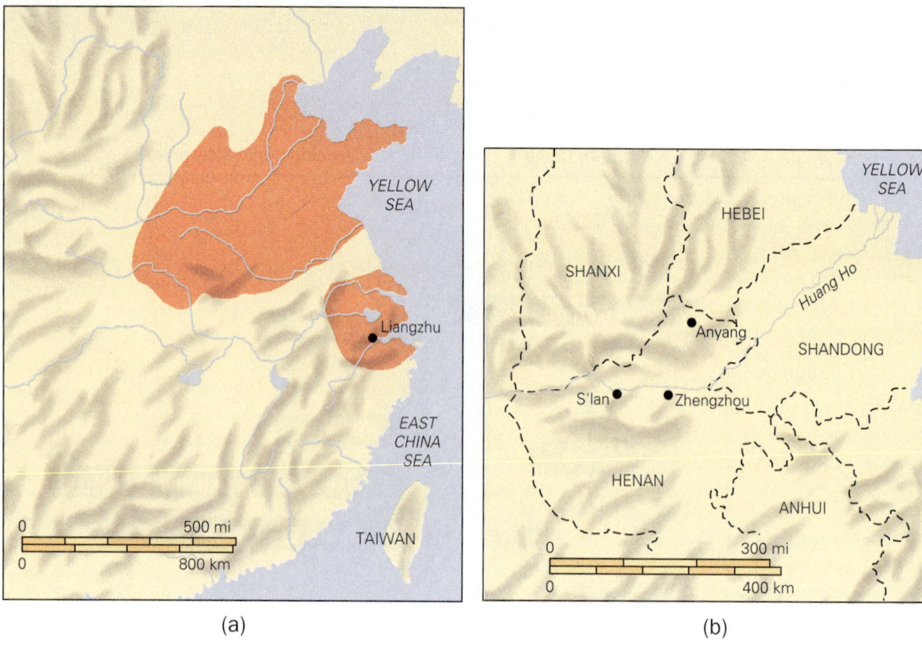

FIGURE 18.1 (a) Distribution of farming cultures that immediately preceded Shang civilization in northern China. Each shaded area represents a different regional culture (not described in detail in the text). (b) The approximate distribution of Shang civilization in about 1400 B.C. (Xiao-tun and other royal sites are close to Anyang).

the Indus River, and about a thousand years later than Egyptian and Mesopotamian states.

This section begins with a simple discussion of the increasingly complex farming societies of 4000 B.C., from which the first small states emerged. This is a follow-on from the narrative in Chapter 12, where we described earlier farming societies. As in the west, the roots of Chinese civilization, its technology and institutions, lie in earlier cultures.

The big problem with Chinese civilization is reconciling legends of the early dynasties of the north and what we know from archaeology. The identification of the Shang and Zhou dynasties is well established. That of the Xia is still uncertain, although recent discoveries, so far unpublished, may throw new light on the problem. Xia, Shang, and Zhou were competing dynasties, as volatile as those in Mesopotamia or Mesoamerica, making it hard to discern what happened when and to whom.

With the Shang civilization, we are on firmer ground, for the archaeological evidence is more plentiful. Here we see the essential characteristics of early Chinese civilization, notably the dispersed nature of the settlement pattern in earlier times, with the elite living in seclusion in royal compounds, surrounded by outlying settlements and a large rural population.

This Xiao-tun structure is a good example of a more imposing Shang dwelling, while the shoulder blades used in divination (illustrated in Figure 18.2) remind us that early Chinese leadership was based firmly in the abilities of the ruler to intercede with revered ancestors. There was, in a sense, a social contract between ruler and subjects, based on his intermediary abilities, and on putative kin ties between the elite and the commoner. As we say in the text, the "Green Circle" farmers surrounded the ruler and

FIGURE 18.3 Reconstruction of a structure from the ceremonial area at Xiao-tun, Anyang, in Henan province. Throughout Chinese history, the nobility lived apart from commoners.

supported the state. Just as with the Maya, described in Chapter 21, the relationship between them depended on spiritual as much as material factors, even if a vast cultural social chasm separated them.

The Tomb of Shihuangdi

If there is to be a spectacular discovery to rival Tutankhamun and the Moche Lords of Sipán in the twenty-first century, the Emperor Qin Shihuangdi's tomb will be it. The Chinese have probed carefully around the margins, but have wisely left the huge burial mound for the future, when they feel they have the experience, the technology, and the financial resources to tackle it. Just as with the Egyptian pyramids, the mound is merely part of an enormous mortuary precinct, of which only small parts are known, most notably the terracotta regiment. Some of the figures have gone overseas on museum exhibits. Even separated from their original setting, they are strangely haunting, and very humanlike. Whoever crafted them had a wonderful sense of the human form, and of the slavish devotion to the emperor that the regiment symbolizes. The mind boggles at the riches and treasure trove of information that lies within the now much-eroded burial mound—but much depends on how much looting has taken place since 221 B.C.

chapter 19

HITTITES, MINOANS, AND MYCENAEANS

The Chapter in Review

- Small towns became growing economic centers in parts of Anatolia as early as 3600 B.C.
- Communities like Çatalhöyük failed to develop the necessary administrative and social mechanisms to cope with the increased complexity of the settlement and its trading activities. The town failed, and Anatolians of the fifth millennium B.C. reverted to village life.
- Small fortified villages flourished in the fourth millennium B.C. One of them, Troy I, dates to just after 3000 B.C. Troy II, founded in about 2300 B.C., was a fortified town with more elaborate architecture and fine gold and bronze metallurgy.
- By this time, the Anatolians were trading widely over the highlands and into the Aegean, and chieftaincies were scattered over mineral-rich areas. About 1900 B.C., the Assyrians set up a trading colony at Kanesh in central Anatolia.
- The Hittites assumed power in Anatolia in about 1650 B.C. They held a vital place in the history of their time, for they played the Assyrians off against the Egyptians.
- Hittite power was based on diplomatic and trading skills until about 1200 B.C., when international trade in the eastern Mediterranean collapsed and a period of confusion, partly the work of the Sea Peoples, ensued.
- The state of Israel was born during this interregnum, among agricultural and herding peoples in the highlands behind the eastern Mediterranean coast.
- Farming settlements developed in Greece and the Aegean islands before 5000 B.C. There were radical changes in the late second millennium B.C., when the cultivation of the olive and the grapevine became widespread and the trading of minerals, stoneware, and other products expanded rapidly.
- Numerous small towns flourished throughout the Aegean and eastern Greece by 2500 B.C., linked by regular trading routes.
- The Minoan civilization of Crete developed in about 2000 B.C. and lasted until approximately 1450 B.C. The great volcanic explosion of its satellite island, Santorini, in the seventeenth century B.C., may have weakened Minoan power for a while.
- After 1400 B.C., the center of civilization passed to the mainland, where the Mycenaeans flourished until 1150 B.C. Mycenaean civilization collapsed as a result of internal dissension and possibly the exhaustion of agricultural land.
- Trading activities continued to expand in the Aegean after the decline of Mycenae. Small city-states flourished, unifying only in the face of a common danger, such as the Persian invasions of the fifth century B.C.

- The Athenians enjoyed a long period of supremacy among city-states, the period of classical Greek civilization in the fifth century B.C. Alexander the Great built an enormous empire across Southwest Asia, of which Greece was part, in the late fourth century B.C.
- The Roman Empire, which followed, marks the entry of the entire Mediterranean area into historic times. Developing from Villanovan and Etruscan roots in Italy, Imperial Roman power was based on the ruins of Alexander's empire.

Key Cultures and Sites

Alaçahöyük	Kanesh	Mycenae
Anemospilia	Knossos	Santorini
Boghazköy	Mari	Sesklo
Etruscan civilization	Minoan civilization	Uluburun
Hissarlik	Mycenaean civilization	Villanovan culture

Introductory Comments

Chapter 19 is a complicated journey through an increasingly complex eastern Mediterranean world. For the most part, the chapter follows a chronological gradient, but we do go forward and backward with the Hittites and Minoans. This is inevitable, given the need to go back in time to trace the beginnings of two civilizations, one after the other.

This chapter has three broad parts:

- Anatolia and the Hittite civilization covers not only the rise of Hittite culture but the complex eastern Mediterranean world in which it flourished, where great powers competed for control of trade routes.
- The Aegean and Greece describes the Minoan and Mycenaean civilizations, and the roots of Classical Greek civilization.
- Finally, a brief section builds on the two earlier narratives and discusses Etruscan civilization and the Romans.

We are now dealing with a closely interconnected Mediterranean world, where the fate of every state was tied to its neighbors and to the fortunes of civilizations at considerable distances.

Now Start Reading . . .

Figure 19.1 covers the sites and civilizations in Chapter 19. You might also want to refer to Table 15.1, which places the societies described here in a broad chronological perspective.

Anatolia and the Hittites

The towns that failed . . . this is the litany at the beginning of this section, for important ritual and trading centers like Çatalhöyük failed to develop the mechanisms needed to handle the massive social change needed to create cities from towns. As we see here, this all happened later, culminating in Assyrian merchant colonies at places like Kanesh and Hittite civilization.

FIGURE 19.1 Sites and cultures mentioned in this chapter.

We still know surprisingly little about the Hittites from archaeology, because relatively little excavation has been carried out. But, thanks to written records from El Amarna in Egypt and the Battle of Kadesh (1286 B.C.), we do know that they were major players in eastern Mediterranean politics, together with Egypt and Mitanni. They have come down in history as the first people to smelt iron on a large scale. This was a discovery of great strategic and economic importance, for iron ore is abundant nearly everywhere and the working edges on tools made from it are much tougher than those of bronze.

The Uluburun shipwreck is very relevant to this section, for the cargo is a capsule of the startlingly complex international trade of the day. The experts believe that the Uluburun ship may have carried a royal cargo, given its enormous value—enough copper and tin to equip a regiment alone. An uninsured loss, and the financial effects must have been severe.

Figure 19.3 gives an impression of just how far-flung this trade was and is worth examining closely, especially as this commerce was one of the backbones of the Bronze Age world of the day.

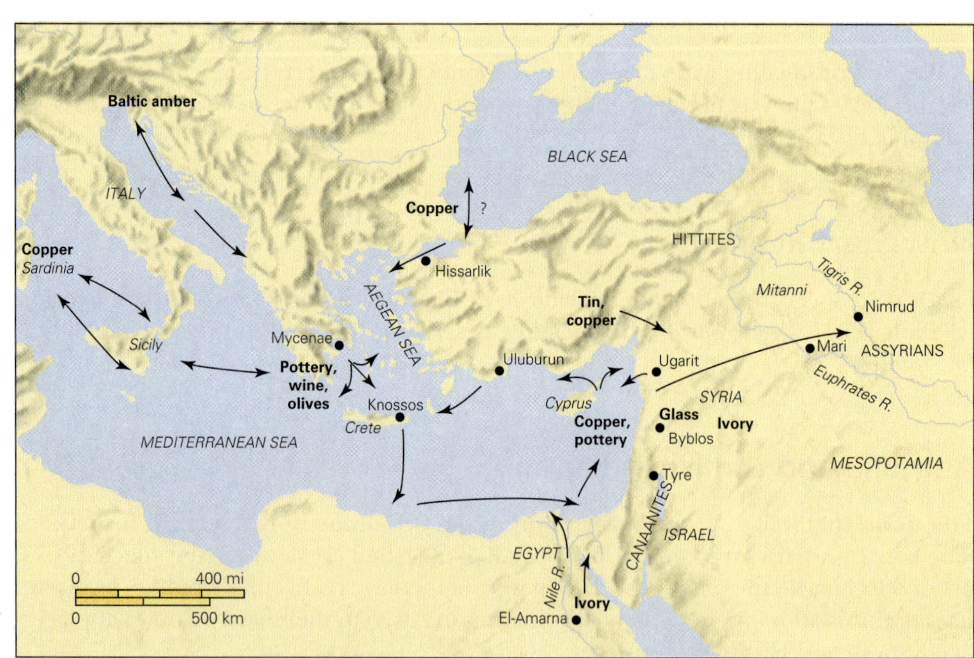

FIGURE 19.3 The balance of power in Southwest Asia in the second millennium B.C.: Egypt, Mitanni, and the Hittite Empire, showing major trade routes.

Notes

This section ends with the fall of the Hittites and the emergence of the Phoenicians as major players in Mediterranean commerce. No one really knows why there were troubled times in 1200 B.C. Some experts suspect that widespread chaos erupted when a series of well-documented droughts (known from pollen and lake cores) settled over southwestern Asia, with catastrophic results.

Minoans and Mycenaeans

This section is devoted to an analysis of the Minoan and Mycenaean civilization, again societies with deep indigenous roots. We show how the olive and the vine played a major role in the expansion of Aegean trade.

Both Minoan and Mycenaean civilizations were palace-based, that is to say they were not urban states, but patchworks of smaller kingdoms based on palaces. Knossos was the largest of the Minoan palaces, and, according to Homer, famed throughout the Aegean world.

The discussion of both civilizations is straightforward enough, but there are plenty of controversies. One surrounds the famous Santorini eruption, which may have devastated Minoan society. Or did it? The date of the cataclysm (it was nothing less) may be as early as 1688 or as late as 1450 B.C., but more likely the earlier of the two readings. Experts differ as to the severity of the impact of the eruption on Minoan life on nearby Crete. But, if the earlier date is correct, then Minoan civilization certainly reached new heights after the cataclysm.

(Incidentally, if you travel to Greece, please do not fail to visit Santorini. The crater itself is most spectacular, and the buried Minoan village at Akrotiri still preserves two-story buildings under meters of volcanic ash. It's well worth a visit.)

Controversy also revolves around the extent to which Homer's *Iliad* and *Odyssey* reflect life in Mycenaean times, as Heinreich Schliemann claimed back in the 1870s. Everyone agrees that Homer wrote in later times, long after the siege of Troy, but the oral traditions he set down may well reflect some folk memories of Bronze Age life and of the flamboyant, militaristic civilizations of the time.

Mycenaean script has been deciphered, notably by a British architect, the late Michael Ventris. Most of it is concerned with commercial transactions, inventories, and offerings.

Talking of offerings, the Mycenaean shrine on the island of Melos in the Aegean Sea is a really excellent example of the investigation of a religious building.

FIGURE 19.11 Impression of a warrior wielding an axe against an enemy with a dagger, from an engraved ring, shaft graves, Mycenae.

dipae mezoe tiriowee **2**

(larger-sized goblet with three handles 2)

FIGURE 19.12 Mycenaean script. Above, a tablet from the Palace of Nestor at Pylos in western Greece, bearing an inventory of goblets and cauldrons. Below, a specimen listing: "Larger sized goblet with three handles 2."

The Shrine at Phylakopi

Unlike the Egyptians or Sumerians, neither the Minoans nor Mycenaeans built large temples. Much of their religion unfolded in village and domestic settings. Colin Renfrew's excavation of a humble town shrine at Phylakopi is a finer example of the challenges of basically investigating the intangible from inconspicuous finds. The reconstruction in Figure 19.13 shows the end result of a dig and careful artifact analysis. It involved meticulous plotting of the positions of individual artifacts exposed in the excavation, combined with a very careful three-dimensional reconstruction of the foundations, crumbled walls, and small rooms.

We still know little of Minoan and Mycenaean religion, but much of it seems to have been concerned with fertility, and involved female fertility deities. It certainly bore no resemblance to the large-scale state religions of Egypt and Mesopotamia, and, in many respects, may have been a concern of household and individual as much as the larger

FIGURE 19.13 Reconstruction of the shrine at Phylakopi, Melos.

Notes

---

community. There are signs of human sacrifice at Knossos and Anemospilia, described in the text. Minoan and Mycenaean religion was also very different from later Classical religions and pantheons, although some of the roots of such gods and goddesses as Zeus, Poseidon, and Athena may have lain in much earlier beliefs.

Etruscans and Romans

This section rounds off the chapter and is self explanatory. It also serves as a link to the later stages of Chapter 20, which takes us into temperate Europe for the first time since Chapter 10.

chapter

EUROPE BEFORE THE ROMANS

The Chapter in Review

- Copper working developed in southeast Europe by about 4600 B.C., and soon afterward in Spain and northern Italy.
- The new technology flourished because of a demand for fine metal ornaments. It was a logical outgrowth of earlier stone and ceramic technologies. Its more widespread use coincides with the spread of Beaker and Battle Ax artifacts throughout much of Europe.
- Bronze working began at an unknown date but was widespread in what is now the Czech Republic by 2000 B.C., as part of the Unetice culture.
- The trading networks of earlier times expanded to meet the increased indigenous demand for metal artifacts during a period of rapid technological change after 1700 B.C. Some rich chieftaincies developed in the temperate zones.
- About 1800 B.C., new Urnfield burial customs and more advanced bronze-working techniques spread over much of central and western Europe. These were associated with an intensification of trading activity and greater social ranking, which resulted in an elite warrior class.
- After 1000 B.C., ironworking techniques spread into temperate Europe and diffused through the Hallstatt and La Tène cultural traditions during the first millennium B.C.

Key Cultures and Sites

Dereivka	Kurgan culture	La Tène culture
Fyn	Pazyryk	Unetice
Hallstatt culture	Similaun	Urnfield cultures
Hascherkeller	Stonehenge	Varna

Introductory Comments

This is the story of Europe and its response to an increasingly sophisticated Mediterranean world, starting with the development of metallurgy and ending with the Roman general Julius Caesar's conquest of Gaul in the first century B.C.

Here's the sequence of the narrative:

- The first part of the chapter covers the development of copper working and its consequences.

- The second section covers the European Bronze Age and the appearance of warrior societies—a momentous change for local society.
- The third section surveys the steppe peoples and describes a Europe increasingly in contact with the Mediterranean world, where iron comes into common use.

European prehistory is very complicated, with numerous local cultures and hundreds of important sites, which defy even experts to place in a larger context. Chapter 20 offers a simple distillation of the basic issues and trends—for more detail, please turn to the Guide to Further Reading, which will take you into the specialist literature and its many arcane, but often important, debates.

Now Start Reading . . .

This map provides a simple geography. You should also glance again at Table 15.1, which places the developments in this chapter in a wider context. In other words, what happened to whom when?

The Beginnings of Metallurgy

Did copper working develop outside Europe or did it result from indigenous initiative? The Renfrew and Tringham argument that local expertise at pot making was the stimulus for local metallurgy is a compelling one. I believe that they are correct. Also

FIGURE 20.1 Europe, 3500 to 2500 B.C. While extreme western and northwestern Europe remained the territory of stone-using farmers, copper working spread in central Europe and bronze came into use in Southwest Asia and peripheral regions. The building of communal tombs was widespread in the west, but more mobile lifeways developed in central Europe and on the eastern steppes. This new pattern expanded into surrounding areas.

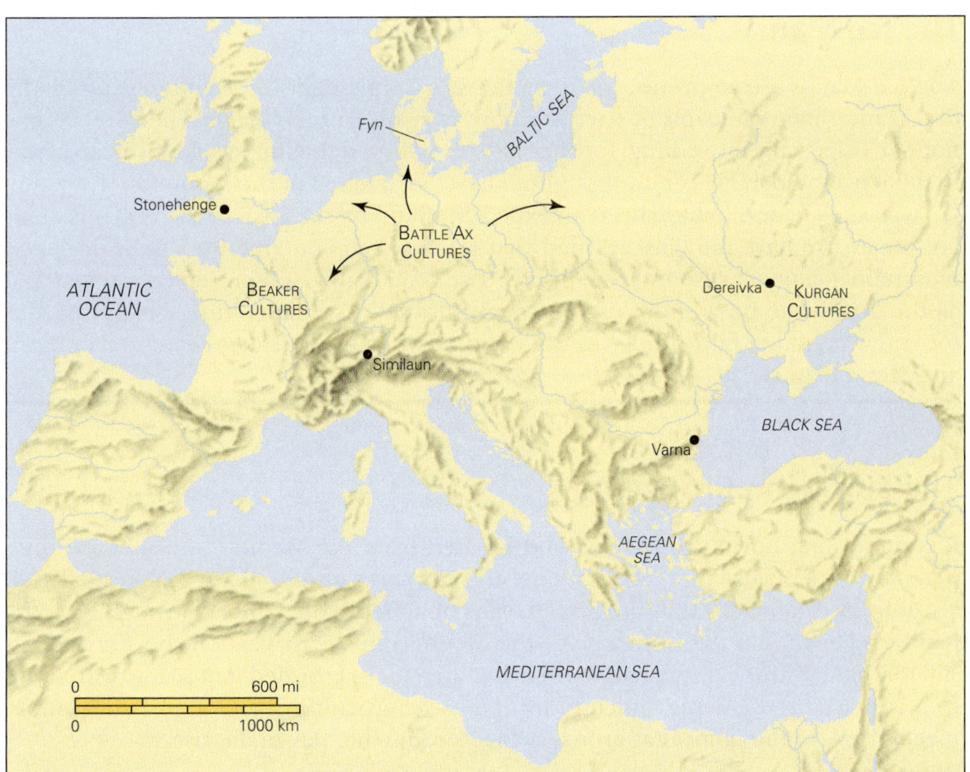

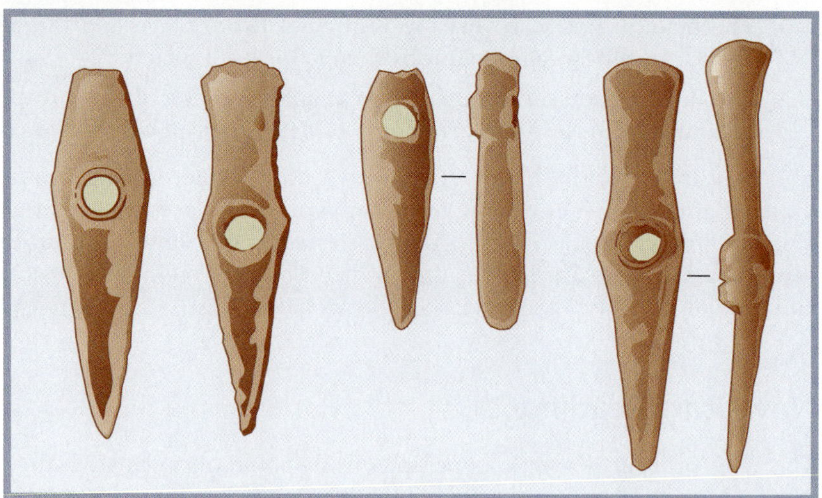

FIGURE 20.3 Simple copper axe heads from the Czech Republic (one-third actual size).

remember Renfrew's point about the social conditions for the widespread use of metal objects. Copper started off as a prestigious, predominantly ornamental metal, and, like gold, was probably used to produce prestigious ornaments, signs of rank.

The "Battle Axes and Beakers" section describes how local copper sources were all-important after 3500 B.C. I make a distinction between the Battle Axe and Beaker peoples, which is probably a totally artificial one. The important innovations were smaller houses instead of the communal longhouses of earlier times, the first appearance of the plow, which allowed the cultivation of heavier soils, and a series of important responses to changing circumstances.

Figure 20.3 illustrates some typical, very simple copper artifacts of the day.

The Ice Man

The Ice Man is a true prehistoric detective story, which gets more interesting by the day, as international teams of scientists pore over his frozen corpse. The latest revelations are especially interesting, for they have established that he was shot with an arrow in the left shoulder. He is now thought to have been killed in the mountains by an unknown assailant and to have been an expert hunter—on the basis of the remains of his last meals. We have only just learned that his stomach contained traces of deer and mountain goat meat, also traces of grains. The remarkably well-preserved artifacts and clothing with the body show just how sophisticated material culture was during this formative period of European society—the time when the first states emerged in Egypt and Mesopotamia.

The European Bronze Age

It is interesting how Europe remained isolated from the Mediterranean world until well on in the Bronze Age, to all intents and purposes until well after 2000 B.C. You'll recall from Chapter 19 that the Mycenaeans obtained Baltic amber through hand-to-hand exchange, but the influence of the Mediterranean civilizations on Europe was still minimal. European societies were living on a more crowded landscape, with more closely placed settlements, much more intensive agriculture, and a great deal more metallurgy—to the point that bronze artifacts came into day-to-day use.

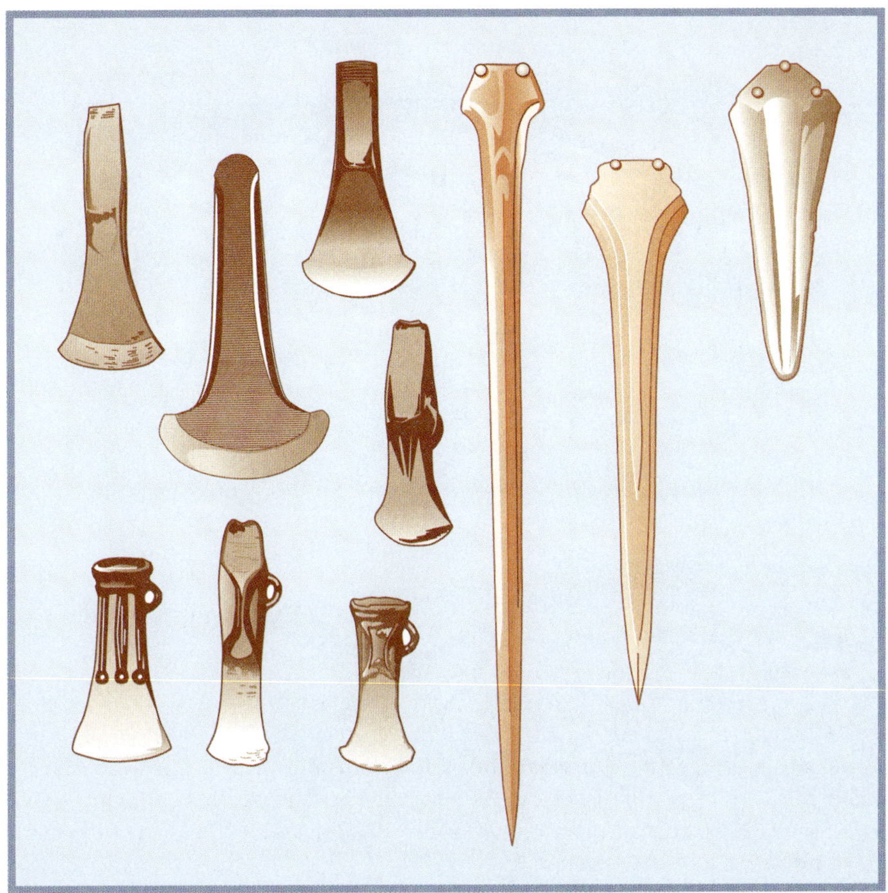

FIGURE 20.6 Copper and bronze implements from Britain. Left, simple flat axes and flanged and socketed axes (one-third actual size). Right, dagger and sword blades (one-fourth actual size). Although both copper and gold were used for ornaments, copper also formed effective utilitarian agricultural implements and weapons.

As Figure 20.6 shows, bronze also came into use for weaponry, as well as farming tools. Note the effects of increased food surpluses, reflected by more investment in monumental architecture, such as Stonehenge, and also in greater social ranking, intensified trade and warfare. The section "Bronze Age warriors" summarizes many of the changes, which resulted in more consolidated agriculture over much of Europe, the exploitation of heavier soils, and more cattle herding. The roots of the Europe known to the Romans go back to these Bronze Age centuries.

The Wasserburg-Buchau site on Germany's Federsee is a good example of a fortified settlement, occupied at a time of territorial disputes. Like all European settlements of the time, Wasserburg-Buchau changed constantly in response to new circumstances, among them were defense needs, climatic shifts, and new leadership.

In the "Scythians and Other Steppe Peoples" section, we discuss the flamboyant, nomadic cultures of eastern Europe and Eurasia, which were a constant threat to Greek and Roman civilization. The horse was first domesticated in this general region, where wild herds abounded.

Finally, the coming of iron in the hands of the Hallstatt culture of the eighth and seventh centuries B.C. Ironworking spread rapidly down long-established trade routes, at a time when European chieftains were trading, albeit sporadically, with merchants from the Mediterranean to the south. There was a steady demand for wine in Europe,

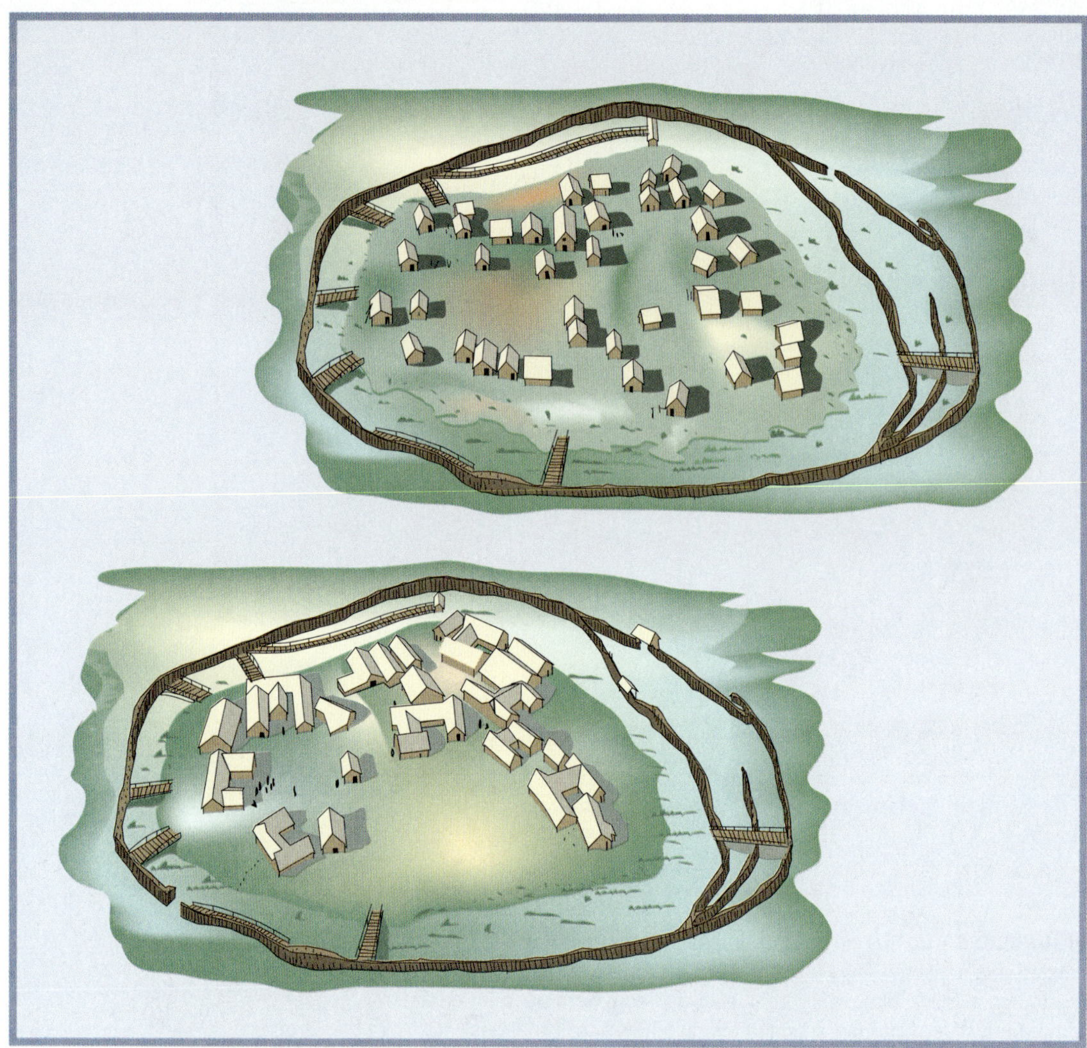

FIGURE 20.9 Bronze Age lakeside settlement at Wasserburg-Buchau, Federsee, Germany. The village was set in marshy ground and first occupied in about 1100 B.C., at a time when climatic change may have put pressure on good agricultural land. Fortified settlements may have been a response to territorial disputes. Top, the village was oval, and was surrounded by a wooden palisade, with 38 log-cabinlike structures inside. Bottom, somewhat later, the village was rebuilt with large rectangular buildings, some joined to make H-shaped or L-shaped houses. The settlement was eventually destroyed by fire.

which came up the Rhone valley from the Marseilles region of southern France. The La Tène people, who submerged the Hallstatt, spread across Europe by the late fifth century B.C. They were Celtic-speakers, and their magnificent iron and bronze technology survived into Roman times. A patchwork of small kingdoms and fortified towns developed, whose rulers fought vigorously against an invading Rome.

FIGURE 20.10 Approximate distribution of Urnfield cultures in Europe.

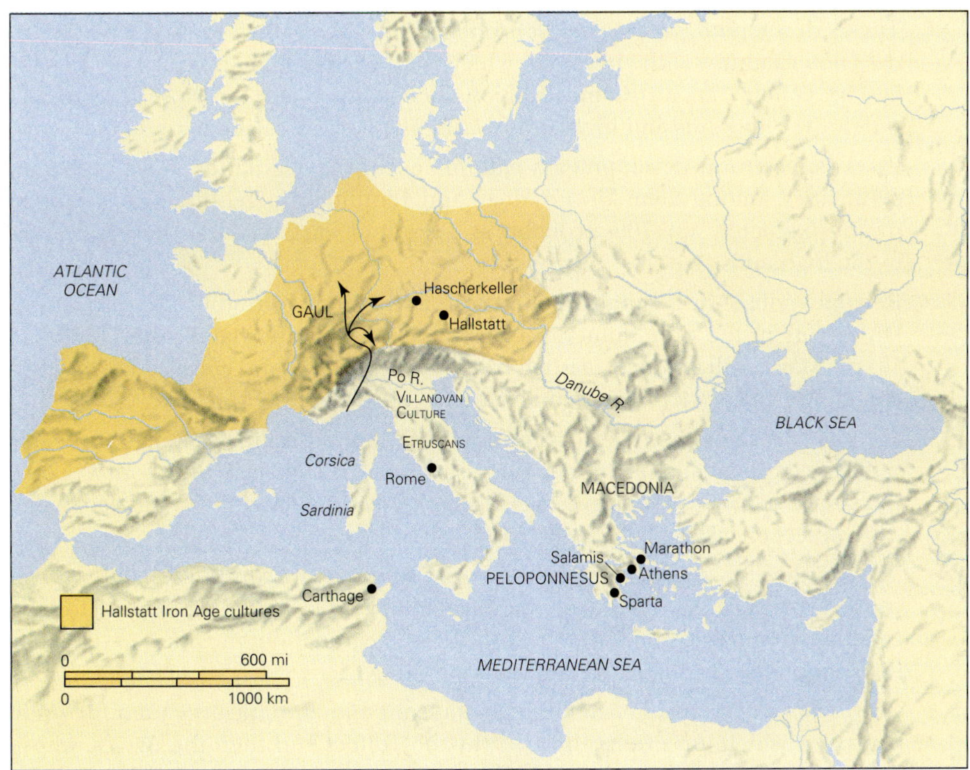

FIGURE 20.11 Distribution of the Hallstatt Iron Age cultures (shaded area) in Europe during the eighth to fifth centuries B.C.

c h a p t e r 

21

MESOAMERICAN CIVILIZATIONS

The Chapter in Review

- The Preclassic period of Mesoamerican prehistory lasted from approximately 2000 B.C. to A.D. 250, a period of major cultural change in both lowlands and highlands.
- Sedentary villages traded with each other in raw materials and exotic objects. These exchange networks became increasingly complex and eventually came under the monopolistic control of larger villages. Increasing social complexity went hand in hand with the appearance of the first public buildings and the evidence of social stratification.
- These developments are well chronicled in the Valley of Oaxaca and in the Olmec culture of the lowlands, which flourished from approximately 1500 to 500 B.C. Olmec art styles and religious beliefs were among those that spread widely over lowlands and highlands during the late Preclassic period.
- Preclassic cultural developments culminated in the highlands in a number of great cities, among them Monte Albán and Teotihuacán. Teotihuacán collapsed by approximately A.D. 700, probably as a result of warfare with other rival states in the highlands.
- Religious ideologies, ritual organization, and extensive trading networks were key factors in the development of Maya society in the lowlands after 1000 B.C. Classic Maya civilization flourished from A.D. 250 to 900 and consisted of an ever-changing patchwork of competing states.
- Maya glyphs show that Maya civilization was far from uniform. Religious beliefs rather than political or economic interests unified the Maya. Until about A.D. 600, the largest states were in northeast Petén, with a multicenter polity headed by the "Sky" rulers of Tikal.
- Maya civilization reached its height in the southern lowlands after the seventh century, collapsing suddenly in the Yucatán after A.D. 900. The reasons for the collapse are still uncertain, but environmental degradation, pressure on the labor force, and food shortages were doubtless among them.
- Teotihuacán's collapse in the highlands resulted in a political vacuum for some centuries, which was eventually filled by the Toltecs and then the Aztecs, whose civilization was dominant in the Valley of Mexico at the time of the Spanish Conquest in A.D. 1519.

Key Cultures and Sites

Aguateca
Aztec civilization
Cerros
Calakmuhl
Caracol
Chichén Itzá
Colha
Copán
Cuello
Dos Pilos
El Mirador
La Venta
Maya civilization
Mayapán
Monte Albán
Nakbe
Olmec civilization
Palenque
San José Mogote
San Lorenzo
Tamarindo
Tenochtitlán
Teotihuacán
Tikal
Toltec civilization
Tula
Uaxactún

Introductory Comments

Part V explores native American civilizations, Chapter 21 being devoted to Mesoamerica. To many people, this immediately suggests the Maya civilization, the most flamboyant and best known of all ancient American civilizations. As we shall see, however, the Maya are but a tiny part of a much more elaborate mosaic of Mesoamerican civilization.

Once again, we take a chronological journey, beginning with the origins of civilization in the Veracruz lowlands. And here again, just as in Mesopotamia, we see small city states becoming larger, culminating in the great empire of the Aztecs, an uneasy patchwork of tribute states overthrown by Spaniard Hernan Cortés in A.D. 1519–21.

The narrative can be broken down into four parts:

- Beginnings, where we discuss Preclassic societies and especially the Olmec.
- The Valley of Oaxaca and Teotihuacán, which rose to power at about the same time, and were contemporary with . . .
- The Maya civilization of the lowlands, which receives the most attention in this chapter.
- And, finally, the Toltec and Aztec civilizations of the highlands, the latter cut off by the Spanish Conquest.

I organized this chapter as chronologically as possible, but also took account of geography. Through the long history of Mesoamerican civilization, there were contacts between highlands and lowlands. But it was not until Aztec times that the two zones came under a simply political authority. Even then, civilization in both areas, while maintaining many similarities, developed its own beliefs, culture, and institutions.

Lastly, a reminder that the term "Mesoamerica," both highlands and lowlands, refers to that area of Central America where states arose. The term is commonly used in scholarly circles.

Village Farming and the Preclassic

Start with a close look at this table, which shows the relationships between the different societies described in Chapter 19. After 500 B.C. or so, many of them developed alongside one another and were in regular contact. Thus, some understanding of the chronological relationships is important. In the right-hand column, all but one shows some developments elsewhere, among them the Moche and Inca civilizations described in Chapter 22.

You might want to Post-it this table for reference.

TABLE 21.1

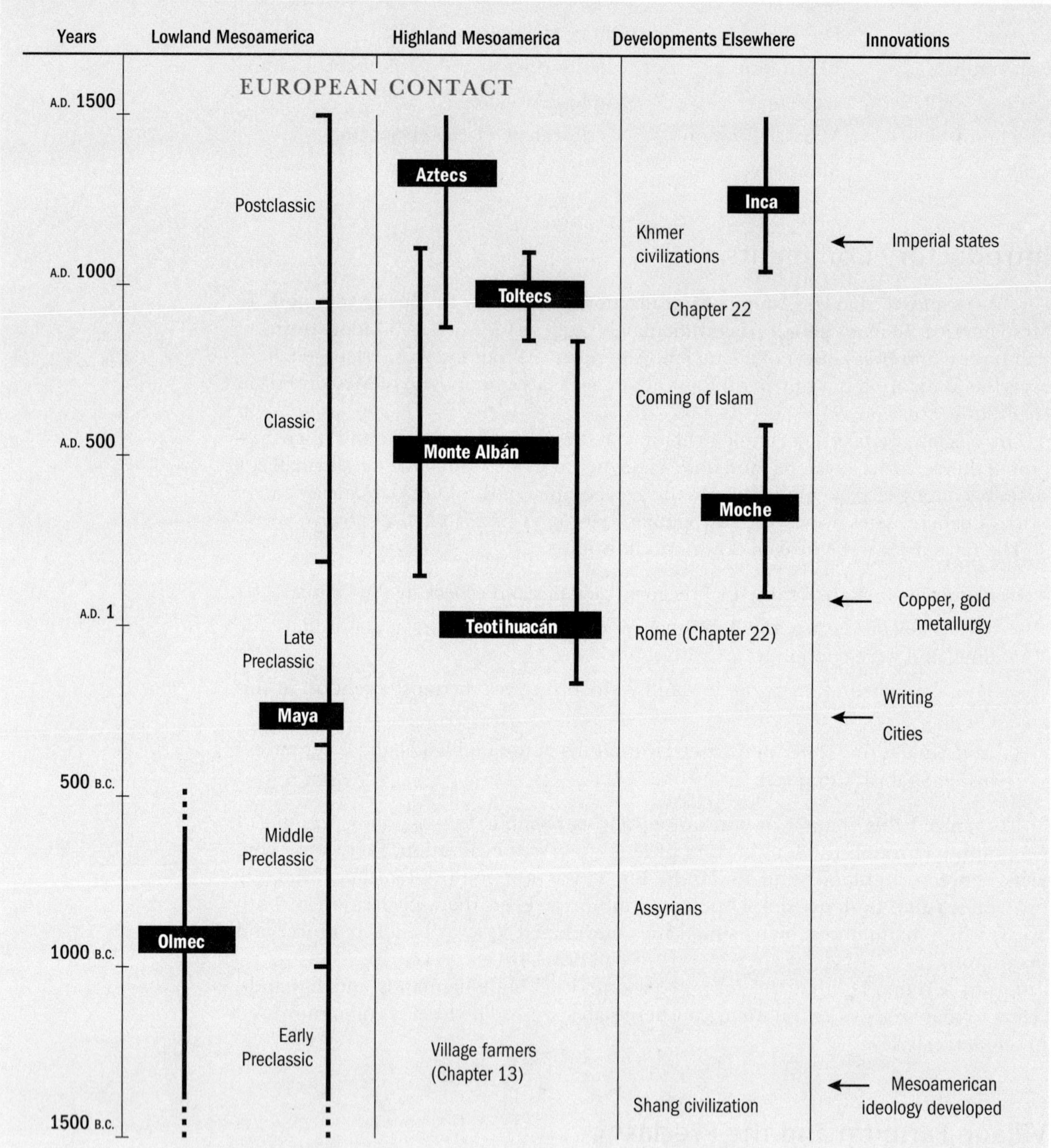

Figure 21.1 shows major sites and the distribution of Olmec and Teotihuacano spheres of influence in the lowlands and highlands, respectively. The distributions are somewhat misleading, as both had a pervasive influence on much of Mesoamerica. Many of the ideas formulated by their rulers and priests endured into later centuries, among them notions of a layered cosmos, human sacrifice, shamanism and kingship, militarism, and art and architectural styles.

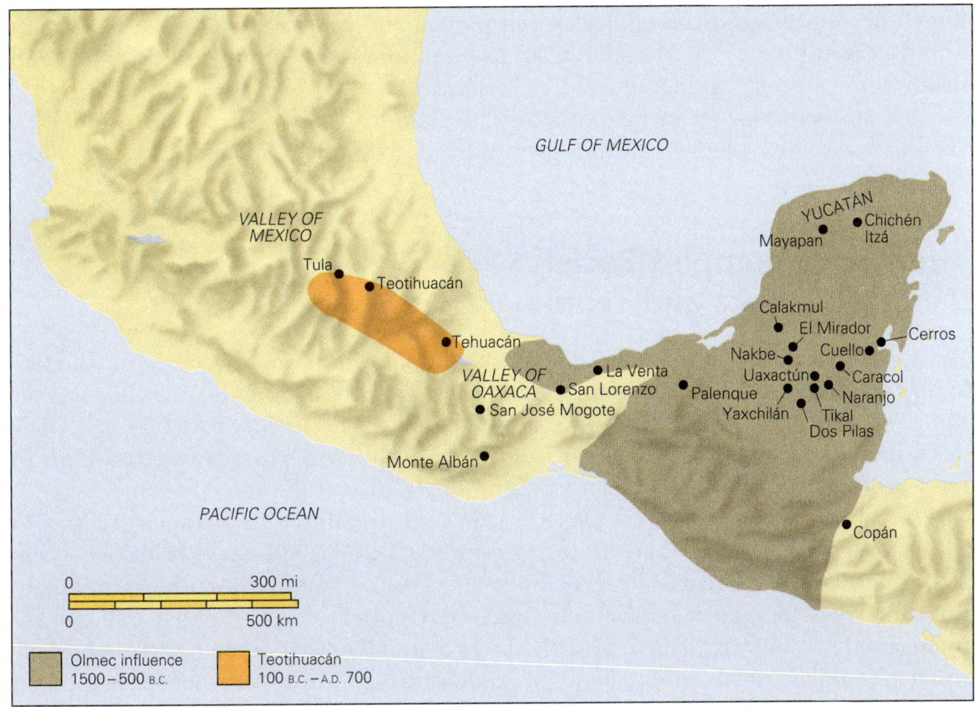

FIGURE 21.1 Mesoamerican archaeological sites mentioned in this chapter. Approximate distributions of two cultural traditions are shown.

Our story begins with village farming, with a diverse environment where many different agricultural methods were in use. One of the great issues of Maya archaeology still revolves around how they supported such dense populations, given the inherently low fertility of lowland tropical soils. In both lowlands and highlands, swamp gardens played an important role in feeding large numbers of people, for they could produce several crops a year, as opposed to the single, much lesser yielding output of dry fields, harvested once a year after the rains.

The emergence of social and political complexity in the Veracruz lowlands followed a somewhat similar path to that in Mesopotamia, Egypt, and elsewhere, where small chiefdoms appeared, competed with one another, and then transformed themselves into larger political units through competition, diplomacy, trade, and warfare.

A generation ago, people still thought of the Olmec as the "mother civilization" of Mesoamerica. But more recent research has dispelled that myth. Rather, the Olmec were a series of chiefdoms, which were a crucible for the development of flamboyant religious beliefs and art styles. It also served as well as public religious performance on open spaces surrounded by mounds and pyramids, cultural traditions that were to persist, albeit in modified form, for over 2,500 years. I think that Arthur Demarest's characterization of the Olmec as "lattices of interaction" is an accurate one. In reality,

FIGURE 21.3 La Venta, Site 4: Layout of the major structures.

the Olmec was more of a complex of ceremonial and religious usages than a civilization. But its influence on Mesoamerican civilization was enormous, and its rulers and institutions revered, among others, by Maya lords.

This shows the layout of La Venta and the notion of open spaces surrounded by artificial mounds, platforms, and pyramids, so pervasive in later Mesoamerican civilization.

The Rise of Complex Society: Valley of Oaxaca and Teotihuacán

We are lucky in that both the Valley of Oaxaca and Teotihuacán are better known archaeologically than most of Mesoamerica. University of Michigan archaeologists Kent Flannery and Joyce Marcus have devoted much of their careers to Oaxaca. Their work has produced major advances in our understanding of both the transition to food production and the rise of civilization.

The important moment in Oaxaca came, as I point out, between 1200 and 1150 B.C., when certain lineages became prominent in village life, eventually becoming associated with hereditary rulers. Flannery quotes the work of Jonathan Friedman, published over 20 years ago, where he develops a model for the emergence of authority in Southeast Asian villages. This model is compelling in Mesoamerica, especially when combined, as it is, with analyses of ideology from art. This is a classic example of good research on the archaeology of the intangible.

Monte Alban and Teotihuacán were rivals, but apparently amiable ones. Such was the volume of trade between them that archaeologists have identified an Oaxacan quarter at the latter city. This section of the chapter is simple narrative and requires little comment here.

Here's a schematic of the major ceremonial precincts. If you visit, start with the pyramids, then walk down the wide Street of the Dead to the Temple of Quetzalcoatl, with its intricate façade of the Feathered Serpent and the Rain God. If you follow this route, you'll also follow the direction in which the city expanded.

No one knows why Teotihuacán's rulers became more secular, and more militaristic. In so doing, however, they established a tradition of militarism and human sacrifice that was to endure into Aztec times. The collapse of the great city is also a mystery,

FIGURE 21.8 (a) Plan of the major public buildings at Teotihuacán.

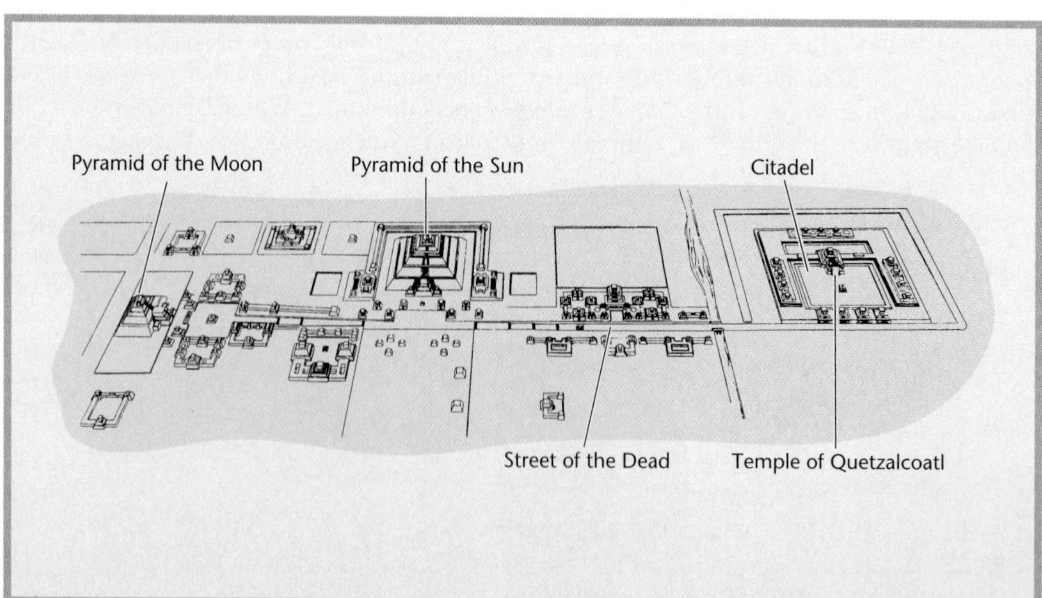

Notes

---

although there has been recent speculation that it resulted in part from major droughts, which caused havoc with the swamp gardens that supported much of the city's population.

Maya Civilization

This is the core of Chapter 21, for the Maya are the best known of all Mesoamerican civilizations, largely as a result of the decipherment of their script in the 1980s. Nothing short of a revolution in Maya research has followed, and continues to this day.

Our discussion follows a chronological thread, with the theme of kingship a prominent one:

- "Maya origins" summarizes what we know about early Maya chiefdoms from sites like Cuello, then the rise of Nakbe and El Mirador, the first great Maya cities. Figure 21.9b is a reconstruction of the central precincts of El Mirador.
- Kingship and political organization. Here I discuss the rise of Maya kingship, the central institution of their society, just as it was in Egyptian civilization. I also show how there were close links between kingship and the passage of time, measured with the intricate Maya calendar, illustrated in Figure 21.10.

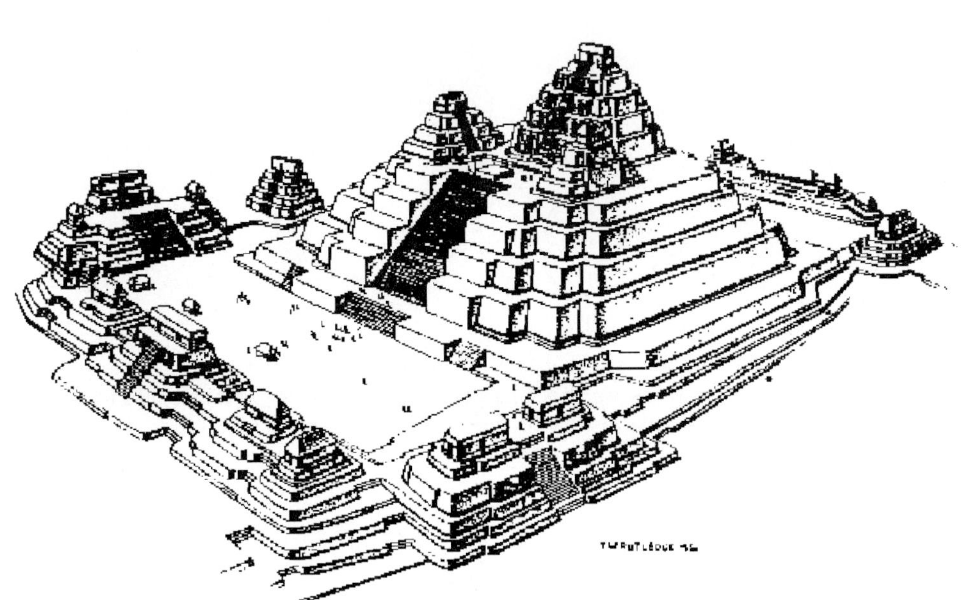

FIGURE 21.9
(b) El Mirador, Petén: Reconstruction of the Tigre complex of buildings and platforms. The entire complex dates to the Preclassic period, c. 100 B.C. to A.D. 50.

(a)

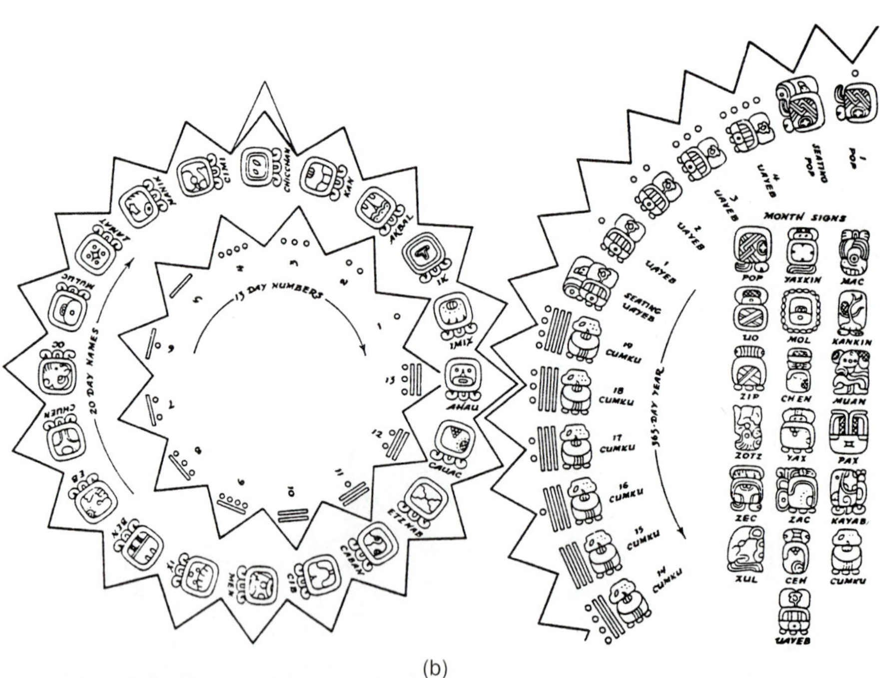

(b)

FIGURE 21.10 The Maya calendar. (a) A Venus calendar depicted on stone tablets with glyphs, mythological figures, warriors, and gods. (b) The Maya calendar comprised two interlocking cycles. The left wheel is the 260-day *tzolkin,* the sacred calendar with 13 numbers (inner wheel) and 20 day names (outer wheel). The right-hand wheel is the *haab,* or secular cycle, with 20 months of 18 days each.

Notes

• Next, I discuss Maya political organization, and stress that their civilization was far from uniform. I think that Joyce Marcus has developed a convincing model for a quadripartite structure, which is worth remembering.

• Maya political history. Here I tread on new and controversial ground. This account is a political history, written mainly from evidence acquired from glyphs, where, for the first time, we can identify specific lords, like Pacal the Great from Palenque. (Examples of glyphs and inscriptions appear in Figures 21.11, 21.13, and 21.15.) I have somewhat submerged the archaeology here, as I think it's more important that you get a general grasp of what happened to whom and when. If you want more archaeology, please refer to the Guide to Further Reading.

FIGURE 21.11 Maya glyphs. Left, the Leiden Plate, a jade plaque that shows a Maya lord trampling a captive underfoot. Right, the reverse side shows the Long Count (the Maya count of years) date in glyphs: 8.14.3.1.12, a day in the year A.D. 320. Height: 21.6 cm (8.5 inches).

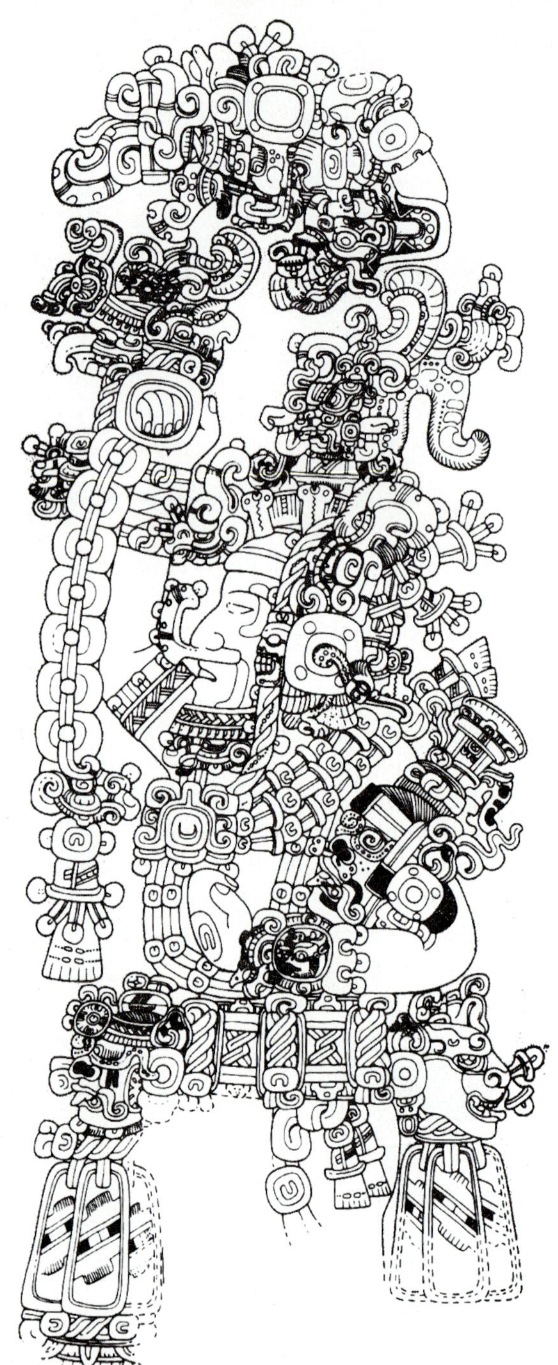

FIGURE 21.13 Lord Stormy Sky of Tikal is depicted on Stela 31 at Tikal, together with his parentage. The lord died on February 19, 456.

Copán Stairway

The Copán box describes the excavation and restoration of the famous Hieroglyphic Stairway, which is self-explanatory. It's an excellent example of a combining of archaeological and glyph research to restore a powerful, but transitory political statement by a Maya lord. This kind of approach to Maya sites large and small is a form of multidisciplinary team research that has great promise for the future.

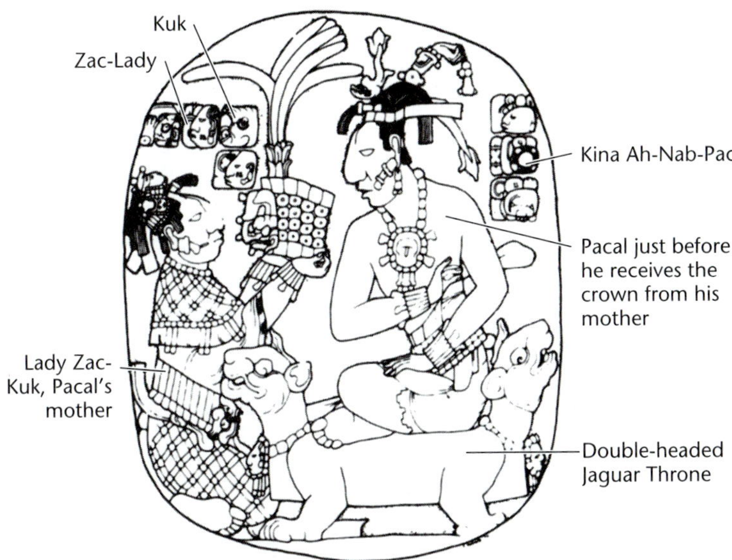

FIGURE 21.15 Pacal the Great (A.D. 603 to 683), ruler of Palenque, reigned for 67 years. This oval tablet commemorates his receipt of the crown from his mother, Lady Zac-Kuk. By using the name of a Maya goddess to refer to his mother, Pacal declared her to be the equivalent of a mother of the gods, making him divine offspring. (After Schele and Freidel, 1990.)

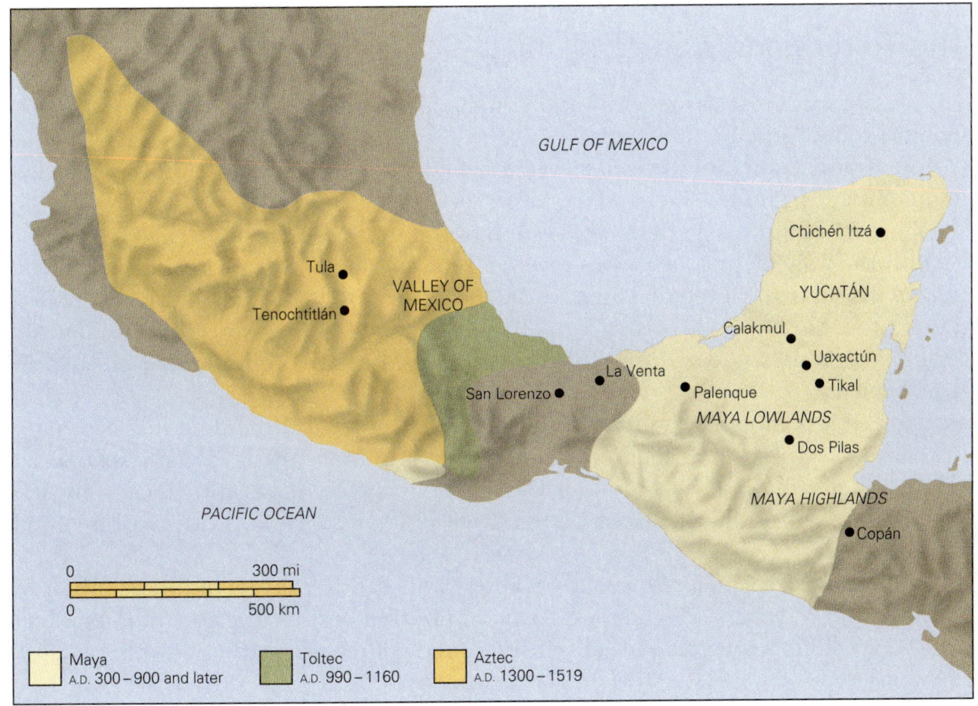

FIGURE 21.19 Distribution of Classic Maya, Toltec, and Aztec civilizations. (The Toltec and Aztec areas overlap.)

- The Maya collapse. Liters of ink have been spilled on this controversial subject. Here I can but summarize the issue and stress that many factors were involved. There is a superb discussion in David Webster's new book on the collapse listed in the Guide to Further Reading (2002), which you should consult for a full critical analysis. Let's stress that the collapse occurred only in the *southern* lowlands, for Maya civilization continued to flourish in the northern Yucatán until the Spanish Conquest.

You should refer to this map for the remainder of the chapter.

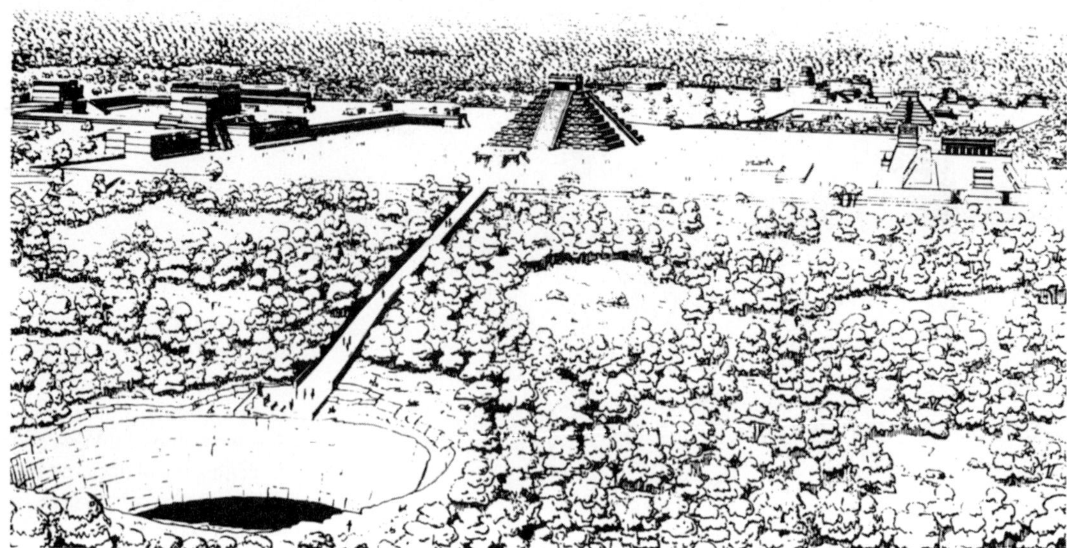

FIGURE 21.21a Chichén Itzá. Reconstructed view of the site and the Sacred Cenote, a limestone sinkhole where sacrificial offerings were made.

The Toltecs and Aztecs

The closing section describes civilization on the highlands after the fall of Teotihuacán, first the Toltecs and then the Aztecs.

Toltec civilization lasted only a few centuries, but its influence apparently extended to the lowlands, and to Chichén Itzá.

Figure 21.21a gives a general impression of this great center.

Both the Toltecs and the Aztecs revered Teotihuacán and its long vanished rulers. Indeed the Aztecs believed that their world, the world of the Fifth Sun, had been created there, atop the Pyramid of the Sun. In like manner, they revered the militaristic Toltecs—to be descended from Toltec nobility was to have considerable prestige in Aztec society.

Again, this is straightforward narrative, which requires little comment. Please note that Aztec civilization was far from monolithic, little more than a loosely structured patchwork of tribute states—which is why Cortés was able to overthrow Aztec civilization so easily. Shrewdly, he played on the dissatisfactions of subject rulers, who joined his army.

The entire Mesoamerican world collapsed with the overthrow of Tenochtitlán in 1521. Within a decade, all traces of Aztec civilization and its ancient traditions had vanished, ending a long chapter of Central American history.

chapter

ANDEAN STATES

The Chapter in Review

- The earliest complex societies of coastal Peru may have developed as a result of the intensive exploitation of maritime resources, especially small fish easily netted from canoes.
- In time, abundant food surpluses, growing population densities, and larger settlements may have preadapted coastal people to intensive irrigation agriculture. These societies were organized in increasingly complex ways.
- During the Initial Period of Peruvian prehistory, large monumental structures appeared, many of them U-shaped, just before and during the transition toward greater dependence on maize agriculture. This was also a period of continuous interaction and extensive trade between the coast and the highlands.
- This florescence of social complexity, new art traditions, and monumental architecture coincided with the emergence of several small polities in river valleys on the coast. The culmination of this trend is seen in various local traditions, among them the famous Chavín style.
- Chavín de Huantár, once thought to have been the source of Peruvian civilization, is now known to be a late manifestation of cultural trends that began as early as 2000 B.C.
- After the Early Horizon ended in about 200 B.C, a series of coastal kingdoms of the so-called Middle Horizon developed between 200 B.C. and A.D. 600, and lasted until about A.D. 1000, the political and economic influence of which spread beyond their immediate valley homelands.
- These states included Moche and Nasca, remarkable for their fine pottery styles, expert metal alloying, and gold metallurgy. They flourished in the first millennium A.D.
- About A.D. 1375, Chimu, with its great capital at Chan Chan on the northern coast, dominated a wide area of the lowlands. Its compounds reflect a stratified state with many expert craftspeople and a complex material culture.
- During the Late Horizon of Peruvian prehistory (A.D. 1400 to 1534), there was unification of the highlands and the lowlands under the Inca Empire, which may have emerged as early as A.D. 1200 and lasted until the Spanish Conquest in 1532–1534.
- The Inca rulers were masters of bureaucracy and military organization. They governed a highly structured state—one, however, that was so weakened by civil war and disease that it fell easily to the conquistador Francisco Pizarro and his small army of adventurers.

Key Cultures and Sites

Cerro Arena	El Paraíso	Middle Horizon	Sechin
Cerro Blanco	Huaca Florida	Moche	Sicán
Chavín	Huaca Prieta	Pachacamac	Sipán
Chavín de Huantár	Huaricoto	Pampa Grande	Tiwanaku
Chimu	Late Horizon	Paracas	Tucume
Chiripa	Late Intermediate period	Pukara	Wari
Cuzco	Machu Picchu		
Early Horizon			

Introductory Comments

As with Mesoamerica, the environmental contrasts in the Andean region are very striking, indeed even more so. The story of Andean civilization is a case of triumph against extreme environments—utter aridity on the coast, near-vertical mountain slopes in the highlands. This is also the story of two poles of Andean civilization, the one on Peru's North Coast, the other far to the south, around Lake Titicaca and on the southern highlands.

As always, the chapter is organized chronologically, as much as this is possible. It divides into three broad parts:

- Beginnings. Here we discuss the "maritime foundations" hypothesis and the first more complex civilizations to appear on the coast. We end with an analysis of the Chavín, the very important Early Horizon, when ideas and art styles spread widely over lowlands and highlands.
- The next section alternates between the northern and southern poles of Andean civilization. First, we journey to the southern highlands, to look briefly at the earliest more complex societies around Lake Titicaca, before returning to the North Coast to describe the spectacular Moche state. We end back in the south, with Tiwanaku and Wari.
- The last section begins with the successor kingdoms to the Moche on the North Coast, then chronicles the rise of the Inca empire and the Late Horizon. The chapter (and the book) end with Francisco Pizarro's conquest of Tawantinsuyu, the Inca "Land of the Four Quarters."

Finally, a reminder that the term "Andean" refers to that area of South America where states arose.

Now Start Reading . . .

As with Chapter 21, the map and table provide locations and a guide to the chronological relationships between the societies described. For your convenience, I have included the chronology of Mesoamerican civilizations in the second column from the right.

The first section begins with a description of the Andean environment and its dramatic contrasts, and makes the point that Andean civilization diverged along many pathways. Then I assess the celebrated "maritime foundations" hypothesis, proposed by archaeologist Michael Moseley in the 1970s, critiqued sporadically, but still holding center stage. He argues, and I think that he is right, that the Peruvian coast with its rich fisheries was a major factor in the appearance of Andean civilization. The bounty of fish provided a stable dietary base in a land where agriculture depended on carefully husbanded irrigation schemes and mountain runoff.

The "maritime foundations" hypothesis cannot explain how civilization arose everywhere in South America, because of the great environmental diversity involved. But it

FIGURE 22.1 Archaeological sites mentioned in this chapter. Approximate distributions of various traditions are also shown. Some sites in coastal river valleys are omitted from the map. Their general location is clear from the text.

certainly provides a useful working model for the coast. Here, as elsewhere in the world, food surpluses, to support the labor involved in public works, were very important—fish meal was part of the solution.

From the "maritime foundations," we move on to a quick summary of the major sites that document this transitional period on the coast. The architecture provides a convincing case for the central importance of an emerging ideology for coastal civilization. Certainly the building of major centers like Huaca Florida required both sizable food surpluses and considerable organizational abilities.

I discuss the Early Horizon and Chavín at some length. Ever since Julio Tello described the art style in 1943, Chavín has been seen as a turning moment in Andean history. Since then, more field researches have confirmed the importance of the art tradition, but show that the Early Horizon was a long period of cultural change and political adjustment.

Lastly, a brief mention of the importance of textiles rounds off this section.

Southern and Northern Poles of Civilization: Moche and Tiwanaku

The first great climax of Andean civilization unfolded during the first millennium A.D., with the Moche and Tiwanaku states at the northern and southern poles of the Andean world.

TABLE 22.1

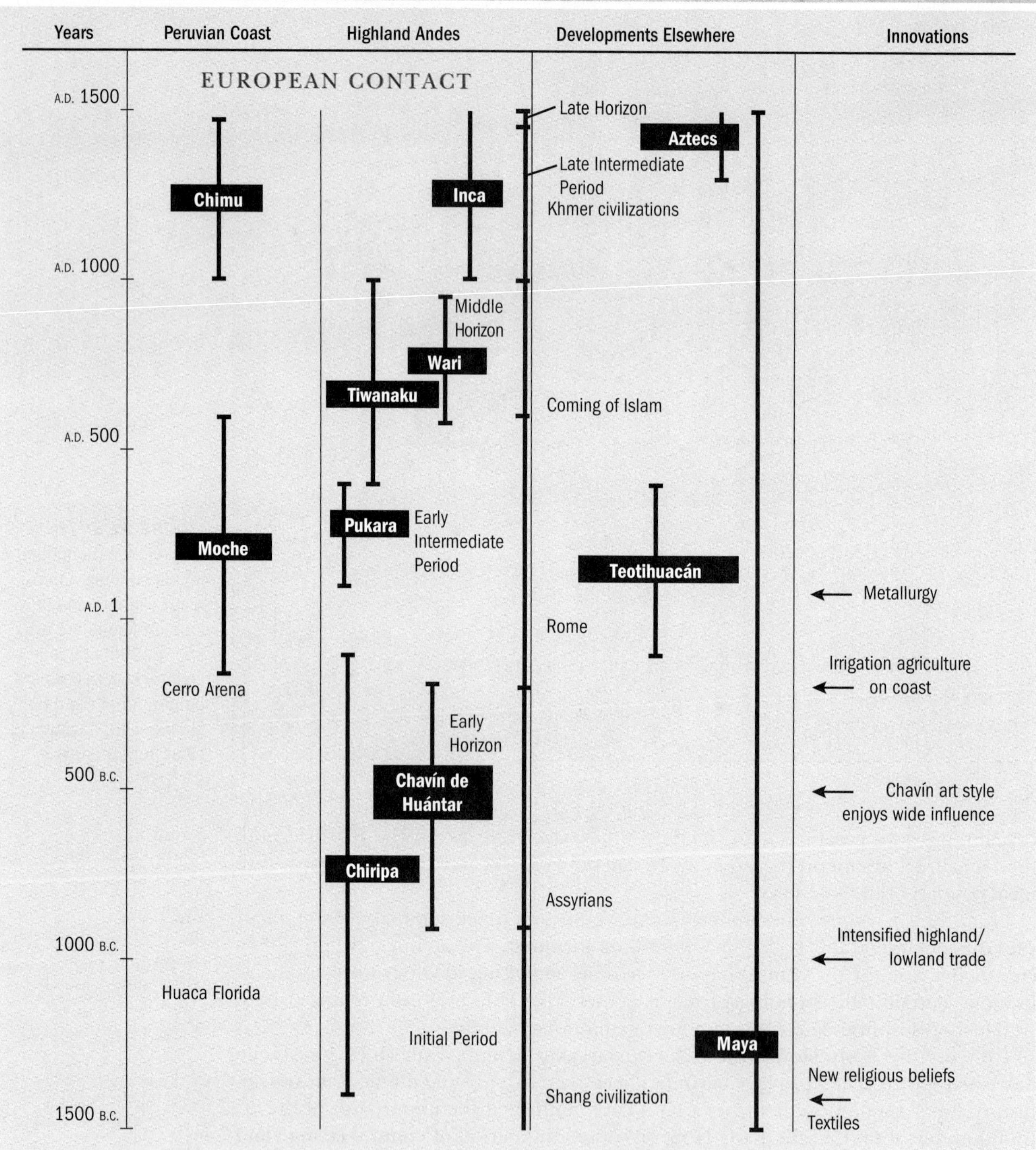

• First we briefly visit Chiripa and Pukara near Lake Titicaca at the southern pole of civilization, before returning to the North Coast and the flamboyant Moche civilization.

• The Moche. . . . The Lords of Sipán and El Niños dominate any discussion of Moche civilization.

Lords of Sipán

The Sipán lords were one of the great archaeological discoveries of the twentieth century. In my view, the finds from their tombs rival, if not surpass, those from the sepulcher of Tutankhamun in Egypt. As the Sipán tombs are about the only undisturbed royal burials from the Moche state, it is not surprising that the interpretation of their significance dominates any discussion of their society, especially since earlier knowledge of the Moche came almost entirely from painted pots. If you ever have a chance to see an exhibit of the finds, it is worth traveling a long way to see them. The artifacts and ornaments overwhelm you with their magnificence. When I saw the exhibit at UCLA, they had a life-size mannequin dressed in the full regalia, which shone bright in the ceiling lights. One could imagine a Sipán lord appearing in public atop a pyramid, the setting sun glittering on his regalia, epitomizing the sun god. Like the great pyramids at Teotihuacán, the sense of awe must have been overpowering—as it was intended to be. And you can be sure that his public appearances, like those of the Egyptian pharaohs, were carefully choreographed and rationed for maximum impact.

The Sipán discoveries tell us much about Moche governance, about a rigid, hierarchical state ruled by a few noble families. In recent years, a mass of new data has accumulated about intense El Niños, which struck the North Coast at crucial moments during the centuries of Moche rule. This is a very rare instance where the influence of a short-term climatic event on an ancient civilization can be documented in some detail. The lesson is obvious—Moche society was so rigid and unbending that it was hard for its lords to adjust to disaster, to an event that could wipe out centuries of irrigation works in a few hours.

- Now we return to the southern pole of Andean civilization—to Wari and Tiwanaku. Straightforward narrative here, which does not really do justice to Tiwanaku, a still little-known state. Some of the most interesting research surrounds Tiwanaku's raised field agriculture, which was revived using archaeological evidence, with dramatic success. It is thought that drought may have been a major factor in the collapse of the Tiwanaku state. The reconstruction of ancient raised fields near Lake Titicaca represents one of the few occasions when archaeology has come to the service of modern-day society. Unfortunately, many of these experiments are foundering because the local people lack the resources to keep the fields going, which is a tragedy, for raised fields produce extraordinary potato yields in a harsh, frost-ridden environment.

Sicán, Chimu, and the Inca empire

It seems that the North Coast people did not learn from the harsh experience of the Moche, for they made few changes to the structure of their societies, or apparently, to their agricultural methods. The Lords of Sicán, who rose from the ashes of Moche, perpetuated the same ideologies. So did the rulers of Chimor, the Chimu state, which arose around A.D. 1375, just as the Inca were rising from obscurity on the highlands.

This final section of Chapter 21 describes how the Chimu developed such institutions as split inheritance and the honoring of the royal mummy, as well as the *mit'a* tax and road construction, all of which were to become integral parts of Tawantinsuyu. (Also known as the "Land of the Four Quarters," which converged on the Inca capital at Cuzco.) My account highlights the strengths and weaknesses of the Inca empire, and ends with the Spanish Conquest.

Once again, the incoming Spaniards were able to take advantage of a fatal weakness of pre-Columbian civilization—factionalism and succession disputes, as well as an empire decimated by smallpox and other exotic diseases that arrived in advance of the conquistadors. Here, again, our description barely scratches the surface of a complex subject, for tremendous advances in our knowledge of Inca civilization have come in recent years.

The End of Prehistory

And so we reach the end of *People of the Earth,* and of our long journey through the seven million years of hominid evolution and human prehistory. The Inca civilization collapsed at the beginning of the European Age of Discovery, which resulted in the spread of an increasingly industrialized Western civilization to all corners of the world during the next four centuries, with unprecedented disruptions to the modern-day descendants of ancient societies all over the globe.

There is an Epilogue to this *Guide,* which follows. This is purely for your information—about archaeology and careers, for those who may be contemplating a life studying the past.

May you enjoy your explorations of the world of archaeology!

epilogue

ALL ABOUT BECOMING AN ARCHAEOLOGIST

Over the years, many people ask me how one can become an archaeologist, and what training is involved. They are also curious about job opportunities. I do all I can to discourage people from becoming archaeologists, for there are already too many of us. So, some years ago, I wrote the frank statement that follows and published it in several texts. I thought that it would be helpful to reprint it here.

I became an archaeologist by sheer accident, having entered Cambridge University in England without any idea of potential careers. I was admitted on the condition I studied anything except Greek and Latin, for which I had no aptitude whatsoever! So, I took a list of potential subjects and chose archaeology and anthropology on a whim with no intention of making it a career. My first lecturer was a Stone Age archaeologist named Miles Burkitt, who was famous for his classroom stories. He had studied late Ice Age rock art under a legendary French archaeologist named Henri Breuil before 1910, the first scholar to copy the art systematically—and had the stories to match the experience. Burkitt's enthusiastic reminiscences triggered my interest in the past. By chance, while still an undergraduate, I met another famous archaeologist, the African prehistorian Desmond Clark, and ended up working in a museum in Central Africa after I graduated. I have been an archaeologist ever since, a career choice I have never regretted.

Archaeology as a Profession

I gave up saying I was an archaeologist at cocktail parties after learning the hard way! Say you are an archaeologist and immediately your questioner brightens up. "How exciting! What a fascinating job," your new acquaintance almost invariably says. They think you are some kind of Indiana Jones, perpetually traveling to remote lands in search of some archaeological Holy Grail. When you tell them you study stone tools and recently spent three months searching for fossil rodents (which is usually the truth), their eyes glaze over and they often do not believe you. There's another scenario, too, where the questioner's eyes light up when they learn of your occupation and he or she asks you, confidentially: "Is it true that the Egyptian Sphinx is 12,000 years old?" Or, "What about the Lost Continent of Atlantis? Isn't it in the Bahamas?" Or, most common of all: "What's the latest on the Dead Sea Scrolls?" I must confess I am a coward and say I am a historian, which, in a sense, I am. My interlocutor soon loses interest.

Archaeology still has an aura of romance and spectacular discovery about it, which probably accounts for why many of you took the course that assigned this book in the first place. You learn pretty fast that modern-day archaeology, while often fascinating and sometimes conducted in remote lands, is a highly technical discipline where spectacular discoveries are few and far between. An Indiana Jones-like personality is certainly not a qualification for archaeology; indeed, it has never been. Today's archaeologist is about as far from Professor Jones as you can get and probably works a long way from the halls of academe.

What, then, are the qualities that make a good archaeologist in these days of highly specialized research and wide diversity of career options? Qualities of character are as important as academic qualifications, which we discuss subsequently, for you will never become rich as an archaeologist. This is a profession that has its own unique rewards. Money is not one of them.

Anyone wanting to become an archaeologist needs far more than academic credentials (covered below). Here are some essentials:

- *Enthusiasm,* indeed a passion for archaeology and the past, is the baseline for anyone who enters this field. The best archaeologists are those with the kind of fire in their bellies that enables them to raise money, overcome major practical obstacles, and carry out their work.
- *Infinite patience* to carry out fieldwork and other research that can involve slow-moving repetitive tasks and dealing with sometimes difficult people.
- *A mind that thrives on detail,* since a great deal of archaeology is minutiae—small attributes of stone tools and potsherds, analyzing computerized data, studying tiny details of the past for weeks on end.
- *Adaptability,* an ability to put up with long journeys, sometimes uncomfortable fieldwork, and often primitive living conditions. You need to be fit enough to walk long distances and to thrive on improvisation under difficult conditions. Imagine, for example, filing Land Rover wheel bearings out of nails when you are several hundred miles from a service station so you can get home. I know archaeologists who have done that. They had to.
- *Good organizational skills,* since a great deal of archaeology is logistics and organization, of field crews, site archives, even camp kitchens. A good mind for organization is a great asset.
- *Cultural sensitivity and good people skills* are essential. Many of archaeology's most successful practitioners invest enormous amounts of time in cultivating people and communicating with Native Americans and other cultural groups. This is one reason why a background in anthropology is so important to an archaeologist.
- *A commitment to ethical archaeology* is also necessary. Do not become an archaeologist unless you are prepared to adhere to the ethical standards demanded of such professionals, some of which are spelled out in this book.
- *A sense of humor* may seem self-evident, but it is vital, for many archaeologists take themselves far too seriously. Have you ever spent a week writing a paper, then had your computer implode before you have backed up your text? Moments like that beset all field research. That's why archaeologists need senses of humor, because sometimes everything that can go wrong goes wrong—all at once.

The most important considerations are commitment and enthusiasm, which will carry you through almost anything.

Deciding to Become an Archaeologist

I became an archaeologist almost by chance, for the occasional fieldwork experiences I had as an undergraduate were interesting and left me wanting more. You can ease your way into the field up to the point when you apply to graduate school and have a great time doing so.

Almost everyone I meet who is contemplating a career in archaeology either encountered the subject in high school or became interested as a result of taking an introductory course at college or university. What, then, should you do next once your appetite for the past is whetted?

First, take more courses in archaeology at the upper division level from as broad a cross-section of instructors as possible. Begin with an advanced method and theory course (if that does not turn you off, then you know you are on to something, for such courses are not remarkable for their excitement!). Then take a selection of area courses, so you find out what general areas of specialty interest you and what do not. Remember, if you apply to graduate school, you will need some specific interest as the potential focus of your degree.

Second, give yourself as thorough and as broad an education in general biological and cultural anthropology as possible, both to focus your interests and to see if living people interest you more than dead ones.

Third, take as many courses as you can in related disciplines, so that you emerge with strongly developed multidisciplinary interests. The most important and fascinating problems in archaeology, for example, the origins of agriculture, can be approached only from a multidisciplinary perspective. Much CRM archaeology is strongly multidisciplinary.

Last, gain significant field and laboratory experience while still an undergraduate. Such experience looks good on graduate applications, especially if it is broadly based. Even more important, it allows you to experience the challenges, discomforts, and realities of field and laboratory work before they become your job (and you should think of graduate school as a job).

If you take the trouble to acquire a broad-based experience of archaeology in your undergraduate years, you will be well equipped for graduate education and its pathways to a professional career. Do not consider applying to a graduate program unless you have well above average grades, a specific interest that coincides with that of the department you are applying to, and people to write letters of recommendation for you, *who really know you and your academic potential well.*

Gaining Fieldwork Experience

"How do I go on a dig?" I am asked this question dozens of times a year, especially when I teach the introductory archaeology course. The good news is that there are more opportunities to go in the field as an undergraduate then ever before, provided you are prepared to make the effort to find them. Begin by taking your department's field course, if it offers one, then look further afield, using personal contacts and departmental bulletin boards as a start. The World Wide Web is a useful source of information on such opportunities. You can attend a university field school. The most popular and rigorous field schools are in heavy demand and are filled by competitive application, sometimes by graduate students. General field schools are worthwhile because they combine excavation, laboratory analysis, and academic instruction into one intensive experience. And the camaraderie among participants in such digs can be memorable. Many of my students receive their first fieldwork experience by working as laborers on local CRM projects. Many of them begin as volunteers and are later paid for their work. It is worth checking with any private-sector CRM firms in your area, or consult your instructor, who may have contacts.

If you want to gain field experience, check carefully that you will learn something on the excavation or survey. Some summer excavations, which, obviously I cannot name, especially in the Mediterranean, are notorious for using unwitting students as unskilled labor!

Career Opportunities

This is not a good time to become an academic archaeologist, for jobs are rare and the competition intense. But it is certainly an excellent moment to consider a career in government or the private sector, both of which effectively administer or carry out most archaeology in North America.

Academic Archaeology. Academic archaeology is shrinking. A generation ago, almost all archaeologists were faculty members at academic institutions or worked in museums or research institutions. Purely academic archaeology still dominates both undergraduate and graduate training, and there are many people who enter graduate school with the resolute ambition of becoming a "traditional" research scholar. But growth in academic positions is now very slow. Some programs are even shrinking.

Most archaeology in North America and many parts of Europe is now conducted as CRM projects, much of it mandated by law. This means that most (but certainly not all) academic archaeology in American universities is carried out overseas, most commonly in Europe, Mesoamerica, or the Andes. Over the years, this means that there is intense competition for the rare vacant academic jobs in such well-trodden areas as Mesoamerica and even more applicants for academic positions in North American archaeology.

A recent study of American archaeologists found that only about 35 percent worked in academia, and the number is shrinking every year. The moral is simple: If you want to become an academic archaeologist, beware of overspecializing or of working in too-crowded fields and have other qualifications such as CRM or computer skills at your disposal.

Museum jobs are rare, especially those that are purely research positions. A career in museum work is rewarding but hard to come by and requires specialized training in conservation, exhibits, curation, or some other aspect of collections care in addition to academic training.

Cultural Resource Management and Public Archaeology. These offer almost open-ended opportunities to those who are seeking a career managing and saving the archaeological record. Time was when academic archaeologists looked down on their CRM colleagues and considered them second-rate intellectual citizens. The reverse has been true, too, for I have met CRM archaeologists who consider academics tweed-suited dilettantes! All this is nonsense, of course, for all archaeologists are concerned with careful stewardship of the human past. The greatest opportunities in archaeology during the next century lie in the public archaeology arena and the private sector, where the challenges are far more demanding than the traditional academic concerns. Adopting to this reality will lead to many changes in undergraduate and graduate curricula in coming years.

If you are interested in public archaeology or CRM, you have the choice of either working in government, or for some form of organization engaged in CRM activity, which can be either a nonprofit group perhaps attached to a museum, college, or university or a for-profit company operating entirely in the private sector. The latter come in many forms and sizes, with larger companies offering the best opportunities and career potential, especially for entry-level archaeologists. Most public archaeology activity operates through government, although a few private-sector firms also specialize in this work. If you choose to work in the public sector, you can find opportunities in many federal government agencies, among them the National Park Service and the Bureau of Land Management. Many archaeologists work for state archaeological surveys and other such organizations. Historical societies, such as that in Ohio, often employ archaeologists.

Whichever career track you choose, you will need a sound background in academic archaeology and fieldwork experience as well as suitable degrees to follow a career in these areas. Although you may receive some background training in CRM or public archaeology during your undergraduate or graduate career, much of your training will come on the job or through specialized courses taken as part of your work.

Whatever your interests in professional archaeology, I strongly advise you to obtain a background and experience in CRM field and laboratory work as part of your training.

Academic Qualifications and Graduate School

An undergraduate degree in archaeology qualifies you to work as a gopher on a CRM excavation or an academic dig and little else, except for giving you a better knowledge than most people have of the human past—not something to denigrate as a source of enlightenment and enjoyment in later life. Many people work on CRM projects for a number of years and live in motels: they even have their own informal newsletter!

Any form of permanent position in archaeology requires a minimum of an M.A. (Master of Arts), which will qualify you for many government and private-sector positions. All academic positions at research universities, and, increasingly, teaching posts require a Ph.D.

Typically, an M.A. in archaeology requires two years of course work and some form of field or data-based paper and, at some institutions, an oral examination. The M.A. may have a specialized slant, such as CRM or historic preservation, but most are general degrees, which prepare you to teach at some two- or four-year colleges and universities and open you to many CRM or government opportunities. The advantage of the M.A. degree is that it gives you a broad background in archaeology, which is essential for any professional. It is the qualification of choice for many government and CRM or public archaeology positions.

The Ph.D is a specialized research degree, which qualifies you as a faculty member to teach at a research university and at many institutions that stress teaching and not research. This is the professional "ticket" for academic archaeologists and is certainly desirable for someone entering government or the private sector, where complex research projects abound and management decisions are often needed. The typical Ph.D program requires at least two years of comprehensive seminar, course, and field training, followed by comprehensive examinations (written and often oral), M.A. papers, then a formal research proposal and a period of intensive fieldwork that, in written form, constitutes the Ph.D. thesis. The average doctoral program takes about seven years to complete and turns you into a highly specialized professional, with some teaching and research experience. After these seven years, you then have to find a job in a highly competitive marketplace. Yes, it is a daunting prospect to face seven years or more of genteel poverty, but the intellectual and personal rewards are considerable for someone with a true passion for archaeology and academic research.

Thoughts on NOT Becoming a Professional Archaeologist

Over many years of teaching archaeology, I have introduced thousands of people to the subject. Only a handful have become professional archaeologists. Most students who pass through my courses go on to an enormous variety of careers—Army rangers, bureaucrats, international businesspeople, lawyers, politicians, real estate tycoons, teachers, and even chefs and pastry cooks. At least two of my former students are in jail! But every one of them is aware of archaeology and its role in the contemporary world, of the remarkable achievements of our ancient forebears. This is by far the most important teaching that I do, of far greater significance than any amount of professional training I may give graduate students.

My task as a beginning teacher is not to recruit people to the field, to create an "in-group" who know all about radiocarbon dating, the archaeology of the central Ohio Valley or eastern Siberia, but to help create what the National Science Foundation calls "an informed citizenry." Many of my students end up with no interest in archaeology whatsoever; they find it boring and irrelevant to their lives (this quite apart from finding me tiresome!). But you can be sure they have heard of the subject and its remarkable achievements and have decided where it fits in their lives. This is, after all, one of the objectives of an undergraduate education.

Having said this, many people take a single course in archaeology and develop an active interest in the subject that endures through the rest of their lives. If you are one of these individuals, you can stay involved, at least tangentially, with archaeology in many ways.

Archaeology depends on informed amateur archaeologists (often called "avocationals"), who volunteer on excavations, in laboratories, and in museums. Many highly important contributions to archaeology come from amateur archaeologists, often members of local archaeological societies, who participate in digs and keep an eye out for new discoveries in their areas. There is a strong traditional of amateur scholarship in archaeology, especially in Europe, where some avocationals have become world authorities on specialized subjects such as ancient rabbit keeping or specific pottery forms—and they publish regularly in academic journals.

Archaeology could not function without volunteers, whether on Earthwatch-supported excavations or through quiet work behind the scenes cataloging artifacts or running lecture programs. If you have a serious interest in volunteering and pursuing archaeology on a regular basis as an amateur, there are many ways to become involved through local organizations such as colleges, museums, archaeological societies and chapters of the Archaeological Institute of America. In these days of highly specialized research and professional scholarship, it is easy to say that there is no place for amateurs. This arrogant statement is nonsense and misses the point. Amateurs bring an extraordinary range of skills to archaeology. During my career, I have worked with, among others, an accountant (who straightened out my excavation books), an architect, a professional photographer and artist (who was a godsend in the field), a jeweler (who analyzed gold beads for me), and an expert on slash-and-burn agriculture (who had a passion for environmental history). Your talents are invaluable, and don't take no for an answer! I showed this passage to a colleague, who pointed out that some of his students have gone on to highly successful and lucrative careers in business. Their quiet philanthropy has endowed professorships, paid for excavations, and supported students. Enough said!

Many people develop an interest in the past, which comes to the fore when they travel. Their background in archaeology obtained as an undergraduate enables them to visit famous sites all over the world as an informed observer and to enjoy the achievements of ancient peoples to the fullest. My files are full of postcards and letters from obscure places and well-known sites, like one mailed from Stonehenge: "Thank you for introducing me to archaeology," it reads. "I enjoyed Stonehenge so much more after taking your course." This postcard made my day, for archaeology cannot survive without the involvement and enthusiasm not just of professionals, but of everyone interested in the past. We are all stewards of a priceless and finite resource, which is vanishing before our eyes.

Credits

Chapter 1 Renfrew and Bahn, *Archaeology: Theories, Methods and Practice.* Copyright 2000. Reprinted with permission: *5.* N. de G. Davies, *The Rock Tombs of El-Amarna,* vol. 6, Pl. IV (London: Egypt Exploration Society, 1908): *6.*

Chapter 3 From John Gowlett in Robert Foley, *Hominid Evolution and Community Ecology.* Copyright © 1984. Reprinted with the permission of Academic Press: *29.* Reprinted by permission of Royal Anthropological Institute of Great Britain: *30* (*top*). Reprinted by permission of Professor J. Desmond Clark: *30* (*bottom*). From Robert Foley, *Hominid Evolution and Community Ecology.* Copyright © 1984. Reprinted with the permission of Academic Press: *31.* From *Mankind in the Making,* 2nd edition by W. W. Howells, copyright © 1959 by William Howells. Used by permission of Doubleday, a division of Random House, Inc.: *33* (*bottom*). Jacques Bordaz, *Tools of the Old and New Stone Age.* American Museum of Natural History: *36.* Eric Higgs and John Coles, *The Archaeology of Early Man* (London: Faber and Faber). Reprinted by permission: *37.*

Chapter 4 After Karl Butzer, *Environment and Archaeology,* 3/e. Copyright 1974. Reprinted by permission of Dr. Karl Butzer: *46.* Clive Gamble and Chris Stringer, *The Search for the Neanderthals.* Copyright © 1990. Reprinted by permission of Thames & Hudson: *51* (*top*). Courtesy Antiquity and Dr. James Adovasio, Archaeology Unit, Mercyhurst College: *51* (*bottom*). C. B. M. McBurney, "Early Man in the Soviet Union." © The British Academy 1976. Reproduced by permission from Proceedings of the British Academy, Vol. LXI (1975): *52.*

Chapter 5 Brian Fagan, *The Great Journey.* Copyright 1987, London: Thames & Hudson. Reprinted by permission: *59.* From *Prehistory of North America* by Jesse D. Jennings. Copyright © 1989 by Jesse D. Jennings. Reprinted by permission of Mayfield Publishing Company: *60.*

Chapter 7 Courtesy Jacques Bordaz: *74.* O Bar-Josef and A. Belfer-Cohen, "The Origins of Sedentism and Farming Communities in the Levant," *Journal of World Prehistory* 3(4): 460. Reprinted with the permission of Kluwer Academic/Plenum Publishers: *76* (*top*). Donald O. Henry, *Foraging to Agriculture: The Levant at the End of the Ice Age.* Copyright © 1989. Reprinted by permission of the University of Pennsylvania Press: *76* (*bottom*). Dorothy Garrod, *The Stone Age of Mount Carmel,* Vol. 1. Copyright 1937. Reprinted by permission of Thames & Hudson: *77.*

Chapter 8 Bruce D. Smith, *The Origins of Agriculture.* Copyright 1984, New York: Scientific American Library. Reprinted by permission of the author: *80.* Reprinted by permission of Dr. Gordon Hillman: *82.* Reprinted by permission of Dr. Gordon Hillman: *83.*

Chapter 9 James Mellaart, *Catal Hoyuk.* Copyright 1967 (London: Thames & Hudson): *91* (*top*). James Mellaart, *Catal Hoyuk.* Copyright 1967 (London: Thames & Hudson): *91* (*bottom*).

Chapter 10 Derek Roe, *Prehistory.* Copyright 1970 University of California Press. Reprinted by permission. Also reproduced with permission of Palgrave Macmillan: *96* (*top*). Grahame Clark, *World Prehistory,* 3/e, p. 140. Copyright © 1977. Reprinted by permission of Cambridge University Press: *96* (*bottom*). Derek Roe, *Prehistory.* Copyright 1970 University of California Press. Reprinted by permission. Also reproduced with permission of Palgrave Macmillan: *97* (*bottom*). Redrawn from Stuart Piggott, *Ancient Europe* (Edinburgh: Edinburgh University Press, 1965). Copyright © 1965 by Stuart Piggott. Reprinted with the permission of Stewart F. Sanderson and Alison M. Sanderson: *98.*

Chapter 12 Bruce D. Smith, *The Origins of Agriculture.* Copyright 1984, New York: Scientific American Library. Reprinted by permission of the author: *106.* K. C. Chang, *The Archaeology of Ancient China,* 3/e. Copyright © 1977. Reprinted by permission of Yale University Press: *107* (*top*). K. C. Chang: *107* (*bottom left* and *right*). K. C. Chang, *The Archaeology of Ancient China,* 3/e. Copyright © 1977. Reprinted by permission of Yale University Press: *108* (*bottom*).

Chapter 13 Richard I. Ford, ed., *Prehistoric Food Production in North America.* Museum of Anthropology, University of Michigan, Ann Arbor. Reprinted by permission: *114. Introduction to American Archaeology, Vol. 2 South America* by Gordon R. Willey. Copyright © 1971. Reprinted by permission of Pearson Education, Inc., Upper Saddle River, NJ: *116.*

Chapter 15 Courtesy Oriental Institute, University of Chicago: *126.* Max Mallowan, *Early Mesopotamia and Iran.* Copyright 1965. Reprinted by permission of Thames & Hudson: *127.* Samuel Noah Kramer, "The Sumerians," *Scientific American* (October 1957). Reprinted by permission of the University of Chicago Press: *128.*

Chapter 16 Barry Kemp, *Ancient Egypt: The Anatomy of a Civilization* (London: Routledge). Copyright 1989. Reprinted by permission: *134.* Courtesy Peter Garlake and the British Institute in Eastern Africa, Nairobi, Kenya: *138.*

Chapter 17 Charles Higham, *Archaeology of Mainland Southeast Asia.* Copyright © 1989. Reprinted by permission of Cambridge University Press: *142.*

Chapter 18 China Friendship Society: *146* (*bottom*).

Chapter 19 Redrawn from Stuart Piggott, *Ancient Europe* (Edinburgh: Edinburgh University Press, 1965). Copyright © 1965 by Stuart Piggott. Reprinted with the permission of Stewart F. Sanderson and Alison M. Sanderson: *152* (*top*). Andrew Robinson, *The Story of Writing.* Copyright 1995. Reprinted by permission of Thames & Hudson: *152* (*bottom*). Reproduced with permission of the British School at Athens: *153.*

Chapter 20 Redrawn from Stuart Piggott, *Ancient Europe* (Edinburgh: Edinburgh University Press, 1965). Copyright © 1965 by Stuart Piggott. Reprinted with the permission of Stewart F. Sanderson and Alison M. Sanderson: *156.* From R. F. Tylecote, *The Prehistory of Metallurgy in the British Isles.* Copyright © 1986. Reprinted with the permission of R. F. Tylecote and IOM Communications, Ltd.: *157.* Bryony and John Coles, *People of the Wetlands* (London: Thames & Hudson). Copyright 1989. Reprinted by permission of the author: *158.*

Chapter 21 Jeremy A. Sabloff, *Cities of Ancient Mexico.* Copyright 1989. Reprinted by permission of Thames & Hudson: *164.* Ray Matheny: *165.* Sachsische Landesbibliothek: *166* (*top*). Michael Coe, *The Maya.* Copyright 1993. Reprinted by permission of Thames & Hudson: *167.* Reprinted by permission of the University of Pennsylvania Museum of Archaeology and Anthropology: *168.* From *A Forest of Kings* by Linda Schele and David Freidel. Copyright © 1990 by Linda Schele and David Freidel. Reprinted by permission of HarperCollins Publishers, Inc.: *169* (*top*).